BARACK OBAMA AND THE JIM CROW MEDIA

The Return of the Nigger Breakers

Ishmael Reed

BARACK OBAMA

AND

THE JIM CROW MEDIA

The Return of the Nigger Breakers

Essays

Baraka
Books

Montreal

Library and Archives Canada Cataloguing in Publication

Reed, Ishmael, 1938-
    Barack Obama and the Jim Crow media: the return of the nigger
breakers / Ishmael Reed.

ISBN 978-0-9812405-9-6 (bound).—ISBN 978-0-9812405-7-2 (pbk.)

    1. Obama, Barack--In mass media. 2. Racism in mass media—United States. 3. Mass media and race relations—United States. 4. African Americans in mass media. 5. United States—Race relations. 6. Racism—United States.

I. Title.
E907.R43 2010   973.932092   C2010-900854-5

Cover by Pascal Bariault, Studio C1C4, based on an idea by Ishmael Reed
Book design by Folio infographie
Copy editing by Robin Philpot and Casey Roberts

Legal Deposit, 2nd quarter, 2010
Bibliothèque et Archives nationales du Québec
Library and Archives Canada

Published by Baraka Books of Montreal.
6977, rue Lacroix
Montréal, Québec H4E 2V4
Telephone: 514-808-8504
info@barakabooks.com   www.barakabooks.com

This book is dedicated to the Maynard Dynasty, Dori, David and Alex, and to Timothy and Tennessee Reed whose second books-in-progress are *Nightmares During The Day* and *Home of the X Challenged* and in memory of Joyce Engelson and Nancy Maynard.

"Notable East Bay residents hail Obama era's dawn

As America awoke to a new chapter of history Wednesday, some notable East Bay residents offered their views on what the Obama victory and presidency might mean.

Poet, essayist and novelist Ishmael Reed, 70, of Oakland, said he was in a Mexican restaurant with a largely black clientele Tuesday night when television networks began announcing Obama's win.

'There was spontaneous cheering, a real outpouring of joy and emotion,' he said. 'Drove to downtown Oakland and people were honking horns and cheering, and I told my spouse and daughter that this must've been what it was like in the South when the Emancipation Proclamation had been declared.'

But Reed said the initial enthusiasm may wane for some.

'A lot of people are going to be disillusioned because Obama is a centrist, even conservative in some areas,' he said. 'I don't expect drastic and radical changes under his administration. But I think it has great symbolic value that might trickle down to the black and Hispanic younger generation. I hope it gets through to the kids who shoot it out on my streets.'

Reed said Obama seems emblematic of the *new black aesthetic* described in Trey Ellis' landmark essay almost two decades ago.

'Obama's the leader of a post-race generation,' he said. 'I look at this sort of like a Nelson Mandela-type administration of reconciliation, but the economic power will still be in the hands of whites. Obama got more money from Wall Street than McCain, and those people are not social-ists no matter what Mrs. Palin says.

'Some of these people who were cheering last night, who were dancing in the streets all over the world, are in for a big surprise.'"

The Oakland Tribune, November 8, 2008

"If we're able to stop Obama on this it will be his Waterloo. It will break him."

Senator Jim DeMint

Contents

Foreword

The Media's lack of diversity skews news judgment. To the more than 7,000 minority journalists who massed in Washington last week for a meeting rooted in their long fight to make the staffs of the nation's newsgathering organizations more diverse, the newsrooms of this city's national press corps must have looked like enemy bunkers.

By DeWayne Wickham Posted 8/9/2004 9:43 PM

When my novel *Flight To Canada* was published in 1976, I could not have imagined that I would live to see the time when the points of view of African Americans in the media and elsewhere would be so marginalized that I would be in the position of the nineteenth-century fugitive slave orator. That I would have to take an intellectual Black Rock ferry across the river into Canada in order to make my case because, in the words of my agent, no American publisher would publish this book.

I'm among the lucky ones. Great African-American journalists, like Pulitzer Prize winner Les Payne, have lost their columns in major American newspapers, which have seen their news rooms emptied of the presence of black, Hispanic, Asian-American and Native-American journalists except for those who adhere to the line promoted by the multinationals, who control the American media, and right-wing and neo-conservative think tanks. That line is that the problems confronting black and other Americans are not structural and institutional but a result of their behavior, or as put by Jamaican American Orlando Patterson, one of the few African Americans invited to appear on the pages of *The New York Times* Op-Ed page, most of whom aim their "tough love" at blacks, exclusively, their lack of "internal cultural reformation."

This oversimplification is refuted by studies and reports printed in the *Times* showing, for example, bias toward blacks and Hispanics in the mortgage industry, which has cost black homeowners billions in home equity and denied millions of blacks home ownership, homes being the chief asset of white Americans, one that allows them to send their children to college and to open businesses. For a while, the press tried to blame the economic crisis on blacks, a claim refuted by Nobel Prize winning economist, Paul Krugman, appearing on C-Span's *The Washington Journal* on June 26, 2009. Indeed, the state with the most mortgage foreclosures is Nevada, a state with a small black population.

Isn't it ironic? A media that scolded the Jim Crow South in the 1960s now finds itself hosting the bird. Jim Crow in the South meant separate but unequal facilities. It meant that any white woman who accused a black man of rape was believed.

In the media it means that whites get the choice billion-dollar media equipment and the rest of us get the blogs. It means all-white media juries disguised as panels and debates evaluating the behavior of not only the blacks and Hispanics but also celebrities and the president of the United States. Not just cable television but web browsers like AOL and YAHOO peddle "news" almost daily about black celebrities, usually athletes, caught in scandals, an attempt to entertain their white subscribers. AOL's expert on black culture and history is intellectual mercenary Dinesh D'Souza.

In terms of its attempt to build a media that "looks like America," the media are as white as a KKK picnic. In terms of diversity, it's fifty years behind Mississippi, that much maligned state that has a higher percentage of blacks with power than CBS. Mississippi is among five states with the highest number of black elected officials; Old Miss has a higher percentage of black enrollment than many northern and western colleges and universities.

Serious black intellectuals have vanished from publishing and a younger generation of black male authors has found greater success in Germany than in the United States. Hollywood, which has always poisoned American race relations, except for brief interludes, is producing movies like *Precious*, movies so foul in their representation of blacks they make D.W. Griffith seem like a progressive. As I write this, the motion picture academy, whose board of governors is entirely white, has nominated this foul project for six Oscars[*]. To add to this insult, *The Wire*, which portrays blacks as degenerates, produced by David Simon, a producer who has claimed the ghetto as his own private moneymaking reserve, is being taught in the African-American Studies department at Harvard. According to *The New York Times*, January 4, 2010, "For the 40th anniversary of the death of the Rev. Dr. Martin Luther King, Jr., when Dr. Wilson gathered scholars, activists and the show's creator to analyze the series' impact, he did not mince words: 'it has done more to enhance our understanding of the challenges of urban life and the problems of urban inequality than any other media event or scholarly publications, including studies by social scientists,'" which is like a Native-American scholar inviting a producer of one of John Wayne's westerns and describing these westerns as having "done more to enhance our understanding," of Native American life than any study offered by social scientists.

Ms. Laura Miller's comment in *Salon.com* sums up the attitude of the establishment media, progressive, right, left and mainstream, toward the views of what might be regarded as rogue intellectuals or what Quincy Troupe calls "Unreconstructed Negroes" like me on a number of issues including the candidacy of Barack Obama. Reviewing my essay about Mark Twain's *Huckleberry Finn*, Ms. Laura gave me a tongue lashing in the progressive *Salon.com*, whose editor, Joan Walsh, a guest on many all-white media panels, where she poses as a progressive, believes that the all-white jury, which acquitted four white policemen who murdered Amadou Diallo, was justified in reaching their decision.

Ms. Laura said that my essay style was "rowdy" and that my writings were "diatribes." This is because I opposed the notion that there were no heroes or villains during the slavery period, the line that is being used

---

[*] The Directors Guild of America reports that just 4 percent of its director membership is black. The Writers Guild of America says that 4.5 percent of members employed as television writers and 3.2 percent of members employed as film writers are black (2007). Paris Barclay, Director-Showrunner of "In Treatment" and co-chair of the DGA's Diversity Task Force, estimates that up to 82 percent of all episodes in television are "directed by Caucasian men."

to peddle post-race products like the work of Kara Walker. Post-racism is another mass delusion under which many Americans are laboring. If Ms. Laura were acquainted with the history of African-American literature she would know that black writers, especially the males, have been called "rowdy," "bitter," "paranoid" and accused of writing only diatribes for over one hundred years. Even elegant James Baldwin was called "antagonistic." When it comes to black literature, Ms. Laura Miller and her friend Michiko Kakutani of *The New York Times* prefer melodramas in which angelic do-no-wrong black heroines are surrounded by cruel and "evil"—Alice Walker's word for the brothers—black men. Ms. Kakutani is so eager to accept stereotypes about black life that she celebrated a fake black ghetto "memoir," *Love And Consequences,* written by Margaret Jones, a white woman. Now even the black women who serve up this kind of writing are being challenged by white women writers like Kathryn Stockett who not only copycat this style, like Elvis copycatted James Brown, but make more money doing it. This has caused outrage among some black women writers one of whom called this style "Neo-Mammy." Yet, some of these same writers made no protest when *The Color Purple* and *What's Love Got To Do With It* were manhandled by white producers, directors and script writers resulting in the black male perpetrators being represented in a worse manner than in the original texts.

But even with the dismissal of my work by powerful critics like Ms. Laura Miller, unlike other black writers, I have not been silenced. I have my own zine, at *IshmaelReedpub.com,* and a blog at the *San Francisco Chronicle.* Lee Froehlich at *Playboy* has published a number of my essays and *CounterPunch* has been open to my views. In fact, many of the essays in this book were published originally at *Counterpunch.org.* They cover the candidacy of Barack Obama and the first year of his presidency.

Obama compares himself to Abraham Lincoln and in at least one way that is true. During research for my novel, *Flight To Canada*, I examined some of the media coverage of Lincoln, especially from Confederate newspapers, and was taken aback by the vitriol that often referred to the president as an ape (one of the favorite descriptions of President Obama by his enemies).

Before I was appointed chair of the PEN Oakland Media Committee, by chairperson and PEN President Floyd Salas, and before that, assigned to respond to a tough-love letter aimed at blacks printed in *Esquire*, I would have been surprised at such a description of a black man of Obama's distinction, but since examining the media coverage of blacks and Hispanics and other minorities over the years, and having covered such portrayals in two books of essays, *Airing Dirty Laundry*, and *Mixing It Up, Taking On The Media Bullies*, I have discovered that these portrayals are par for the course, and are aimed not only at the underclass, but the middle class and the upper classes as well. There was no difference between the way the press assailed Reginald Lewis, the African-American head of a billion-dollar corporation, and the vehemence the same press accords a crack-dealing street thug.

The media are a segregated white-owned enterprise with billions of dollars at their disposal. Their revenue stream is based upon holding unpopular groups to scorn and ridicule, a formula for ratings that dates to the early days of the mass media. Mexican Americans, Chinese and Japanese Americans, and Jewish Americans and even Italian Americans have taken turns being the targets of their abuse. Now it's the Muslims. But among ethnic groups, it's the African Americans who have been the permanent 24/7 group that is subjected to the media take down. The token black, Hispanic and Asian-American commentators are those found non-threatening to the media's white subscribers and submissive to the editorial line coming from the top. They are like the black servants in *Gone With The Wind* who remained loyal to their masters even when the Union troops were approaching the city. George Bush received two percent of the black vote and it often seems that all two percent have jobs as commentators in the media. Two of the favorite black regulars on cable, Bob Christie and Joe Watkins, actually worked for Bush and Cheney. Dan Rather, formerly of CBS news, as a newsman who was tea-bagged and swift-boated out of his job, has warned about the undue influence of corporations upon news content. WMR reported:

> On September 16, Dan Rather, the former anchor of the CBS Evening News, warned that today's news is shaped by very powerful corporate network owners who "are in bed with powerful political interests" that

are influenced by government regulatory interests. [See breakdown below.]

Rather spoke at a National Press Club remembrance of his colleague Walter Cronkite, his predecessor in the CBS Evening News anchor chair, and Don Hewitt, the late producer of 60 Minutes.

Rather revealed that in his conversations with Cronkite, the late anchor also believed that corporate interests were shaping the news to the detriment of objective journalism.

Not only are the media influenced by their corporate owners but are also under pressure from advertisers. Janine Jackson and Peter Hart of *FAIR, Fairness & Accuracy in Reporting*, pointed out that:

A 2001 survey by the Project for Excellence in Journalism (*Columbia Journalism Review*, 11-12/01) found that 53 percent of local news directors "reported advertisers try to tell them what to air and not to air, and they say the problem is growing." (...)

In a 2000 Pew Center for the People & the Press poll of 287 reporters, editors and news executives, about one-third of respondents said that news that would "hurt the financial interests" of the media organization or an advertiser goes unreported. Forty-one percent said they themselves have avoided stories, or softened the tone on stories, to benefit their media company's interests. Among investigative reporters, a majority (61 percent) thought that corporate owners exert at least a fair amount of influence on news decisions.

Peter Phillips, assistant professor of Sociology at Sonoma State University and director of Project Censored, a media research organization, has detailed "Corporate influence in the newsroom:"

Eleven influential media corporations in the United States—General Electric Company (NBC), Viacom Inc. (cable), The Walt Disney Company (ABC), Time Warner Inc. (CNN), Westinghouse Electric Corporation (CBS), The News Corporation Ltd. (Fox), Gannett Co. Inc., Knight-Ridder Inc., New York Times Co., Washington Post Co., and the Times Mirror Co.—now represent a major portion of the news information systems in the United States. Many people have no other source of news and information than these 11 corporations.

Collectively, these 11 corporations had 155 directors in 1996, and the directors accounted for 144 directorships on the boards of Fortune 1000 corporations in the United States. These directors are the media elite of the world. While they may not agree on abortion and other domestic issues, they do represent the collective vested interests of a significant portion of corporate America and share a common commitment to free market capitalism, economic growth, internationally protected copyrights, and a government dedicated to protecting their interests.

These 11 media organizations have interlocking directorships with each other through 36 other Fortune 1000 corporations creating a solid network of overlapping interests and affiliations. All 11 media corporations have direct links with at least two of the other top media organizations. General Electric, owner of NBC, has the highest rate of shared affiliations with 17 direct corporate links to nine of 10 other media corporations.

Given this interlocked media network, it is more than safe to say that major media in the United States effectively represent the interests of corporate America, and that the media elite are the watchdogs of acceptable ideological messages, the parameters of news and information content, and the general use of media resources.

Do the media elite directly censor the news? Without being privy to insider conversations, it is difficult to prove direct censorship by management of particular stories in the news. But clearly an organizational tendency will be to comply with the general corporate culture, and career-minded journalists and editors sharing this common corporate culture will create what direct censorship cannot, a general compliance with the attitudes, wishes, and expectations of the media elite and in turn corporate America.

Keeping democracy safe in America requires an informed electorate and a strong watchdog press. But major media today are tending to favor news stories on sex scandals, celebrity events, and crime, leaving less or little room for analytical news on important social issues. If privately owned commercial media will not meet the task of keeping democracy safe then it is time for a strong public supported national news system.

Are we to believe that General Electric's selling of health insurance doesn't influence the position of MSNBC's Joe Scarborough on the issue?

Moreover, are the liberal and right-wing media the only outfits that omit the points of view of African Americans, Hispanics, Asian Americans and others who are not former speechwriters for Dick Cheney, or token columnists at *The National Review*?

As of this writing, the progressive network, Pacifica, is under fire by black media activists like Joseph Anderson and M.O.I. JR aka JR Valrey for its lack of inclusion and NPR, which is touted as a liberal network, is being criticized by the National Association of Black Journalists for firing black journalists and canceling black shows.

When the National Association of Black Journalists protested the firings of blacks from National Public Radio, Vivian Schiller, NPR's chair and CEO said, in an attempt to stonewall the NABJ, that "the definition of diversity includes not only race and ethnicity, but also socioeconomic background, political perspective, gender and sexual identity, age, geography, point of view and a multitude of other factors that may not be obvious or measured." Ms. Schiller must have adopted Gloria Steinem's proposition that "gender" is the most "restrictive" element in American life. White gender that is! The white feminists and their surrogates didn't care about the Central Park Five, whom they helped to send to prison for a crime that they didn't commit, even though their mothers belonged to the same gender as they. Ms Schiller probably believes that her condition is worse than that of Emmett Till. Apparently Ms. Schiller isn't aware that among the groups she mentioned, whites are at the top of the hierarchical ladder. When it comes to playing the race card, whites continue to hold all of the aces and so with the kind of absence of black journalists except those who mimic the views of the media owners (the only on-air African-American commentator at National Public Radio is right-winger Juan Williams, who is also a Fox contributor), President Obama continues to be reviewed by all-white panels, and whatever gains his programs might achieve, for them, he will always come up short or even fail. His children will be the targets of vicious comments. Juan Williams called his spouse, Michelle, "Stokely Carmichael in a dress."

From Monday to Friday, October 26 through 30, 2009, there was good news for the economy. It was announced that that the stimulus plan had saved or created 640,000 jobs. (On November 30, Paul Krugman, media-designated Obama critic and Nobel Prize winning economist, had to admit that, "Basically, we started out with a year that matched the Great Depression, but have since pulled back a bit from the edge of the abyss.") Ford Motor Company announced a profit of nearly a billion dollars due

partially to the administration's "cash for clunkers" program. Home buying increased by 6.1 percent, the most since 2006. Construction spending
rose. Manufacturing grew for the third straight month. The GDP came
in at an annualized rate of 5.7 percent during the fourth quarter of 2009.
A few weeks later GM announced that it would repay the government's
bailout money five years ahead of schedule.

This news didn't diminish the steady flow of criticism emanating from
Obama's adversaries on talk shows and panels that aired the following
Sunday—shows that have been criticized over the years for lacking black
representation or for using tokens. On *Meet The Press* it was Tavis Smiley,
who had been outed by a blog called *TheRoot* for being the advance man
for Wells Fargo in its successful attempt to sell toxic mortgage loans to
inner city residents. He said that maybe those who during the campaign
said that Barack Obama lacked the experience to be president were right.
Appearing on CNN's *State of the Union*, on Sunday, Mary Matalin ridiculed the president's programs and repeated the GOP talking point that
the public was opposed to the administration's public option plan, even
though there was a consensus among those polled that the majority of
the public was for it. (On the following Monday, William Kristol, a guest
on *The Washington Journal*, echoed Matalin's talking point and was also
allowed to create an "American public" that rivaled that reflected in the
polls, without being challenged by the moderator.) Ms. Matalin's presence
on a panel on which the majority followed the line introduced by *Saturday
Night Live*, a comedy show, was an example of how even Obama's fiercest
enemies are given time to weigh in on the president's alleged failure.

Saturday Night Live, on October 3, opened with Fred Armisen as
President Obama, delivering an address from the Oval Office. "When
you look at my record," he said, "it's very clear what I've done so far, and
that is nothing." During the following week and months the show, a comedy show mind you, was cited around the clock as proof that President
Obama hadn't accomplished anything.

Whether this was a result of journalistic lethargy, an unwillingness to
consult the facts, or whether it was talking points required of pundits by
the media owners, the *Saturday Night Live* writers—who tend to be
white—were wrong. What are the facts? *The St. Petersburg Times'*

PolitiFact.com's Truth-O-Meter listed promises that Obama had made. They included:

15:   Create a foreclosure prevention fund for homeowners;

33:   Establish a credit bill of rights;

36:   Expand loan programs for small businesses;

58:   Expand eligibility for State Children's Health Insurance Fund (SCHIP);

76:   Expand funding to train primary care provides and public health practitioners;

77:   Increase funding to expand community based prevention programs;

88:   Sign the UN Convention on the Rights of Persons with Disabilities;

110: Assure the Veterans Administration budget is prepared as "must-pass" legislation;

119: Appoint a special adviser to the president on violence against women;

125: Direct military leaders to end war in Iraq;

222: Grant Americans unrestricted rights to visit family and send money to Cuba;

239: Release presidential records;

269: Increase funding for national parks and forests;

290: Push for enactment of the Matthew Shepard Act, which expands hate crime laws to include sexual orientation and other factors;

327: Support increased funding for NEA;

337: Use the International Space Station for fundamental biological and physical research;

346: Appoint an assistant to the president for science and technology policy;

359: Rebuild schools in New Orleans;

371: Fund a major expansion of AmeriCorps;

411: Work to overturn *Ledbetter* vs. *Goodyear*;

435: Create new criminal penalties for mortgage fraud;

452: Weatherize 1 million homes per year;

459: Enact tax credit for consumers for plug-in hybrid cars;

480: Support high-speed rail;

500: Increase funding for the Environmental Protection Agency;

507: Extend unemployment insurance benefits and temporarily suspend
     taxes on those benefits;

513: Reverse restrictions on stem cell research.

Did nothing? All of these promises were kept. Yet, the mainstream cable news channels used the *Saturday Night Live* comic interpretation as a hook that was even picked up by progressives. Typical was Ed Schultz, of Air America, who criticized Obama for his lack of "aggression," with the knowledge that a black "aggressive" president becomes to his enemies an "angry black man" and one who, as Glenn Beck of Fox said, hates white people. On November 9, 2009, Keith Olbermann cited an interview conducted with Rupert Murdoch by an Australian newspaper during which Rupert Murdoch agreed with Glenn Beck that Obama was a racist.) If criticism of Obama from the white right and mainstream weren't enough, some of Obama's harshest criticisms came from *The Huffington Post*, *Salon.com* and Air America which, on November 5, invited listeners to judge Obama's first year. Most of the respondents and the guest host Nicole Sandler gave him a failing grade. She gave her opinion that Bush was a more effective president, an idea offered by comedian Bill Maher, begrudgingly, yet fifty-seven percent of Americans polled during that November period held that Obama was more effective than Bush.

That afternoon, progressive talk show host Ed Schultz's guest was an admitted conservative who trashed Obama's economic program, a program that most economists credited with having saved the country from a depression.

The left said that they wanted Obama to be more like Lyndon Johnson, forgetting apparently that Johnson's aggressive foreign policy got him into trouble. Brent Budowsky of *The Hill* was brought on by progressive Air America to criticize Obama's performance during his first year in office. Go to *The Hill* website and one will find the black point of view represented by two right-wingers Ron Christie and Armstrong Williams, former aide to Strom Thurmond, a segregationist everywhere but in bed. (On November 16, *The New York Times* acknowledged that the criticism of Obama was coming from both the right and the left.) Accompanying the photo was that of three hosts, one of whom plays liberal, Chris Matthews, and two progressives, Keith Olbermann and Rachel Maddow, all-white. In the same section was an article about *Newsweek*'s problems. All three executives pictured were white including the managing editor, Jon Meecham, who believes that the country is center right (even though it rejected John McCain, who campaigned from the center right) and that Billy Graham looks like God.

After Democratic losses in November 2009 in Virginia and New Jersey, the segregated media was once again speaking of Obama's bad week and the failure of his administration and pronouncing victory for the tea-baggers whose challenge to the Republican establishment led to the election of the first Democratic congressman from New York's 23rd district in over one hundred years. Even with losses in both New Jersey and Virginia, where the candidate for governor ran as an Obama Republican, Obama's poll numbers remained high.

Despite the encouraging news of the week ending on October 30, the Sunday show panels, which have been criticized for their lack of minority representation, continued their yearlong criticism of the Obama administration. Much attention was given to Senator Joseph Lieberman, who threatened to block health legislation if a public option were included. The commentators didn't reveal that Lieberman has received over two million dollars from the insurance industry and that his wife has lobbied on behalf of the health insurance industry. After making predictions about Obama's failures—predictions that weren't borne out—you'd think that members of the Jim Crow media fraternity would be more cautious. For weeks they were predicting that a health bill would come out of the House, minus public option. A bill with a public option passed the House despite the prediction of a CNN newswoman who, the night before, predicted that it wouldn't.

Though few black women reporters and commentators are seen on television, white women are plentiful both on national and local television. They are among those who appear on camera to lash out at Obama. I've mentioned Mary Matalin, editor of one of the most abominable books about the president. She receives gentle treatment when she is brought on to comment about the president's alleged failures. This woman worked for Dick Cheney who advocated the torture of prisoners and is suspected of outing a CIA agent, Valerie Plame, a treasonable offense. During the August 5, 2008 edition of Fox News' *Fox & Friends*, Fox News contributor Bob Beckel said to Jerome Corsi, author of the book *The Obama Nation*, edited by Matalin:

"You said that Barack Obama supported a bill that allowed mothers to kill their babies even after they were born. Now, were they gonna use knives, guns, or how were they gonna do that? And do you actually believe that to be true?" Corsi responded, "Well, it's true," and asserted that "Obama, on the floor of the Illinois state Senate, said that woman had an absolute right to abortion, to kill the baby even if it survived that abortion." In fact, during the floor debate on the bill Corsi was discussing—which opponents said was unnecessary, as the Illinois criminal code unequivocally prohibits killing children, and said that it posed a threat to abortion rights—Obama never said any such thing, as *Media Matters* noted in response to similar false claims by Corsi in several media appearances.

Beckel later brought up several controversial comments by Corsi:

"Can I give you a couple other Corsi comments just so that people can understand the person writing this book? Corsi on Muslims: 'Ragheads are boy-bumpers and clearly are woman-haters.'" Beckel further said, "Corsi on—you called 'John Effing Commie Kerry. He married Teresa then he became a Jew.' You say about Hillary Clinton, 'Fat Hog' Clinton." Later in the discussion, Beckel asked Corsi, about his comment about Hillary Clinton. Corsi had said "Anybody asked Hillary why she couldn't stop B. J. Bill being satisfied? She's a lesbo." Beckel asked, "When did you say that?" Corsi responded, "Bob, I never defend these comments. They're ancient history," and claimed, "Ad hominem attacks on me are a fairly low way of trying to get to the substance of what I'm saying." Beckel later stated, "Doctor, I have looked through a good part of your book. All I can tell you is, you say you have 600 sources. Most of those sources are people who have right-wing agendas who are against Barack Obama." Beckel also said to Corsi: "[I]f you're holding yourself out here to be an expert on Barack Obama and say the kinds of things you've said, you have to understand why some of us question not only your standing, not only the accuracy of your book, but also your history."

Mary Matalin, editor of the book, defended this scurrilous rubbish. The fact that she is awarded hours of TV time to criticize the president is a disgrace and shows how low Jonathan Klein, CNN president, will stoop to get ratings.

With the election of a black president, the media have become a sort of white power government in exile taking its lead from Fox News. When President Obama and his team began to treat Fox News as an arm of the Republican Party, the "mainstream" media rallied to defend Fox and even suggested that their criticism of Fox would only serve to improve Fox's ratings. Wrong again.

Eric Boehlert of *Media Matters* wrote:

...we saw nearly universal agreement among media elites that the White House decision to publicly call out Fox News was monumentally dumb, thin-skinned, short-sighted, and uncivil. [Paging the etiquette police!]

Everyone said so. Therefore pundits were certain that Fox News' ratings were way up and that Obama and his aides had made a huge tactical blunder. The ratings angle simply provided statistical ammunition for what the Beltway press corps already knew to be the truth: Fact-checking Fox News, in the immortal words of *The Washington Post*'s CW-loving Sally Quinn, was "absolutely crazy."

Except it turns out none of that was true. There was no viewer stampede toward Fox News.

From Fox, MSNBC, where a man who has a history of making racist and anti-Semitic remarks, Pat Buchanan, has been given unlimited time to criticize the president, to CNN, that features a man who designed a racist ad for Senator Jesse Helms, Alex Castellanos, and a professional scapegoater of African Americans, William Bennett, Obama faces a rogue's gallery of pundits with a history of racist comments and campaigns against blacks. Bennett was rewarded with a regular CNN spot after his remark that if you were to abort black babies the crime rate would decline (apparently unaware that seventy percent of the crimes in the U.S. are committed by whites). Relying apparently on the short memory of the American public, Bennett is allowed to criticize the president's economic plans. Bennett, a constant critic of black family values, has been exposed as such a gambling addict that his losses at one point totaled eight million dollars, which is pertinent because Republicans are always comparing the way individual citizens manage their personal budgets with the way "tax and spend" Democrats manage the government.

Glenn Beck was hired by CNN after he called the survivors of Katrina "scumbags." Another example of how talk show culture influences politics was the announcement of the Palin-backed conservative candidate for New York's 23rd district congressional seat, Doug Hoffman, that Fox News host Glenn Beck was his inspiration. He lost. During the week of November 16, the Anti-Defamation League blasted Beck for his demagogic and inflammatory attacks on the president in an alarming report about the growing anti-Obama rage that is being promoted partially by the media.

> Although much of the recent anti-government anger has been generated by a combination of partisan politics, grass-roots activists, and extreme groups and movements, the mainstream media has also played a role in promoting anti-government anger and pandering to people who believe that the Obama administration is illegitimate or even fascistic.

> The most important mainstream media figure who has repeatedly helped to stoke the fires of anti-government anger is right-wing media host Glenn Beck, who has a TV show on FOX News and a popular syndicated radio show. While other conservative media hosts, such as Rush Limbaugh and Sean Hannity, routinely attack Obama and his administration, typically on partisan grounds, they have usually dismissed or refused to give a platform to the conspiracy theorists and anti-government extremists. This has not been the case with Glenn Beck. Beck and his guests have made a habit of demonizing President Obama and promoting conspiracy theories about his administration.

Much of the animus directed at Obama from Fox is meant to destroy his administration according to court documents filed by Sandra Guzman, a former Fox employee. *Gawker* reported:

> The 38-page complaint was filed by former employee Sandra Guzman, and she claims she was fired in retaliation, after publicly condemning a racist cartoon published in the paper depicting President Obama as a dead chimpanzee. (…)

> Guzman's complaint also states that "Charles Hurt, the *Post*'s Washington D.C. Bureau Chief told Guzman that the Murdoch-owned *Post*'s 'goal is to destroy Barack Obama. We don't want him to succeed.'"

> Rupert Murdoch also owns Fox News, which Fox News' Senior Vice President for Programming, Bill Shine recently admitted had the goal of being "the voice of opposition" to the Obama administration. Murdoch also

stated in a recent interview that he agrees with Glenn Beck that President Obama is a racist.

The allegations in Guzman's lawsuit, if true, paint Rupert Murdoch-owned newspapers and media outlets, as having a set agenda to slant news coverage to bring down the Obama administration.

When minority American journalists met at a convention in 2004, the media were termed the enemy. With the removal of black, Hispanic and Asian-American journalists from the media groups whose members voted overwhelmingly for Barack Obama, the president continues to be judged by all-white commentary, a punditry which includes members of the Imus Alumni, those loyal to Don Imus, who was fired for calling black female members of a basketball team "nappy-headed hos." Howard Kurtz, David Gregory, Joe Scarborough, Pat Buchanan and others remained loyal to Imus until the end. And though this book is critical of Obama's chastising of African Americans, Africans, Rev. Jeremiah Wright, Henry Louis Gates, Jr., and Kanye West in order to please a white constituency, the Sister Souljah strategy, I am the first to acknowledge that it took great courage for him and his family to campaign for a job that even General Colin Powell's family declined for fear of his being murdered. Just as the American media is the enemy of blacks and Latinos, Obama's candidacy and presidency have been treated with a similar hostility, (not only from the right but the left, as Bush could always count on Fox) that at least one newspaper, *Boston Globe*, has commented that through their actions they have increased the threats on the president's life. "Threatening language has also found its way into talk radio broadcasts and social networking websites, raising fears that individuals not normally considered threats to the president could be incited to violence."

This book ends however on an optimistic note, the author having witnessed the heroic efforts of members of a younger generation in their David versus Goliath effort, by using modern and ancient techniques to combat a corporate giant, the mainstream American media in decline and continuing to poison the American mind even amidst its death groans. Jackie Jones, a reporter for *BlackAmericaWeb.com*, was on point when she said: "Cyber-news is increasingly informing traditional media coverage and providing more lenses through which to view our world."

Introduction

A niche market could be defined as a component that gives your business power. A niche market allows you to define whom you are marketing to. When you know who you are marketing to it's easy to determine where your marketing energy and dollars should be spent.

Laura Lake
"Defining Your Niche Market
A Critical Step in Small Business Marketing"

Many associate the term Nigger Breaker with the incidents recounted by Frederick Douglass in his autobiography, *Narrative of the Life of Frederick Douglass*, where he gives an account of his beatings by a professional Nigger Breaker named Edward Covey until he fought back. Yet Nigger Breakers were not an American invention. When I visited a famous slave fort in Ghana, I was shown a dungeon where rebellious blacks were held.

I was also informed by our guide that race mixing, the American practice that has, in the minds of some, led to the rise of a new race in America, began before the ships departed from this fort. The white crew helped themselves to the female prisoners at the slave castle and probably en route to the South as well.

Though thought of as a custom that perished with the "emancipation" of blacks, Nigger Breaking persists in subtler forms. The fact that black young people are punished by the criminal justice system for crimes that, if they were committed by white youth, would be considered pranks, in the opinion of Sheriff Michael Hennessey of San Francisco, can be seen as a form of Nigger Breaking. These youth not only supply the prison industrial complex with human merchandise but capricious incarceration is a manner by which the more assertive of these youth might be chastened. The fact that two hundred thousand inmates, probably a low number, are raped in the gulags that pass as prisons is ignored even by progressives who've spent thousands of hours of air time and print space complaining about the accommodations accorded members of bin Laden's staff.

Another form of Nigger Breaking is to publicly humiliate a prominent black person as a way of sending a message to blacks, which was the assessment of MSNBC's Ed Schultz about the ratings-boosting marathon coverage of the Michael Vick case, the football player who was convicted for his part in a dog-fighting operation. Schultz is one of a handful of white on-air commentators who speaks about race with anything approaching candor. There was more coverage by the corporate media of the Vick case than that accorded the millions of deaths resulting from the embargo of Iraq, and invasions of Middle East countries.

The pillorying of ex-Washington mayor, Marion Barry, is a good example of how a prominent black individual is used to cast collective ridicule on the black male population. When I suggested in my play *Savage Wilds* that the former black mayor of Washington had been singled out for his cocaine use because cocaine was the recreational drug of Washington's political and media elite, I was called "paranoid" by Elizabeth Kastor of *The Washington Post*. Now that a number of prominent white politicians have admitted, even boasted, about their cocaine use, including two candidates for New York district attorney in the 2009 race, perhaps my diagnosis by the *Post*'s reporter was premature. On October 22, Steve Kastenbaum reported on CNN that it was "no secret that cocaine was rampant on Wall Street during the 1970s and 80s," yet a member of their CNN panel of experts, William Bennett, then Drug Czar, presented drug use as primarily a black problem, which is how CNN treated it and continues treating it. White teenagers and middle class whites being admitted to emergency rooms and overdosing on cocaine are one or two-day stories relegated to a few columns in the rear of the newspaper, while the identities of black juveniles are often exposed on television whereas those of white juveniles are pixeled out. Here again, the double standard by which the criminal justice system judges white and black crime was exposed. Most incarcerated blacks are there because of non-violent drug crimes and some are doing long terms as a result of New York State's Draconian Rockefeller drug laws.

Though, traditionally, Nigger Breakers have been white, with immigration, other groups have joined them. An example is the Mexican-American gangs who were recently busted for attempting to expel African Americans from a public housing project in Los Angeles.

And not all Nigger Breakers are thugs. Dinesh D'Souza came to prominence as one of former Treasury Secretary William Simon's counter policy wonks. Simon believed that the public debate had been overrun by radicals and that it needed to be balanced by conservative voices. D'Souza was aligned with the right-wing *The Dartmouth Review*, which reveled in sophomoric racist hi-jinks with D'Souza often joining in, nothing original, just the old racist shenanigans like mocking the black dialect.

Both he and Simon were embarrassed about defending *The Dartmouth Review* when a former president of Dartmouth, American Book Awards winner James O. Freedman, leveled charges of anti-Semitism at it. Turned out that the *Review* was guilty. After the publication of his book *The End of Racism*, which was endorsed by The American Enterprise Institute, a far-right think tank that is awarded a hefty amount of airtime by cable, two black conservatives quit the institute, one calling him the Mark Fuhrman of public policy. Mark Fuhrman was the Los Angeles policeman whose racist views were exposed during the O.J. Simpson case.

D'Souza's attacks on blacks were often silly and offensive but when he wrote a book accusing some white people of treason, some of those who had praised him greeted the book with ridicule. He'd forgotten his original assignment. Like many of those who've received good money to fault blacks for society's woes, the Jewish commentators who are silent about the abuse of Jewish women here and abroad (On October 14, 2009, *The New York Times* ran a story about child abuse in the Orthodox community: said that it had been covered up), Dinesh D' Souza has ignored the problems of those who share his ethnic background, for example, the million child prostitutes who walk the streets of Mumbai, the city of his birth. No money in it? His book, *The End Of Racism* is a blown-up scissors and paste job that is based on the idea that affirmative action is a black program, a false premise, and that blacks are at the bottom of the genetic tree, Asians and whites at the top branches, Hispanics in the middle, millions of whom are blacks, a fact about which he seems to be ignorant. And, oh yeah, there is no African Shakespeare. Well, people all over the world have story-telling traditions which include all of the techniques one associates with this art—metaphors, similes, irony, etc.—and if Dinesh wasn't so bound to the idea that a superficial knowledge of a handful of European traditions makes one smart and if he were the least bit adventuresome, he might enjoy some of it. African stories were transmitted to this hemisphere, including forms that are ancestors of such popular styles as Hip Hop. I find these stories more interesting than the work of Saul Bellow.

Of course, without the Muslims, major parts of the European traditions might have been lost, including the novel. I once thought that there was such a thing as "Eurocentrism" until I traveled to Europe (West Asia) and found things to be more complicated than what D'Souza and his hero Allan Bloom make it out to be. (Bloom's knowledge of "the ancients" was challenged by a real Greek Scholar, Martha Nussbaum, and Bloom himself was involved in a scandal involving blacks toward the end of his life. Regardless of his reckless moral behavior, exposed by his friend, Saul Bellow, in his novel *Ravelstein*, Gertrude Himmelfarb, a member of neocon America's first family, while critical of black morals, defended Bloom.)

The intellectual mercenary and Nigger Breaker like D' Souza presents a greater danger to minorities than the street thugs who commit hate crimes. Minorities have little capability to counter the propaganda and smears that emanate from think tanks and the media, and even academia. With the firing and buyouts of minority journalists, their access to the media has been diminished even more. Unlike the hoodlums who write swastikas on the doors of synagogues or the ruffians, usually young white males, who bash gays, kill Hispanics and are acquitted by white juries with nothing like the continuing outrage that accompanied the acquittal of O.J. Simpson, the ideas of Dinesh D' Souza and Charles Murray, author of *The Bell Curve*, influence public policy. Murray is another example of a writer who redirects stereotypes from his group, in this case the Scots Irish, to blacks. When Vice President Cheney got into trouble for his joke about having Cheneys on both sides of the family and not even being from West Virginia, he was referring to the incest libel that's been aimed at the Scots Irish. Sponsors of Murray, D'Souza and John McWhorter, front man for the eugenics-minded Manhattan Institute, are funded by, in some cases, billionaires, like William Scaife, the Pittsburgh billionaire who is helping to fund the "grass roots" tea-bagger spectacle, and along with the media, which have billions at their disposal, have formed the main opposition to President Obama. During August 2009, the power of these money people, who have been able to buy opinion, reached an influence way beyond the dreams of William Simon. They were able to design faux grass roots organizations and demonstrations using insurance industry-backed front organizations like Freedom Works and Americans for Prosperity.

Blacks have chosen many ways to fight back against the Nigger Breakers. From using the machete against whole families in Haiti or murdering a whole bunch of people like Nat Turner and his associates to using subtler ways. Barack Obama uses wit, wile and irony to embarrass the low-grade mentality of the 9/12 demonstrators, the tea baggers whose numbers have been magnified by 24/7 cable news because people yelling and screaming makes exciting television. Right-wing commentators at Fox gave those who rudely interrupted congresspersons at town halls during August of 2009 more strength than their actual numbers, and MSNBC, which is falsely cast as Fox's liberal opposition, awarded them more exposure by denouncing the demonstrations. On October 14, when a spokesperson for tea-party demonstrators said that over a million people turned out to demonstrate against the polices of the Obama administration, he wasn't challenged by Chris Matthews on whose show he appeared. The actual number was sixty thousand. While the media exaggerate the numbers of those who believe that the president was born in Kenya, Southerners mostly—while President Obama receives high favorability ratings in the rest of the country, his favorability percentage in the South is twenty-eight percent—the left has always protested the media's tendency to undercount the numbers of their demonstrations, which have, in the case of the many anti-war demonstrations, drawn hundreds of thousands. While individual gun toters and deathers were interviewed on cable, rarely did one see someone as far left as these demonstrators are far right. Indeed, demonstrators who picketed insurance companies, whose opposition to a public option has created a situation where, according to a Harvard study, forty-five thousand Americans die each year because of a lack of coverage, have been ignored.

Some of the fiercest and most hostile and racist trash has been aimed at the young president, and not only by the usual suspects, those who view the president as a monkey, a witch doctor with a bone in his nose (an image created by neurosurgeon and Fox "expert" David McKalip), and someone who would paint the White House black, or use the White House lawn to grow watermelons, but also by prominent members of the Republican Party including Sarah Palin, who was the candidate who called the president, who is a centrist, a socialist, and was the person who referred to the health plan advocated by the White House as one that would include death panels.

So desperate are the cable networks for niche-market viewers that Sarah Palin is treated as a serious person even though her demagoguery increased the threats to the president's life, and her support among the public is twenty-eight percent, a fact that seemed to have been ignored by prominent supporters of Mrs. Palin like Tina Brown and Mika Brzezinski. Sarah Palin was the designated Nigger Breaker of the McCain campaign. But as I point out in this book, during his campaign and during these months of his presidency Obama has had to maneuver through a gauntlet of Nigger Breakers—right, left, Republican and Democratic— who used the repertory of ancient stereotypes about black people against the president.

While ex-President Bush could always rely on the support of Fox and other right-wing commentators, Obama is getting it from both sides, some of his harshest criticism coming from the left, indeed the first attempt to break him came from his own party. In a manner similar to how Mary Matalin's author, swift-boater Jerome Corsi, sought to portray Barack Obama, Mrs. Clinton's campaign manager, Mark Penn, sought to portray him as a drug user and possibly a drug dealer. After the campaign, the Clinton strategy of depicting Obama as different as the *Other*, and even a possible secret Muslim, was exposed. When asked about Obama's Muslim heritage during the campaign, Mrs. Clinton equivocated.

The McCain campaign dredged up the strategy that was used successfully against Michael Dukakis and Harold Ford, that of showing Obama as a threat to white women and white children. The New Jersey Republican Party even tried to tie him to O.J. Simpson. Not only did Obama become the forty-fifth president of the United States, but also the national psychiatrist or someone like Jesus expelling the demons from the mad man he had encountered at Gardarenes. It was as though some of his opponents were like some mentally disturbed person writing his sentiments on the walls of a padded cell with his feces.

As usual the corporate media was the mob leader. For the media, Obama can't win for losing and often the right wing sets the agenda for the mainstream media.

Take the response to Barack Obama winning the Nobel Peace Prize. *Media Matters* wrote:

> The volume emanating from the right quickly impacted more mainstream reporters. *Time*'s Simon Robinson penned an online piece explaining how the award could prove politically harmful to the president, and Nancy Gibbs wrote a widely circulated article for *Time* as well, this one explaining why the Nobel was "the last thing [Obama] needs." She's right... we all know the Nobel Prize is something that should be avoided, you know, like cancer. Sigh.

> It wasn't long before the calls started for Obama to turn down the award, from a variety of sources. Malkin, CBS' Chip Reid, *Time*'s Mark Halperin, John Bolton, *Slate.com*'s Mickey Kaus, *The Weekly Standard*'s Mary Katherine Ham, and *The Atlantic*'s Jeffery Goldberg all echoed the theme, among others.

Can Nigger Breakers be black? I would consider right-wing blacks, who continue to be brought on by cable producers who choose black and Hispanic panelists, those least likely to offend their white audience, solely to defame Obama during his campaign and during his presidency, to be Nigger Breakers, especially those from Rev. Moon's newspaper, *The Washington Times*, and Barack Obama became a Nigger Breaker himself when he singled out black men in the United States and Africa for scolding.

He was admired for his placing race in the background. The exception was when he criticized Rev. Wright, black fathers, African leaders and Henry Louis Gates, Jr. and Kanye West whom he called a jackass. He was applauded even by his critics for that one but when he said that the Boston police acted "stupidly" in the arrest of Harvard professor Henry Louis Gates, Jr., he was met with a national uproar and had to modify his remarks.

(When appearing before a conference of policemen, the officer who violated Gates' rights and lied on his report about the arrest was greeted with a standing ovation. The entire Gates episode was a blow to those who adhere to the fantasy of a post-race United States.)

The purpose of the corporate media, which serve as a sort of home base for the Nigger Breaking operation against Obama, regardless of the opinions of Don Imus Alumni Howard Kurtz and others who pretend that Obama has the media in his pocket, seems to be that of positing a right-of-center United States, while the public that elected a president who campaigned as a liberal and the poll numbers, that shows continued support for the president, presents a left-of-center country. Yet on a Sunday's *This Week*, a Republican operative Nicolle Wallace was unopposed when she talked about Obama's declining poll numbers. His poll numbers had decreased as a result of network television broadcasting attention-grabbing antics of the tea baggers, but on the date of the actual broadcast of ABC's *This Week*, his poll numbers had rebounded to fifty-six percent. During the fourth week in November, Gallup and Public Policy released polls that offered a break down of Obama's poll numbers along racial lines. While Public Policy found his support among whites to have fallen to forty-two percent, he still maintained high numbers among Hispanics and blacks, sixty-seven percent among Hispanics and seventy-seven percent among blacks. Gallup found seventy-three percent support among non-whites, their term, ninety-one percent and seventy percent among Hispanics. The Hispanics and blacks whom the Jim Crow media bring on camera to diss Obama don't reflect these numbers. (Richard Prince of the Maynard Institute writes: "According to

Election Day exit polls, whites preferred McCain to Obama fifty-five percent to forty-three percent. In exit polls dating to 1972, Democrats have never carried a majority of the white vote.") What the discussion left out was the media's role in Obama's declining numbers by exaggerating the strength of the far-right demonstrators and even assisting them. A Fox News reporter was spotted at the 9/12 demonstration egging on the demonstrators (some of whom, when interviewed by Max Blumenthal, didn't seem to know why they had come to Washington in the first place.)

In October, Fox's John Stossel actually appeared before audiences where he opposed what his sponsor, Americans for Prosperity, called a government insurance plan. *The New York Times'* Charles Blow wrote:

> This was conservatives' seething summer of discontent and unhinged hysteria: town halls, tea parties and tirades. They captured headlines and gained momentum. Misinformation ran amuck. President Obama's approval ratings tumbled. Through it all, Obama maintained a Pollyannaish, laissez-faire disposition. Some found this worrisome. Others, like me, even thought it weak. But maybe not so fast.

> According to Gallup poll results released on Wednesday, the president's approval rating has stopped falling and has leveled out in the low-50 percents, about the same as Ronald Reagan's and Bill Clinton's at this point in their presidencies (both two-termers, lest we forget).

An example of how the media have presented a few loud demonstrators to represent the thinking of the public occurred on October 13. After a conservative health bill passed a Senate committee, CNN's Tom Foreman used footage of the same tea baggers rudely interrupting congresspersons to announce that the public was against the legislation. This was the theme of the cable shows and even Sunday talk shows that feign seriousness. On this issue and others the wealthy individuals who lurk behind the talk show screamers and who obey a gentleman's agreement not to criticize each other, use their ownership of the airwaves to construct a false reality. They got us coming and going. Not only do they own the media, but finance the think tank "policy analysts" who are frequent guests on their shows. This is why Obama continues to be judged by all-white panels on CNN's *State of the Union*, ABC's *This Week*, C-Span's *The Washington Journal*, which provides a service by exposing the abysmal ignorance of some Americans each day, *Fox News Sunday*, NBC's *Meet The Press* and CBS's *Face The Nation*. Given the dearth of those who share the background of those constituencies that voted overwhelmingly for Obama, blacks, Asian Americans, Hispanic Americans, Native Americans and others, President Obama will continue to be judged by an all-white, mostly male, middle-aged jury, some of whom like Alex Castellanos, have designed racist campaigns and others like Mary Matalin who have shepherded scurrilous swift-boat styled propaganda campaigns against the president, and David Gregory, who defended Don Imus's racist outbursts until the very end. On the morning of November 8, 2009, after the House passed a health bill that included a public option, after pundits of the left predicted that it wouldn't up until the night before it passed, David Brooks, one of the most powerful of the country's pundits, with a column in *The New York Times*, was brought on to Imus-defender David Gregory's show, *Meet The Press*, to criticize the president on an all-white (one woman) panel. David Brooks is a neo-con who backed the invasion of Iraq, a multi-trillion-dollar calamity, yet complains about the president's fiscal policies. He says his mentor is the late Irving Kristol and wrote that Bush won in 2004 because he carried states with high "white fertility rates" those who wanted to escape "vulgarity."

How did the public feel about those who shouted down the proponents of health care legislation at the town meetings and who were boosted by the Infotainment media?

> Most Americans say the tone of the debate has been negative. According to the latest weekly News Interest Index survey, conducted September 11-14 among 1,003 adults by the Pew Research Center for the People & the Press, 53 percent say the tone of the debate over health care has been generally rude and disrespectful; 31 percent say it has been generally polite and respectful and 16 percent do not offer an opinion. Among those who say the debate has been rude and disrespectful, most believe that opponents of the health care legislation under consideration are to blame. By a 59 percent to 17 percent margin, more blame opponents than supporters of the legislation; 17 percent volunteer that both groups are to blame. (Pew Research Center, 16 September 2009)

The Huffington Post discovered that one of CNN's panel regulars was in the insurance business. Alex Castellanos, a right-wing Cuban

American. This is the same man who designed the ad showing a black hand taking a job from a white hand, an anti-affirmative action ad, which led to the defeat of a black senatorial candidate, yet CNN uses him to comment on the actions of a black president. If that were not enough, in October it was revealed that Castellanos' firm actually created ads on behalf of the insurance industry that was spending over three hundred million dollars, according to London's *Guardian*, to defeat the public option.

> Alex Castellanos is a regular CNN contributor, but one of Castellanos' secret identities is being the media buyer for one of the ad campaigns bankrolled by America's Health Insurance Plans, a major industry trade group fighting strenuously against health care reform. Castellanos was responsible for placing more than $1 million of AHIP advertising in five states.

CNN said that they didn't know about his ties to the insurance industry.

With the exception of MSNBC's Rachel Maddow, very rarely did the cable networks mention that the insurance industry spent millions to stage these demonstrations. *The Guardian* put the amount at over three hundred fifty million dollars.

> The industry and interest groups have spent $380m (£238m) in recent months influencing healthcare legislation through lobbying, advertising and in direct political contributions to members of Congress. The largest contribution, totaling close to $1.5m, has gone to the chairman of the senate committee drafting the new law.

Barack Obama made a speech in Africa, criticizing African governments for taking bribes. Over here, we call them "campaign contributions."

If cable had been around during the Eisenhower administration, leaders of fringe groups like the John Birch Society would have been given equal time with administration officials. Joe McCarthy would have been designated as the Republican Party's leader. Next to Joe Wilson, McCarthy was eloquent. All Wilson had to do for cable to grant him prominence was to call the president a liar during the president's speech to Congress, which was like taking a piss in public.

The dilemma faced by black intellectuals like me who are sometimes critical of Obama is similar to that faced by some Israeli intellectuals whom I met during my second trip to Israel. Though they found Ariel Sharon's policies abhorrent—given the opposition to the former prime minister by outsiders—they found themselves supporting the odious prime minster.

When blacks see people showing up at Obama rallies with guns and the ugly racist signs aimed at the president; when they are informed of "The Obama Effect," a phrase for the unprecedented arming of whites throughout the nation, and when they are assaulted by a media for which the president can't win for losing—a sort of electronic white-power government in exile—a Republican Party and other assorted Nigger Breakers, who have raised the vilest and most salacious attacks on the president since that directed at Abraham Lincoln by the Confederate media, they find themselves rallying behind one of their own.

Ma and Pa Clinton
Flog Uppity Black Man[*]

(Black public intellectuals and politicians accused the Clinton campaign of using racist tactics against Barack Obama. The Clintons denied the accusation and the media backed them up. But after the campaign, a report about the Clinton strategy was published and it showed that the aim of the campaign was to paint Obama as different. As someone who was not like us. Mark Penn's campaign memo of March 19, 2007 was printed in the August 11, 2008 issue of *The Atlantic*:

> More than anything else, this memo captures the full essence of Mark Penn's campaign strategy—its brilliance and its breathtaking attacks. Penn identified with impressive specificity the very coalition of women and blue-collar workers that Clinton ended up winning a year later. But he also called Obama "unelectable except perhaps against Attila the Hun," and wrote, "I cannot imagine America electing a president during a time of war who is not at his center fundamentally American in his thinking and in his values." Penn proposed targeting Obama's "lack of American roots."

Their effort to break Obama failed, but Clinton supporters' insistence upon painting Clinton as a martyr or someone who was cheated out of the nomination led to the rise of Sarah Palin.)

---

[*] A version of this essay was first published at *Counterpunch.org*, January 14, 2008.

During Bill Clinton's first run for president, I appeared on a New York radio panel with some of his black supporters, including Paul Robeson, Jr., son of the actor and singer. I said that Clinton had character problems. They dismissed my comments and said that I didn't know anything about politics and should stick to writing novels. (Clarence Page, who has a monopoly on the few column inches and airtime made available to black columnists by the corporate media, said the same thing about me. I should stick to creative writing and leave politics alone.)

These criticisms didn't deter me. Writing in *The Baltimore Sun*, I was the first to identify Clinton as a black president as a result of his mimicking a black style. (I said he was the second, since Warren G. Harding never denied the rumors about his black ancestry.) As a result of his ability to imitate the black preaching style, Clinton was able to seduce black audiences, who ignored some of his actions that were unfriendly, even hostile to blacks. His interrupting his campaign to get a mentally disabled black man, Ricky Ray Rector executed. (Did Mrs. Clinton tear up about this act?) His humiliation of Jesse Jackson. His humiliation of Jocelyn Elders and Lani Guinier. The welfare reform bill that has left thousands of women black, white, yellow and brown destitute, prompted Robert Scheer to write in the *San Francisco Chronicle*, "To his everlasting shame as president, Clinton supported and signed welfare legislation that shredded the federal safety net for the poor from which he personally had benefited." (Has Mrs. Clinton shed a tear for these women, or did she oppose her husband's endorsement of this legislation?) His administration saw a high rate of black incarceration as a result of Draconian drug laws that occurred during his regime. He advocated trade agreements that sent thousands of jobs overseas. (Did Mrs. Clinton, with misty eyes, beg him to assess how such trade deals would affect the livelihood of thousands of families, black, white, brown, red and yellow?) He refused to intervene to rescue thousands of Rwandans from genocide. (Did

Mrs. Clinton tearfully beseech her husband to intervene on behalf of her African sisters; did Ms. Gloria Steinem, whose word is so influential among millions of white women that she can be credited by some for changing the outcome of a primary, and maybe an election, marshal these forces to place pressure upon Congress to rescue these black women and girls?) President Clinton also repealed the Glass-Steagall Act, which permitted the kind of wildcat speculation that has led to millions of Americans losing billions in equity.

Carl Bernstein, appearing on Air America Radio on January 9, 2008, described Clinton's New Hampshire attacks on Obama as "petulant." Bill Clinton's behavior demonstrated that regardless of his admiration for jazz, and black preaching, he and his spouse will go South on a black man whom they perceive as being audacious enough to sass Mrs. Clinton. In this respect, he falls in the tradition of the southern demagogue: grinning with and sharing pot likker and cornbread with black folks, while signifying about them before whites. Though his role models are Martin Luther King, Jr. and John F. Kennedy, he has more in common with Georgia's Eugene Talmadge (*The Wild Man From Sugar Creek*), Louisiana's Huey Long, and his brother Earl, Edwin Edwards, who even hinted that he had black ancestry to gain black votes, Alabama's George Wallace, Texas's Pa Fergusor., and "Kissing Jim" Folsom, who wrote, *You Are My Sunshine*. He employs the colorful rhetoric of the southern demagogue, the rustic homilies ("till the last dog dies"), the whiff of corruption.

Having been educated at elite schools where studying the War of the Roses was more important than studying Reconstruction, the under-educated white male punditry and their token white women failed to detect the racial code phrases that both Clintons and their surrogates sent out—codes that, judging from their responses, infuriated blacks, caught immediately. Blacks have been deciphering these hidden messages for four hundred years. They had to in order to survive.

Gloria Steinem perhaps attended the same schools. Her remark that black men received the vote "fifty years before women," in a *New York Times* Op-Ed (January 8, 2008), which some say contributed to Obama's defeat in New Hampshire, ignores the fact that black men were met by white terrorism, including massacres, and economic retaliation when attempting to exercise the franchise. She and her followers, who've spent thousands of hours in graduate school, must have gotten all of their information about Reconstruction from *Gone With The Wind*, where moviegoers are asked to sympathize with a proto-feminist, Scarlett O'Hara, who finally has to fend for herself after years of being doted upon by the unpaid household help. Booker T. Washington, an educator born into slavery, said that young white people had been waited on so that after the war they didn't know how to take care of themselves, and Mary Chesnutt, author of *The Civil War Diaries*, and a friend of Confederate president Jefferson Davis's family, said that upper class Southern white women were so slave dependent that they were "indolent." Steinem and her followers should read, *Redemption, The Last Battle Of The Civil War*, by Nicholas Lemann, which tells the story about how "in 1875, an army of white terrorists in Mississippi led a campaign to 'redeem' their state— to abolish with violence and murder if need be, the newly won civil rights of freed slaves and blacks." Such violence and intimidation was practiced all over the South sometimes resulting in massacres. One of the worst massacres of black men occurred at Colfax, Louisiana, in 1873. Their crime? Attempting to exercise the voting rights awarded to them "fifty years" before white women received theirs. Lemann writes "burning Negroes" met "savage and hellish butchery."

> They were all killed, unarmed, at close range, while begging for mercy. Those who tried to escape, were overtaken, mustered in crowds, made to stand around, and, while in every attitude of humiliation and supplication, were shot down and their bodies mangled and hacked to hasten their death or to satiate the hellish malice of their heartless murderers, even after they were dead.

White posses on horseback rode away from the town, looking for Negroes who had fled, so they could kill them.

Elsewhere in the South, during the Confederate Restoration, black politicians, who were given the right to vote "fifty years before white women," were removed from office by force, many through violence. In Wilmington, North Carolina, black men, who "received the vote fifty years before white women," are the subject of Charles Chesnutt's great novel, *The Marrow of Tradition*:

On Thursday, November 10, 1898, Colonel Alfred Moore Waddell, a Democratic leader in Wilmington, North Carolina mustered a white mob to retaliate for a controversial editorial written by Alexander Manly, editor of the city's black newspaper, the *Daily Record*. The mob burned the newspaper's office and incited a bloody race riot in the city. By the end of the week, at least fourteen black citizens were dead, and much of the city's black leadership had been banished. This massacre further fueled an ongoing statewide disfranchisement campaign designed to crush black political power. Contemporary white chronicles of the event, such as those printed in the *Raleigh News and Observer* and Wilmington's the *Morning Star*, either blamed the African-American community for the violence or justified white actions as necessary to keep the peace. African-American writers produced their own accounts—including fictional examinations—that countered these white supremacist claims and highlighted the heroic struggles of the black community against racist injustice.

Black congressmen, who, as a rule, were better educated than their white colleagues were expelled from Congress.

Either Gloria Steinem hasn't done her homework or, as an ideologue, rejects evidence that's a Google away, and the patriarchal corporate old media, which has appointed her the spokesperson for feminism, permits her ignorance to run rampant over the emails and blogs of the nation and though this white Oprah might have inspired her followers to march lockstep behind her, a progressive like Cindy Sheehan wasn't convinced. She called Mrs. Clinton's crying act, "phony."

Moreover, some of the suffragettes that she and her followers hail as feminist pioneers were racists. Some even endorsed the lynching of black men. In an early clash between a black and white feminist, anti-lynching crusader Ida B. Wells opposed the views of Frances Willard, a suffragette pioneer, who advocated lynching.

As the president of one of America's foremost social reform organizations, Frances Willard called for the protection of the purity of white womanhood from threats to morality and safety. In her attempts to bring Southern women into the Woman's Christian Temperance Union, Frances Willard accepted the rape myth and publicly condoned lynching and the color line in the South. Wells argued that as a Christian reformer, Willard should be speaking out against lynching, but instead seemed to support the position of Southerners.

Ms. Willard's point of view is echoed by Susan Brownmiller's implying that Emmett Till got what he deserved, and the rush to judgment on
the part of New York feminists whose pressure helped to convict the black
and Hispanic kids accused of raping a stockbroker in Central Park. After
DNA proved their innocence—the police promised them if they confessed, they could go home—a *Village Voice* reporter asked the response
of these feminists to this news; only Susan Brownmiller responded.
She said that regardless of the scientific evidence, she still believed that
the children, who spent their youth in jail on the basis of the hysteria
generated by Donald Trump, the press, and leading New York feminists,
were guilty.

Feminist hero, Elizabeth Cady Stanton, offended Frederick Douglass—
an abolitionist woman attempted to prevent his daughter from gaining
entrance to a girls' school—when she referred to black men as "sambos."
She was an unabashed white supremacist. She said in 1867, "[w]ith the
black man we have no new element in government, but with the education and elevation of women, we have a power that is to develop the Saxon
race into a higher and nobler life."

Steinem should read *Race, Rape, and Lynching* by Sandra Gunning,
and Angela Davis's excellent *Women, Culture, & Politics*, which includes
a probing examination of racism in the suffragette movement. The *Times*
allowed only one black feminist to weigh in on Ms. Steinem's comments
about Barack Obama, and how he appealed to white men because they
perceive black males as more "masculine" than they, an offensive stereotype, and one that insults the intelligence of white men, and a comment
which, with hope, doesn't reflect the depth of "progressive" women's
thought.

Do you think that the *Times* would offer Steinem critics like Toni
Morrison Op-Ed space to rebut her? Don't count on it. The criticism of
white feminism by black women has been repressed for over one hundred
years (See: *Black Women Abolitionists, A Study In Activism, 1828-1860*, by
Shirley J. Yee).

I asked Jill Nelson, author of *Finding Martha's Vineyard, Volunteer
Slavery* and *Sexual Healing*, how she felt about Gloria Steinem's use of a
hypothetical black woman to make a point against Obama. She wrote:

I was offended and frankly, surprised, by Gloria Steinem's use of a hypothetical Black woman in her essay supporting Hillary Clinton. I would have liked to think that after all these years struggling in the feminist vineyards, Black women have become more than a hypothetical to be used when white women want to make a point, and a weak one at that, on our backs. It's a device, a distraction, and disingenuous, and fails to hold Hillary Clinton—or for that matter, Barack Obama and the rest of the (male) candidates—responsible for their politics.

On the second day of a convention held at Seneca Falls in 1848, white suffragettes sought to prevent black abolitionist Sojourner Truth from speaking. The scene was described by Frances Dana Gage in Ms. Davis's book:

> "Don't let her speak!" gasped half a dozen in my ear. She moved slowly and solemnly to the front, laid her old bonnet at her feet, and turned her great speaking eyes to me. There was a hissing sound of disapprobation above and below. I rose and announced "Sojourner Truth," and begged the audience to keep silence for a few moments.

Many minority feminists, Asian-American, Hispanic, Native-American and African-American, contend that white middle and upper class feminists' insensitivity to the views and issues deemed important to them persists to this day.

Their proof might be Ms. Steinem's lack of concern about how Mrs. Clinton's war votes affect the lives of thousands of women and girls—her brown sisters—in Iraq and Iran. One hundred and fifty thousand Iraqi people have been killed since the American occupation was ordered by patriarchs in Washington, DC, patriarchs who were responsible for the Welfare Reform Act.

With this in mind, I recently asked Robin Morgan, who was editor of Ms. magazine, where I was called the worst misogynist in America, whether she still held those views. I replied to that accusation that I should be accorded the same respect given to the men who ran the magazine at the time, Lang Communications. The accusation was made by Barbara Smith, a black feminist whom I debated on television and whose bitter comments about the white feminist movement make mine seem timid. She also criticizes the white gay and lesbian movements. She said that when she tried to join the gay and lesbian march on Washington, the leaders told her to get lost. That they weren't interested in black issues. That they wanted to mainstream. About me, she wrote in *The New Republic* magazine, edited by Marty Peretz, a man who once said that black women were "culturally deficient," that my black women characters weren't positive enough. For running afoul of this feminist "blueprint" for writing that she tried to lay on me, her views and those like hers were repudiated by Joyce Joyce, a black critic who deviates from the party line.

I also reminded Ms. Morgan that the *Ms.* editorial staff reflected the old plantation model, even though its founder, Gloria Steinem, said that she's concerned about the progress of black women. White feminists had the juicy editorial Big House positions, while women of color were the editorial kitchen help as contributing editors. A few months later, Ms. Morgan resigned as editor and was replaced by a black woman, but not before taking some potshots, not at misogynists belonging to her ethnic group, whose abuse of women has been a guarded secret according to feminists belonging to that group, but at Mike Tyson and Clarence Thomas (incidentally, when the white women who ran for office as a result of Ms. Anita Hill's testimony against Clarence Thomas arrived in Congress, they voted with the men).

Robin Morgan had her secretary respond to my recent letter and from the letter I gather that Ms. Morgan hasn't changed her mind. I'm a worse misogynist than the men in the Pentagon, and those who passed Clinton's welfare reform bill. I guess that bell hooks, another black feminist, who won't be invited by the men who run the *Times* to respond to Ms. Steinem, was right when she wrote in her book, *Outlaw Culture*, that white feminists are harder on black men than white men, but like other black feminists, from the nineteenth century to the present day, her point has been ignored by the mainstream media, who, when they view feminism, and just about every other subject, all they can see is white! (Except when it's crime, athletics, and having babies out of wedlock!)

Feminists are harder on Ishmael Reed, Ralph Ellison (yes, him too), and even James Baldwin, that gentle soul, than on Philip Roth and Saul Bellow. Harder on Barack Obama than on Bill Clinton, to whom Gloria Steinem, a harsh critic of Clarence Thomas, gave a free pass when he was charged with sexual indiscretions by various women. She said that Bubba was O.K. because when he placed Kathleen Wiley's hand on his penis and she said no, he withdrew it. That when other women said no, he also halted his sexual advances. A letter writer to the *Times* challenged Ms. Steinem's double standard for white and black men:

> Bob Herbert (column, January 29) writes that Gloria Steinem said that even though Paula Jones has filed a sexual harassment suit against President Clinton, Ms. Jones has not claimed that the president had forced himself on her. "He takes no for an answer," Ms. Steinem intones.
>
> Lest we forget, Anita Hill said no to Clarence Thomas. And her accusations nearly derailed his appointment to the Supreme Court.
>
> Patricia Schroeder, the former Congresswoman, did not claim that "somebody may be overstating the case" when Ms. Hill accused Judge Thomas of sexual misconduct, but Ms. Schroeder claims that now in Mr. Herbert's column. Again the left inadvertently exposes its sliding scale of moral indignation.
>
> RAYMOND BATZ
> San Rafael, California, January 29, 1998

Black feminists also charge that white feminists deserted them during the fight against Proposition 209, which ended racial and gender hiring in the state of California, even though affirmative action has benefited white women the most!

They charge that white women were missing in action during the fight against the welfare reform bill. It seems that the cheapest form of solidarity they can express toward their minority sisters is to join in on the attack on Mike Tyson, Kobe Bryant, and Clarence Thomas and Mr. _____, a character in *The Color Purple*, who, for them, represents all black men.

Though Steinem accuses men of being mean to Mrs. Clinton, she expressed no outrage about surrogate Bill Shaheen painting Obama as drug dealer, or the innuendo promoted by Senator Bob Kerrey. Senator Bob Kerrey, who, apparently having made up with the Clintons, was recruited to associate Obama with what the right refers to as "Islamo fascists."

He said, "His name is Barack Hussein Obama, and his father was a Muslim and his paternal grandmother is a Muslim." He added that Obama "spent a little bit of time in a secular madrassa."

You'd think that the New School of Social Research would have fired Kerrey when he admitted to committing atrocities in Vietnam. Now this.

All of these attacks must be what Hillary Clinton meant when she warned her opponents "now the fun begins."

One of the charges made by some black feminists is that white women middle-class movement figures embezzle their oppression. In *The New York Times*, Gloria Steinem's using a hypothetical black woman to do a house cleaning on Obama was what these women must have had in mind. (Philip Roth does the same thing; uses his black maid characters to denounce black history and black studies: "Missa Roth, dese Black Studies ain't doin' nothin' but worrying folks. Whew!") Her using a black woman as a prop must have annoyed Nobel Laureate Toni Morrison who made blistering comments about Ms. Steinem during an interview conducted by novelist Cecil Brown and carried in the University of Massachusetts *Review*, where Ms. Morrison made the harshest comments about Alice Walker's novel *The Color Purple* to date, even harsher than those made by black feminist Professor Trudier Harris, who, as a result of her essay, published in *African American Review*, faced such a hostile backlash from white feminist scholars that she stopped commenting about the novel, which has become a sacred text among white feminists, who are silent about how women are treated among their ethnic groups. Steinem said that had Obama been a black woman, he would not have made as much progress as a presidential candidate and added that white men would prefer voting for a black man over a white woman because they perceived black men as being more masculine than they.

I wrote a response to the *Times* on January 8, 2008:

Dear Times,

Even Dr. Phil would probably snicker at the level of pop psychology employed by Gloria Steinem to explain the attraction of many voters to Senator Barack Obama. For example, she believes that the preference for a black male candidate over a white woman by some white males is based upon their admiration for the black male's "masculine" superiority. "Masculine superiority?" All four of the current heavyweight champions are white as well as last year's MVPs of the NBA were white men.

Moreover, Ms. Steinem is a long time critic of black men as a group. She said that the book, *The Color Purple*, in which one black man commits incest, told "the truth" about black men, the kind of collective blame that's been used against her ethnic group since the time of the Romans.

I also made a reference to her abandonment of a tearful Shirley Chisholm's presidential candidacy after supporting it. If she's so concerned about the political fate of a black woman's presidential bid, why did she desert Ms. Chisholm in favor of the man?

She also said "Gender is probably the most restricting force in American life." The fact that when white women received the vote they experienced little of the violence that accompanied black men being awarded the right to vote, fifty years earlier, suggests that some groups, black men, black women, Hispanics, Asian Americans and American Indians, face more restrictions than white women, whose college enrollment is far higher even than that of white men. (Steinem said that women are never "front runners." How many white women senators are there? How many black?)

Cecil Brown, author of the bestselling *Hey, Dude Where's My Black Studies Department*, wrote:

> I grew up in North Carolina, where I often heard my mother and my aunts speak of the racism of white women against them. Their experience is that of millions of black women who were and are discriminated by white women.
>
> In the Bay Area, where I now live, a professor friend told me, recently, that a white female student told him that she found the use of the expression, "white woman" in his lectures offensive, and asked that he not use it.
>
> Like this student, Ms. Steinem avoids the phrase "white woman," because it historicizes their gender. While she lectures to us about black men, white men, and black women, she can only think of her white women as women.
>
> "It's time to take pride in breaking all the barriers," Ms. Steinem ends her remarks. We have to be able to say: "I'm supporting [Hillary] because she'll be a great president and because she is a woman." But do we dare say that we should support her because she is a white woman?

Our letters were not published, but one written by a black feminist exposed the divide between black and white feminists, one that is rarely aired since white feminists have more access to the media than black ones. White feminists, in their books, report, falsely, a solidarity between them and black women. Among letter writer Karin Kimbrough's comments:

> As a black woman and a feminist, I find it depressing to see Gloria Steinem set up this tired, false debate as to whether a black man or a white woman is more disadvantaged in national politics.

> She cites as evidence that "black men were given the vote a half-century before women of any race were allowed to mark a ballot." So what?

> My parents (who are Ms. Steinem's age) vividly recall racism in the Deep South, including barriers to voting as well as the barriers to many other supposedly granted rights like eating in restaurants, staying in hotels and using public facilities. These were all rights white women actively enjoyed.

Camille Paglia also weighed in:

> Hillary's disdain for masculinity fits right into the classic feminazi package, which is why Hillary acts on Gloria Steinem like catnip. Steinem's fawning, gaseous *New York Times* Op-Ed about her pal Hillary this week speaks volumes about the snobby clubbiness and reactionary sentimentality of the fossilized feminist establishment, which has blessedly fallen off the cultural map in the twenty-first century. History will judge Steinem and company very severely for their ethically obtuse indifference to the stream of working-class women and female subordinates whom Bill Clinton sexually harassed and abused, enabled by look-the-other-way and trash-the-victims Hillary.

An example of the problems that Barack faces as a result of there being few blacks having jobs in the old media occurred during an appearance by a white woman reporter on *The Washington Journal* (January 14, 2008). So pro-Hillary was this reporter, Beth Fouhy, that one woman called and said that she thought that this woman was a Hillary spokesperson, before noticing that she was from the Associated Press. Obviously the media have been infiltrated by Steinem's legions.

Scathing comments about the white feminist movement by black feminists are included in *The Feminist Memoir Project*, edited by Rachel Blau DuPlessis and Ann Snitow. *Times* person Maureen Dowd also challenged

Steinem, who is hard on black guys, but once confessed in the *Times* that she becomes embarrassed when a male of her ethnic group becomes involved in a scandal. Challenging Steinem's argument that "she is supporting Hillary [because] she had no 'masculinity to prove,'" Dowd wrote, "Empirically speaking, her masculinity is precisely what Hillary has been out to prove in her bid for the White House. What else was voting to enable W. to invade Iraq without even reading the National Intelligence Estimate and backing the White House's bellicosity on Iran but proving her masculinity."

Desperate, when the campaign moved into New Hampshire, the Clintons launched the brass knuckles attack on Obama that commentator William Bennett predicted would happen after Mrs. Clinton was upset in Iowa.

His voice shaking with rage, a livid Bill Clinton said that Obama's positions on the war in Iraq were "a fairy tale," and that nominating Obama was "a roll of the dice."

Writing in *The Washington Post* on January 13, 2008, Marjorie Valbrun, voiced the reaction of many blacks to Clinton's performance:

> If anyone needed any proof that the mean Clinton machine is alive and well in this campaign, all they had to do was watch Bill Clinton deliver his angry diatribe against Obama in New Hampshire last week just before the primary. His red-faced anger was clear and a little scary, too. It wasn't what he said but how he said it. His tone was contemptuous of his wife's main challenger, whom he described as a political neophyte who for some reason was being granted a honeymoon with the national media.

> This is the same Bill Clinton who took on Sister Souljah, a young and, at the time, controversial black rapper who made incendiary racial remarks after the Los Angeles race riots. Many people accused Clinton of using the rapper, and an appearance before Jesse Jackson's Rainbow Coalition, as an opportunity to distance himself from Jackson, the ultimate race man. The move helped reinforce his white moderate bona fides.

On January 13, when Tim Russert interrogated Mrs. Clinton as to whether the attacks on Obama by her, her husband, and her surrogates were racist, she filibustered and dismissed such concerns as the one made by Ms. Valbrun and other blacks in a patronizing manner. She falsely accused Obama of comparing himself with JFK and MLK. He didn't. He invoked their names to make a point about hope. How some hopes, considered false by cynics, can be fulfilled.

So offended by what he considered a black man getting "cocky" with his wife, Clinton blew his top. "Cocky" was the word that nuns-educated Bob Herbert used to admonish Obama. Herbert, one of three blacks whom the *Times* views as unlikely to alienate their readership, pointed to an exchange between Obama and Mrs. Clinton. When Mrs. Clinton, during a debate, commented that voters found Obama more "likeable" than Mrs. Clinton, Obama said that Mrs. Clinton was "likeable enough." Obama's reply prompted an Antebellum white man, Karl Rove, to refer to Obama as "a smarmy, prissy little guy taking a slap at her." He said that this exchange threw the primary victory to Mrs. Clinton. Notwithstanding the irony of Karl Rove referring to someone as "smarmy," if a reply as mild and innocuous as Obama's leads to his being flogged by Clinton and reprimanded by one of the Establishment's black tokens, Obama is going to be restricted in his ability to take on the political brawlers and hit persons aligned with Clinton, like Don Imus's buddy, James Carville, a man who sneers at people who live in trailer parks, and who practices a no-holds-barred political strategy.

Both CNN and Carl Bernstein said that Clinton, in the midst of giving this uppity black the required flogging—Clinton's a Jeffersonian and flogging blacks was Jefferson's idea of recreation—had misrepresented Barack's record. Also, those who commented about Hillary Clinton's tearful breakdown missed the commentary that accompanied this calculated attempt at seeming human and personal, which occurred, as Jesse Jackson, Jr. noted in *The Daily News*, when her advisors told her that she should appear to be more human. "Why didn't she cry for the victims of Katrina?" he added.

She said that she didn't want to see the country "go backwards," or "spin out of control," the kind of vision of black rule promoted by D.W. Griffith's *Birth of a Nation*, and neo-Confederate novelist Tom Wolfe's *A Man In Full*. (Unfortunately for Obama, this was during a week that saw post-election violence in Kenya, where Barack's father was born.) Hers was the kind of rhetoric that was used by the Confederates whose rule was restored by Andrew Johnson. Give the black man governing powers and no white woman will be safe. This was Mrs. Clinton's Willie Horton moment.

Bill Clinton's orchestrating his wife's being more personal was a brilliant stroke: one that might doom Obama's candidacy, but will doom the Democrats' chances to win the 2008 election as well. As a Southern demagogue, Bill Clinton calculated that no black man can compete with a white woman's tears, a left over from Old South thinking. Black men have been lynched as a result of the tears of white women. While Jesse Helms, another Southern demagogue, used a black man's hand in an ad that criticized affirmative action, feminist Bill Clinton, who exploited a young woman who held him in awe—and cost Al Gore an election—used his wife's tears, so desperate was he to achieve a third term and redeem his being impeached. But judging from angry black callers into C-Span's *The Washington Journal* the day after the New Hampshire primary and the following day, and from my own non-scientific survey, many blacks finally get it. That they have been snookered by the Clintons. One angry man said that blacks supported Clinton during his marital problems and this is what they get for it. Another man said that he was going to vote for McCain as a way of protesting the Clintons' treatment of Obama. On January 11, an irate black woman called in and said that she had been devoted to the Clintons since the 1990s, but after his attack on Obama, which she likened to "a knife in my chest," and which she described as "low down," she said that if Hillary were nominated, she'd either "vote Republican, or stay home." Calling into the *Journal* on January 13, a black woman from Ohio said that many of her friends were upset with the "subliminally racist" campaign against Obama that the Clintons were conducting. These callers expressed the disgust that thousands of blacks feel about the Clintons' dirty-tricks campaign against Obama, which included sending out mailers making false statements about his view about abortion, and deceptively attributing another mailer, critical of Obama, to John Edwards. This black backlash against the Clintons provides the Republican Party with a golden opportunity to recruit black voters for McCain, but I doubt whether they will seize upon it. After all, while Clinton might have an office in Harlem, McCain has a black daughter!

A black PhD caller said that he found blacks in a barbershop to be more prescient than he. They said that once whites entered the voting booth, they'd vote for the white candidate no matter what they said to the pollster. Some commentators recalled treatment that Harvey Gantt and Tom Bradley received. Pollsters considered both to be shoo-ins for senator from North Carolina and governor of California because whites misled pollsters about how they really intended to vote.

Later in the day of January 8, Larry Sabato of the University of Virginia, appearing on *The Chris Matthews Show*, commented about a previous segment during which Dee Dee Meyers and Pat Buchanan opposed Michael Eric Dyson's argument that white racism was a factor in Obama's New Hampshire defeat. He said, "I think its very naïve, given American history, to automatically dismiss the racial voting theory before it's investigated. There is some evidence that race is one of several factors involved in this upset." Chris Matthews, who, apparently, has taken a new look at racism in the United States, after the Imus debacle, and a couple of other white commentators, including NBC News Political Director, Chuck Todd, agreed with this sentiment that race was a factor. But most white commentators agreed with Pat Buchanan and Dee Dee Meyers, former Clinton press secretary, who said that the difference between the polling that showed Obama with a double digit lead and the actual outcome had nothing to with white voters telling pollsters one thing and voting the opposite. For people like Pat Buchanan, nothing has to do with race, unless he can use race to stir up votes in one of his campaigns.

Predictably, *The New York Times* also followed the line that the racial attitudes of whites had nothing to do with Obama's narrow defeat in New Hampshire, not surprising since the line of *The New York Times*, on the opinion page and elsewhere, is that we have entered a "post-race" period.

Such is the rage of blacks against the Clintons after Iowa and New Hampshire that if Hillary Clinton is nominated, she will not be elected president. Obama and his "Joshua" generation will inherit a party that has lost its way. This would be a new development for the progressive movement since, from the abolitionists to the progressive movements of the twentieth century, black progressives were the followers and not the leaders. When Frederick Douglass, Richard Wright and Ralph Ellison got out of line, the progressives replaced them with other more obedient black spokespersons. After he broke with his progressive sponsors, Richard Wright was assaulted (*The God That Failed* by Koestler, Silone, Wright, etc.).

An uninformed *Times* Op-Ed writer, a colored mind double, said that Obama had gotten farther toward the nomination than any other black. Not true. When Jesse Jackson won the Michigan primary, there was an eruption of panic among the party elite. Ben Wattenberg and others were brought in to smear Jackson with the charge of anti-Semitism and out of this emergency arose the white conservative wing of the party, the Democratic Leadership Council, whose founder, Al From, still brags about how he put black people in their place. Clinton was the Democratic Leadership Council's candidate for president.

The reason for the 1960s rift between the Black Power people and the New Left was because when the black nationalists arrived at Freedom Summer, the Northeastern liberals were giving orders, while the blacks were taking the risks. The black nationalists took control of the movement and dragged Stokely Carmichael, who was devoted to non-violence, kicking and screaming into their ranks, and into their philosophy of armed self-defense, according to Askia Toure, whom Mary King in her book, *Freedom Song*, accuses of purging the Northern liberals from the Student Nonviolent Coordinating Committee. The progressive white women left SNCC, but not before borrowing the SNCC manifesto and using it as their own, according to King. They changed the pronouns and this became the beginning of the modern feminist movement. The reason that much of the feminist movement's fire is aimed at the brothers is because some of these women went away mad (See *Going South* by Debra L. Schultz). Based upon Stokely Carmichael's remark that the position of women in SNCC was "prone," they accused the black men in SNCC of misogyny. According to black women, who were members of SNCC, the white feminists, led by Casey Hayden, took Carmichael's comments out of context. Their views about their clashes with white feminism are printed in *The Trouble Between Us* by Winifred Breines, a book ignored by Mark Leibovich, writing in *The New York Times* on January 13, 2008. He repeated the charge about Carmichael made by white feminists without asking black feminists what they thought. Typical of a member of the Old Media, which takes its cues from those whom the patriarchy has appointed to lead the movement.

If Cynthia McKinney is nominated for president by the Green Party, a test for corporate feminists like Gloria Steinem so concerned about the lack of opportunities for their black sisters, black voters will flock to McKinney by the thousands, which might tip the balance if the contest is close between Mrs. Clinton and her Republican opponent. Others will leave the line for president on the ballot blank. This rage against the Clintons will go unnoticed by the segregated old corporate media, which has more information about the landscape of Mars than trends in the black, Asian-American and Hispanic communities. They rely upon their handful of colored mind doubles who tell them what they want to hear. Modern day Indian scouts. When they're not available, all-white panels instruct each other about who is a racist and who is not, how black people feel, how they are going to vote, continuing what some blacks regard as the white intellectual occupation of the black experience, an attitude that dates all the way back to a letter written by Martin Delaney to Frederick Douglass in 1863, in which he complained about the favorable treatment Douglass gave to Harriet Beecher Stowe's book *Uncle Tom's Cabin*, while ignoring his *Blake or the Huts of America* (1859-1862). "She can not speak for us," he wrote.

Clinton will still receive some support from some black Democratic loyalists, and celebrities although some of them are beginning to distance themselves from the couple after the Iowa and New Hampshire smears against Obama, but a large number of black people, who helped elect Clinton, twice, will defect.

Representative James E. Clyburn, a black congressman from South Carolina, told *The New York Times* (January 11, 2008) that "he may abandon his neutral stance in his state's primary, based in part on comments by Senator Hillary Rodman Clinton about President Lyndon B. Johnson and the Rev. Dr. Martin Luther King, Jr." He and other blacks interpreted Hillary Clinton's remark about the two as implying that Johnson did more for the cause of civil rights than King, who, like Obama, made great speeches.

Also one wonders whether Henry Louis Gates, Jr., media-appointed leader of the Talented Tenth (a phrase that W.E.B. DuBois used to appoint the black elite as the true leaders of the Negro masses, an insult to grassroots leaders like Fannie Lou Hamer), will follow suit. While smearing a number of black male writers as misogynists, in the *Times* and elsewhere, when Bill Clinton was caught with his pants down, Gates, Jr. said we will "go to the wall for this president."

Are the Clintons new in a South where husbands like George Wallace extended their power by getting their wives elected? Hardly. Take the Fergusons.

In Texas there was a couple called the Fergusons, affectionately called "Ma and Pa Ferguson."

Miriam Ferguson was a quiet, private person who preferred to stay home in her big house in Temple, Texas, and take care of her husband, raise her two daughters, and tend to her flower garden.

But in 1923 she was elected governor of Texas, the first woman governor elected in the United States.

Her husband, Jim Ferguson, served two terms as governor, but during his second term he was impeached, which meant he could not run again for public office. So Miriam agreed to run to clear his name and restore the family's honor.

She served two terms as governor: from 1925 to 1927 and from 1933 to 1935. She and her husband became known as "Ma and Pa Ferguson." Her campaign slogan was, "Two Governors for the Price of One."

Remind you of anyone?

The Crazy Rev. Wright[*]

(The Media and the Clinton campaign sought to break candidate Obama by associating him with Rev. Jeremiah Wright. Predictably, Wright's complex theology was reduced to an inflammatory sound bite. So effective was this campaign that Obama had to make a speech denouncing Rev. Wright. Largely ignored by the media were the ties of John McCain, Sarah Palin, and Mrs. Clinton herself to ministers who were authors of controversial comments.)

[*] A version of this essay was first published at Counterpunch.org, March 24, 2008.

Nothing is more uplifting than watching MSNBC's *Morning Joe*, where wealthy Anglicized Irish Americans like Joe Scarborough, Chris Matthews, Tim "Little Russ" Russert and Pat Buchanan hold forth on the topic of race. During the week beginning March 17, 2008, the talk was all about whether Barack Obama should distance himself from Rev. Jeremiah Wright. Presumably in the same manner that they distanced themselves from Don Imus.

Buchanan has been awarded more time to discuss race and the bigotry of Rev. Wright than the scores of black intellectuals and scholars, who could provide some insight. According to *U.S. News & World Report* (January 16, 1992), Pat Buchanan said in 1977 that Hitler was "a political organizer of the first rank," a man of "extraordinary gifts," "great courage" and elements of "genius." Yet there was his sister, Bay Buchanan, debating Roland Martin, one of a handful of token black commentators with any kind of bite. This was on CNN, March 21. She was in a tizzy about the Rev.'s anti-Americanism, yet Hitler, her brother's hero, was responsible for the deaths of one hundred and twenty thousand Americans.

Why doesn't Dan Abrams at MSNBC just go ahead and offer Minister Louis Farrakhan a commentary? Why aren't the Anti-Defamation League and the American Jewish Congress, so quick to pounce upon blacks who say silly anti-Semitic things, all over MSNBC for Buchanan's position as Dan Abram's resident authority on race.

Tim Russert, his colleague, was employed by the late Daniel Moynihan. Moynihan's report on the black family has guided public policy and been cited in hundreds of Op-Eds and editorials. Black intellectuals who opposed Moynihan's report have cited the fact that the majority of women on welfare at the time of the report were white women. In fact it was a Nazi, Tom Metzger, who told Larry King that the average welfare recipient was a white woman whose husband has left her, while neo-cons and black tough-lovers ignore this possibility. Isn't it ironic that one can gain a more accurate picture of welfare in this country from a Nazi than a neo-con? Most of those white welfare recipients were probably Celtic, members of Moynihan's tribe.

It was Daniel Moynihan who accused black women of "speciation," of reproducing mutants, the kind of thing that the Nazis used to say about their victims. Did Russert disown the senator after this remark? Some of those in the media who are now criticizing senator Obama's pastor are Irish Catholics. They dominate the panels on *Morning Joe*. (His token black guests are passive participants, grateful-to-be-on camera types.)

Have these panelists, who are so critical of Rev. Wright, disassociated themselves from a church that had to pay two billion dollars to people who've been sexually abused by priests? Both the last pope and the current one attempted to cover up the scandal. Would they fly to Rome to scold the pope, which is what they demanded of Obama who wasn't even present when Rev. Wright preached about 9/11? Have they had a one-on-one with their priests during which they criticized the church's cover-up of the epidemic of pedophilia infecting the church?

The classic indicator for racism has been the double standard applied to blacks and whites. This still exists for blacks in everyday life. In the criminal justice system, the mortgage lending industry, and the treatment of blacks by the medical industry, etc. Why is Rev. Wright crazy for citing racism in the criminal justice system? The infamous three strikes law where poor people might receive a life sentence for stealing a pizza pie? Even the Bush administration has documented racial profiling. MSNBC's Tucker Carlson flew into a rage when Marc Morial of the Urban League mentioned racial disparities in the criminal justice system. I sent Carlson documentation, including data from the Sentencing Project. He still probably denies it, and his misrepresentations go out unchallenged to millions of viewers. It's appropriate that he and his colleagues dance on variety shows. They're entertainers, not news people. Could you imagine Edward R. Murrow appearing on *Dancing With The Stars*?

When Rev. Wright talks about AIDS being an ethnic weapon, those critics who denounce him haven't examined the speculation that it might have originated in the Koprowski's polio vaccine experiment that was conducted out of Philadelphia. Those who embrace this theory might find some support in the book, *The River: A Journey Back to The Source of HIV and AIDS* by Edward Hooper (Penguin, 2000). A white man wrote this book.

I did a considerable amount of research for my recent off Broadway play, *Body Parts*, which was dismissed by *The New York Times* as "angry." I found that the pharmaceutical companies use Africans to test drugs that might have bad side effects without the knowledge of those being tested. *The Washington Post* did a series about this scandal. A series written by whites. They mention the Tuskegee experiments. According to Harriet Washington in her book *Medical Apartheid*, such experiments that date back to the days of slavery continue. Tuskegee was just the tip of the iceberg. *Medical Apartheid: The Dark History of Medical Experimentation on Black Americans from Colonial Times to the Present* was reviewed in *The Washington Post* on January 7, 2007 by Alondra Nelson under the title "Unequal Treatment: How African Americans have often been the unwitting victims of medical experiments." She wrote:

> J. Marion Sims, a leading nineteenth-century physician and former president of the American Medical Association, developed many of his gynecological treatments through experiments on slave women who were not granted the comfort of anesthesia. Sims's legacy is Janus-faced; he was pitiless with non-consenting research subjects, yet he was among the first doctors of the modern era to emphasize women's health. Other researchers were guiltier of blind ambition than racist intent. Several African Americans, such as Eunice Rivers, the nurse-steward of the Tuskegee study, served as liaisons between scientists and research subjects.
>
> The infringement of black Americans' rights to their own bodies in the name of medical science continued throughout the twentieth century. In 1945, Ebb Cade, an African-American trucker being treated for injuries received in an accident in Tennessee, was surreptitiously placed without his consent into a radiation experiment sponsored by the U.S. Atomic Energy Commission. Black Floridians were deliberately exposed to swarms of mosquitoes carrying yellow fever and other diseases in experiments conducted by the Army and the CIA in the early 1950s. Throughout the 1950s and '60s, black inmates at Philadelphia's Holmesburg Prison were used as research subjects by a University of Pennsylvania dermatologist testing pharmaceuticals and personal hygiene products; some of these subjects report pain and

disfiguration even now. During the 1960s and '70s, black boys were subjected to sometimes paralyzing neurosurgery by a University of Mississippi researcher who believed brain pathology to be the root of the children's supposed hyperactive behavior. In the 1990s, African-American youths in New York were injected with Fenfluramine—half of the deadly, discontinued weight loss drug Fen-Phen—by Columbia researchers investigating a hypothesis about the genetic origins of violence.

With this kind of record, is Rev. Wright paranoid when he speculates that AIDS might be the result of an experiment gone wrong or even, as some black intellectuals assert an ethnic weapon? Given these recorded instances of abuse by the government and private groups, would anybody put it past them? *The New York Times* has carried a series about Eli Lilly's role in distributing a drug called Zyprexa. Seems that the company knew about the dangerous side effects of this drug before they put it on the market. "Eli Lilly, the drug maker, systematically hid the risks and side effects of Zyprexa, its best-selling schizophrenia medicine, a lawyer for the State of Alaska said Wednesday in opening arguments in a lawsuit that contends the drug caused many schizophrenic patients to develop diabetes."

J. B Reed of *Bloomberg News* wrote:

Eli Lilly has faced legal problems over evidence that Zyprexa, a top-selling medicine, tends to cause weight gain and diabetes.

The lawyer, Scott Allen, said that memorandums from Lilly executives showed that the company knew of Zyprexa's dangers soon after the drug was introduced in 1996. But Lilly deliberately played down the side effects, Mr. Allen said, so that sales of Zyprexa would not be hurt.

Lilly's conduct was "reprehensible," Mr. Allen said. In the suit, which is being heard in Alaska state court before Judge Mark Rindner, the state is asking Lilly to pay for the medical expenses of Medicaid patients who have contracted diabetes or other diseases after taking Zyprexa.

Of course when I read that the drug was also used on "disruptive" children, you can imagine where my mind went; probably the same place that Rev. Jeremiah Wright's went.

My oldest daughter, Timothy, a novelist, author of *Showing Out*, has been suffering from schizophrenia since the age of twenty-eight. Every day for her is a challenge. Her psychiatrist only stopped prescribing Zyprexa for her when I told him to stop, having read about the Zyprexa scandal about a year ago. Now Eli Lilly's offering her six thousand dollars, her share of a class action suit, a pittance when compared to the complications from type-one diabetes that she contracted as a result of taking this drug. And *The New York Times* calls me "angry" for taking on the subject of corruption in the pharmaceutical industry. Also, what am I supposed to make of a report that dangerous anti-psychotic drugs are prescribed to black patients suffering from mental illness while white patients are steered into talk therapy?

Rev. Wright proposes that crack was deliberately brought into the inner city by the government. The CIA admitted to having knowledge that U.S. allies brought drugs into the urban areas. The late Gary Webb was ridiculed by the American press for his *Dark Alliance: The CIA, the Contras, and the Crack Cocaine Explosion* yet as Alexander Cockburn and Jeffrey St. Clair disclose in their book *Whiteout: The CIA, Drugs and the Press*, two years after Webb's series ran, the CIA's inspector general confirmed that the agency had in fact been aiding those very same Contra drug-runners (and many more).

Even before the publication of *Dark Alliance*, in the *San Jose Mercury News*, Senator John Kerry found that other government agencies knew about their allies' drug peddling and didn't do anything to stop it.

Don't blacks have a right to ask why? These crack operations may not be affecting the neighborhoods of the rich pundits who dismiss Wright as an anti-American nut but they affect mine and probably those served by Rev. Wright. We had our latest shootout on my block on March 17. It took the Oakland police at least twenty minutes before they arrived. In a *Playboy* article (December 2007), I described my neighbors and me as being among the marooned. We don't receive the kind of police protection or services that white neighborhoods receive. Rev. Wright knows this. Maureen Dowd doesn't. She referred to him as a "wackadoodle," the typical way in which black grievances are treated. We're angry. Paranoid. Politically correct. We're wack jobs. Foreign leaders who complain about American foreign policy are routinely described by the in-bed-with press as peculiar or crazy. Jokes are made about them on comedy shows.

Wasn't Wright conservative when he mentioned just two of the horrendous crimes against humanity committed by the American government? Nagasaki and Hiroshima, attacks that were unique in history because the Japanese are still suffering from the damaging genetic effects of the war. He could have gone all out as Ward Churchill does in his book *A Little Matter of Genocide: Holocaust and Denial in the Americas, 1492 to the Present* (Paperback). He could have reminded them that the West has been bombing Muslim countries since 1911 (see *The History of Bombing* by Sven Lindquist). Wright didn't blame the three thousand casualties at the World Trade Center on the victims (nor did he say that it was an inside job, MSNBC's Willie Geist's lie). The fact that people abroad might be enraged by the country's policies is a difficult message for the American public, which has been kept in a bubble of ignorance by the media and the school curriculums. Three thousand lives were lost as a result of the American invasion of Panama alone. Rick Sanchez of CNN said on March 21, 2008 that some Hispanics warmed to Obama's speech on race because they remember the invasion of Panama and the overthrow of the Allende government in Chile. They might also remember the Reagan administration's support of Contra death squads. While white commentators and politicians were cynical about Obama's speech on race another Hispanic, Gov. Bill Richardson, said that he endorsed Obama as a result of the speech. Sanchez also stepped away from his CNN comfort zone by adding that there were few Latinos represented in the media (during this week, "historian" Tom Brokaw called Hispanics, people who've been here since the 1500s, "Latin Americans"). He's right. The few Asian-American, Hispanic, African-American, and Native-American journalists remaining are being bought out or fired according to Richard Prince of the Maynard Institute. And so what we had that week in March 2008 was a white separatist media criticizing a black nationalist preacher. Multi-deferment chicken hawk types criticizing a Marine. All you have to do is pick up a copy of *The Washingtonian* to see photos of these commentators and Op-Ed writers partying with and smooching up to the people whom they cover.

Air America's Rachel Maddow seems to be the only MSNBC commentator who views the double standard being applied to Obama and other presidential candidates, when she's not interrupted bullied and screamed at by Joe Scarborough who has to carry on like a maniac in order not to meet the same fate as Tucker Carlson. His show was cancelled. If two CNN reporters on the show *Ballot Bowl* surmised that Obama's association with Rev. Wright hurt him, why doesn't Hillary Clinton's association with Billy Graham, her spiritual advisor, hurt her? In a *Time* interview, Hillary Clinton reported that the evangelist "fulfilled a pastoral role during the Monica Lewinsky scandal and helped the First Lady endure the ordeal. At that time, Clinton said, Graham was 'incredibly supportive to me personally. And he was very strong in saying, 'I really understand what you're doing and I support you.' He was just very personally there for me.'"

Billy Graham in a conversation with Richard Nixon described the Jews as "satanic" and offered that they owned the media and peddled pornography. If Mrs. Clinton denounced and rejected Billy Graham, of whom the editor of *Newsweek* Jon Meacham likened to God with his blue eyes, etc., her poll numbers would decline overnight. Jon Meacham was on a Sunday talk show, March 23, 2008, criticizing Rev. Wright and taking some jabs at Obama, part of it laced with sarcasm. He said that now people have found that Obama doesn't "walk on water," maybe because for Meacham only Billy Graham can perform such miracles.

And if that weren't enough, the day before, C-Span's guest was Donald Lambro, *The Washington Times*' chief political correspondent who joined in the media's running loop devoted to criticizing Obama's relationship with his pastor. The Friday before, Diana West, a reporter for the same paper, appearing on the Lou Dobbs show, criticized Michelle Obama and Rev. Wright for their "anti-Americanism," and quoted Victor Davis Hanson, a far-right columnist for the *San Francisco Chronicle*. Their boss is Rev. Sun Myung Moon who warns Korean widows that their husbands will go to hell if they don't give him money. If, for them, Obama should disown Rev. Wright, why are they still working for a religious shakedown artist? Why don't they step away from Rev. Moon's anti-Americanism reported by Robert Parry of *Consortiumnews*:

...Moon's jingle of deep-pocket cash also has caused conservatives to turn a deaf ear toward Moon's recent anti-American diatribes. With growing virulence, Moon has denounced the United States and its democratic principles, often referring to America as "Satanic." But these statements have gone virtually unreported, even though the texts of his sermons are carried on the Internet and their timing has coincided with Bush's warm endorsements of Moon.

"America has become the kingdom of individualism, and its people are individualists," Moon preached in Tarrytown, N. Y., on March 5, 1995. "You must realize that America has become the kingdom of Satan."

In similar remarks to followers on August 4, 1996, Moon vowed that the church's eventual dominance over the United States would be followed by the liquidation of American individualism. "Americans who continue to maintain their privacy and extreme individualism are foolish people," Moon declared. "The world will reject Americans who continue to be so foolish. Once you have this great power of love, which is big enough to swallow entire America, there may be some individuals who complain inside your stomach. However, they will be digested."

During the same sermon, Moon decried assertive American women: "American women have the tendency to consider that women are in the subject position," he said. "However, woman's shape is like that of a receptacle. The concave shape is a receiving shape. Whereas, the convex shape symbolizes giving. (...) Since man contains the seed of life, he should plant it in the deepest place.

"Does woman contain the seed of life? ["No."] Absolutely not. Then if you desire to receive the seed of life, you have to become an absolute object. In order to qualify as an absolute object, you need to demonstrate absolute faith, love and obedience to your subject. Absolute obedience means that you have to negate yourself 100 percent."

(On November 18, *The Washington Post* reported that Richard Miniter, former editorial page editor of *The Washington Times*, had filed a complaint against the paper, charging that he was "coerced" into attending a Unification Church religious ceremony that culminated in a mass wedding conducted by Rev. Sun Myung Moon.)

Diana West and Donald Lambro are applying a double standard for their boss and for Rev. Wright. And why does CNN keep on as a regular the employee of a man who hates our country so much? Does Lou Dobbs agree that the United States is satanic? Does Jonathan Klein, CNN's boss? Where is NOW?

When Richard Cohen appeared on television on March 21, he joined the media chorus in taking offense to the remarks of Rev. Wright. This is the columnist who defended the practice of racial profiling by Washington shopkeepers.

On March 20, the Dalai Lama was the subject of gushing praise by a writer for *Time* magazine where Rev. Wright had been roistered all week on cable. From *Jameswagner.com*: "the Dalai Lama explicitly condemns homosexuality, as well as all oral and anal sex. His stand is close to that of Pope John Paul II, something his Western followers find embarrassing and prefer to ignore. His American publisher even asked him to remove the injunctions against homosexuality from his book, *Ethics for the New Millennium*, for fear they would offend American readers, and the Dalai Lama acquiesced."

Also, why isn't there a running loop about John McCain's relationship with controversial ministers? Are those who control the media easy on him because he plays the father in their fantasies?

What about these "wackadoodles"? The late Jerry Falwell, Pat Robertson and Rev. John Hagee. About 9/11, Falwell said "I really believe that the pagans, and the abortionists, and the feminists, and the gays and lesbians who are actively trying to make that an alternative lifestyle, the ACLU, People For The American Way, all of them who have tried to secularize America. I point the finger in their face and say 'you helped this happen.'"

And Pat Robertson: "I would warn Orlando that you're right in the way of some serious hurricanes, and I don't think I'd be waving those flags in God's face if I were you, this is not a message of hate—this is a message of redemption. But a condition like this will bring about the destruction of your nation. It'll bring about terrorist bombs; it'll bring earthquakes, tornadoes, and possibly a meteor." This was Robertson commenting on "gay days" at Disneyworld.

John McCain's spiritual advisor is Rev. John Hagee. He says that the Roman Catholic Church and Hitler formed an alliance for the purpose of exterminating the Jews. Hurricane Katrina, for him, was God's punishment for a gay rights parade that occurred in New Orleans.

The double standard applied to Obama, the Clintons and Senator McCain and their relationship to controversial pastors is the result of a media gone wild. (On *The View*, Elisabeth Hasselbeck even compared Rev. Wright to Jeffrey Dahmer, the cannibal). A media that, since the O.J. trial, has found that it can make more money from the racial divide than by any of the other fault lines in American life.

While Obama talked to Americans as though they were adults, the media treated the controversy as though it were a video game in which Rev. Wright was the heavy. They OJayed Wright for cash. Martin Luther King, Jr. had a dream. Here's mine. What would happen if all of the whites holding forth in Op-Eds and on cable about race—both in the progressive and corporate media—the middle persons who interpret black America for whites (when they are capable of speaking for themselves), the screenwriters and TV writers who make millions from presenting blacks as scum, and the authors of the fake ghetto books, would just shut the fuck up for a few months and listen. Just listen. Listen to blacks, browns, reds and yellows, people whose views are ignored by the segregated media. Listen, not just to their meek colored mind doubles like an Obama critic, Rev. Rivers, who nobody's ever heard of, but people who will level with them.

In 1957, Doubleday released Richard Wright's *White Man Listen*. In it, he wrote "...the greatest aid that any white Westerner can give Africa is by becoming a missionary right in the heart of the Western world, explaining to his own people what they have done to Africa."

Nobody expects the media to educate the public about Africa. The current coverage is consistent with the images found in the Tarzan movies. It's not going to change. I'll settle for missionary work among the American public. Free them from entrapment by the corporate media, which are causing their brain cells to atrophy. Teach them the other points of views that are smothered by the noise, and trivialized on You Tube. Then maybe they'll understand where the crazy Rev. Wright is coming from.

Springtime for Benedict and Sarah[*]

(For Quincy Troupe's magazine *Black Rennaissance Noire*, I contrasted the treatment of Pope Benedict and Sarah Palin with that accorded Barack Obama. While Rev. Wright was hammered around the clock, Sarah Palin and Benedict were given a free pass. The media were more outraged by a black man's preaching style, which a *Newsweek* writer, with little acquaintance with black culture called "hysterical," than with a Christian leader, Pope Benedict, who continues to cover up the church's pedophilia scandal, one of the worst to hit the Catholic Church since the days of Saint Peter, and one ignored by *The New York Times* recent conservative hire. In January of 2009, the Pope "unexcommunicated" a bishop who has denied the Holocaust.)

* First published in *Black Rennaissance Noire*, Volume 9, Issue 2-3, Fall 2009/Winter 2010.

The responses to the election of the first Celtic-African-American president tested powerful institutions, whose monopoly over how opinion is formed was challenged in a manner rarely seen. In fact these institutions were subjected to what amounted to a grass roots revolt. While the Clinton machine sought to win some Southern states by buying off black preachers, a technique described in *It Can't Happen Here*, their congregations flocked to Barack Obama's candidacy in droves. Clinton supporters among the black leadership had to abandon the candidacy of Mrs. Clinton as they were swept along by the currents arising from below.

Other elements of the religious community compared his election as nothing less than the appearance of the anti-Christ, predicted in the Book of Revelations. A bishop connected to the Vatican said that his election was "apocalyptic," yet the majority of Catholics voted for Obama. The ultra right responded by issuing death threats. Though the Secret Service reported that a rise in death threats against the candidate correlated with the speeches of Sarah Palin, she was still defended by upper and middle class white media feminists like Mika Emilie Leonia Brzezinski, Andrea Mitchell and Tabloid Tina Brown. The have-it-both-ways bent of privileged upper class feminism was revealed in Mrs. Mitchell's comment that vice-presidential candidate Joe Biden would do well in a debate against Sarah Palin because he had a reputation for being "courtly." "Courtly" against a woman who described herself as a "pit-bull." Pit-bulls have been known to maim and kill. Aren't we lucky that Joe McCarthy didn't have a hot body!

His election also demonstrated how out of touch this feminist leadership is not only with minority women and white rank and file women, whose votes supported Obama after predictions that he would lose those votes, but also with the global sisterhood. When Senator Clinton said that she would obliterate Iran, I figured that a lot of her Iranian sisters might be hurt. This military hawk was chosen as Obama's Secretary of State and Madeline Albright a foreign policy advisor. This is the woman who said the deaths of five hundred thousand children as a result of President Clinton's embargo on Iraq was worth it. For his economic council he chose Lawrence Summers who believes that Africa is unpolluted and a good place to store waste. At Harvard Summers made a comment doubting the math and science aptitude of women. President Obama's choice for attorney general spent many hours arranging for the pardon of Marc Rich, but apparently didn't encourage the president to pardon the thousands of blacks who were sent to prison as a result of his 1995 Omnibus Crime Bill, a bill the former president said he regretted.

The Talented Tenth, a term used by W.E.B. DuBois to describe the vanguard of educated blacks who would lead blacks to liberation, performed their usual role of using the election of their fellow Talented Tenther to scold the black "underclass" for their behavior. The rich white men who own the media used these writers to act as a buffer between their white subscribers and blacks whose views might make them uncomfortable. Since these writers have little financial control over media that air their views, they behave as independent contractors for newspapers, cable and think tanks whose sales pitch originates with the penny press of the 1830s, which, like today's media, viewed its market as that of white males. Rev. Barbara Reynolds was fired from *USA Today* for not comforting this demographic; apparently Zambia-born Amy Holmes whom *USA Today* hired did. Ms. Holmes described as a "Republican Strategist" is an all purpose black right-winger who is shuttled from cable show to show when someone is needed to take down black people and President Obama. She and other African-born intellectuals promote the stereotype that the immigrant African intellectuals and writers are acceptable to corporate media and academia because they are less confrontational than traditional black Americans, as one white Louisiana professor told me after a few drinks. We hear very little about African immigrant intellectuals, writers and public intellectuals who have formed an alliance with their African-American counterparts.

Today's media, like the old penny presses, market the moral superiority of whites. Black moral failures are played up while those of whites— widespread drug addiction, unmarried motherhood and crime—are underreported, or when reported, spinned.

When the Republican Party nominated Mrs. Sarah Palin, the head of a dysfunctional family, as vice-presidential candidate, all of a sudden unmarried pregnancy became a hip thing and some of the white pundits gave a glimpse into the dysfunction in the white community, inadvertently.

Obtaining information about what goes on behind the curtains of Mall Land is like it was getting information about unrest behind the Iron Curtain in the old days. Reporting as some of those pundits did on *Morning Joe* that "every family had a case like Bristol Palin" indicates that unmarried motherhood among whites is more widespread than the media reports. After the election it was revealed that the Palin family had splurged on GOP funds for their own fashion interests without Mrs. Palin being called a "welfare queen," and on December 20, 2008, Sherry L. Johnston, the future mother-in-law of Bristol, Mrs. Palin's unmarried daughter, was busted in Wasilla, Alaska, for charges "…in relation to the drug Oxycontin."

Judging from products created by white writers, who have a monopoly over how blacks are depicted in literature, television and the movies, you'd think, if you watched merchandise like *The Wire*, that drugs were a black problem, exclusively. The only difference between a writer like David Simon, whose television series *The Wire* appeals to the feelings of white moral superiority, and a publisher like James Gordon Bennett, whose 1830s newspaper circulated stories of blacks committing cannibalism (a story that makes it into *The New York Times Magazine* section from time to time), is that Simon's profitable enterprise of selling white moral superiority reaches a world-wide audience—an audience that makes judgments about black Americans based on products like his. (As a result of the profits earned by *The Wire*, Allen Hughes, a black filmmaker, has been hired by HBO to do a series about an aging black pimp who is under attack by violent younger pimps. It's to be filmed on location in Oakland where members of other ethnic groups are actually making more money at it; some have been at it since the Gold Rush. Think that HBO would do a story about the customers of black and Asian Oakland prostitutes? Seventy percent are from the suburbs.)

Of the hypocrisy of the white right, neo-cons and even *The Nation* white male writer, who congratulated Obama on his "critique of the black family," Byron York of *The National Review*, a conservative, said that "If the Obamas had a seventeen-year-old daughter who was unmarried and pregnant by a tough-talking black kid, my guess is if they all appeared onstage at a Democratic convention and the delegates were cheering wildly, a number of conservatives might be discussing the issue of dysfunctional black families."

Shortly before the purge of African-American journalists at National Public Radio, neo-Liberal NPR's Michele Norris said on the *Chris Matthews Show* that with the election of Obama, young black men would cease wearing dreadlocks and saggy pants. This comment occurred at the same time that a white gang beat a Hispanic man to death, yet if Ms. Norris did a NPR comment about how the typical hate crime is perpetrated by young white men they wouldn't air it.

What do you think would have happened had partying black or Hispanic youths and not white youths begun a bonfire that caused the destruction of 210 homes of wealthy Southern Californians? I was in Los Angeles when it was discovered that this was the origin of one of the 2008 fires, but the local news that reported the story didn't even identify them. The Associated Press reported:

> A bonfire built by a group of young adults caused a weekend wildfire in Santa Barbara that destroyed 210 homes, including multimillion-dollar mansions, and injured more than two dozen people, authorities said Tuesday. An anonymous tip led to the discovery that ten college students had gathered for a late night hangout at an abandoned property where the fire originated, Santa Barbara County Sheriff Bill Brown said. He declined to say which college the students attended.

As for the white boy who murdered a Hispanic, *The New York Times* just about wrote his defense, a *Times* policy about which complaints were received. In 2000, the New York City Youth Media Study found that white youth guilty of crimes are shown in their yearbook pictures while youthful black and Hispanics are identified by mug shots. This is not only the policy of the *Times* but of cable networks like CNN, which conceals the identity of white youthful perps while exposing those of black or Hispanic youth.

Michelle Bernard, one of the few regular black talking heads on MSNBC and head of an organization that is funded by the far right, the

Independent Women's Forum, congratulated President Obama's singling out blacks for tough-love lectures about "personal responsibility." She said that "personal responsibility" was especially a problem in the black community, the kind of group libel that blacks are subjected to each day by the media. Wish she'd tell that to the parents of those Dallas white middle class teenagers who are overdosing on cheese heroin, a story that barely merited a crawl on CNN, which runs mug shots of blacks all day and designates its crew of female surrogates to lecture black men about their behavior. Bernard is another person whose point of view is restricted by her white employers. Were she to present commentaries with some heft, she'd meet the fate of George Curry, Jack White, Ed Gordon, and the scores of journalists who, according to media watcher Richard Prince, are being shown the door. Fired and bought out.

In their bogus *Black In America* special, an excuse by CNN head Jonathan Klein to draw ratings—he was successful—, Soledad O'Brien scolded a black man for not attending his daughter's birthday party. Here again the old 1830s media strategy of boosting white morality by denigrating that of blacks is used by Jonathan Klein in the same manner that Buffalo Bill sought ticket sales by staging Indian attacks on cabins sheltering virtuous helpless white women.

On July 17, 2009, *The New York Times* pundit Sam Roberts, who once said that blacks are prone to violence, and when I reminded him, didn't remember, quoted Census figures which showed a rise in two-parent households among blacks and a decline in two-parent households among whites, giving support to Andrew Hacker's remark that were Daniel Moynihan around today he'd be writing about "the tangle of pathologies" in the white community. The *Times* also reported that while the rate of incarceration among black women has declined that of white women is on the rise. Obviously, the behaviors of Paris, Lindsay, Britney, the Barbie bandits, and the girls who beat up a schoolmate and broadcast it on You Tube are part of a trend.

Bush supporter Tara Wall, CNN's regular black talking head and Rev. Moon's employee (nothing like seeing Rev. Moon's people on MSNBC and CNN hold forth on Rev. Jeremiah Wright), mentioned that seventy-three percent of black children have been born out of wedlock, a figure that the right has bandied about for decades despite figures from the Centers of Disease Prevention and Control that there's been a significant decline in such births over the last decade. Charles Blow of *The New York Times* and Henry Louis Gates, Jr. on his blog, *TheRoot*, bankrolled by *The Washington Post*, used Obama's election to excoriate blacks again for unmarried motherhood and drug addiction. Both Charles Blow and Henry Louis Gates, Jr. are also apparently unaware that black teenage pregnancy has declined significantly over the last ten years with only a slight up-tick last year. I reminded Blow that these statistics were printed in his newspaper!! *The New York Times*. He didn't reply, which is how the black tough-lovers treat their critics even though some of the academics among them pretend to love the Socratic dialogue. Ninety percent of the white pundits whom I have questioned, including Frank Rich, Richard Lowry, Sam Roberts, Samuel Freedman, Andrew Sullivan—pundits of the right and left—have replied to my questions about their coverage of black issues, but Bob Herbert, Charles Blow and black pundits who soak all of the little opinion oxygen that the conservative media owners allot to blacks feel that they are above debate. The wealthy white men who promulgate their views shield them and the neo-liberals and neo-cons and plain pawns of the right like John McWhorter, Steele, and Connerley. Orlando Patterson, apparently the only African American on the rolodex of the *Times* Op-Ed page editor, hailed Obama's election as a sign that the United States is the greatest democracy since the Greeks, which would probably come as a surprise to the thousands of Greek slaves. On the day after the election *The New York Times* announced in its headline that Obama's election had broken a barrier, yet on the editorial page all of the poets who were invited to chime in were white. Some barriers remain.

Moreover, regardless of how professional tough-lover Juan Williams, a Caribbean American like Orlando Patterson, rates Hispanic behavior above that of blacks, there is a larger drug problem among Hispanics both in terms of addiction and distribution, and Blow and Gates, Jr. might want to know that there are more cases of unmarried motherhood among Hispanics, per thousand, than among blacks, yet President Obama, who uses personal responsibility as code words, told the council of La Raza that he shared the values of the Hispanics. This was a week after the president appeared before a black audience and read the required tough-love speech to black fathers for which he was congratulated by white divorced fathers like Joe Scarborough.

If he'd done the same before a Hispanic audience he would have lost the Hispanic vote. Hispanics are the country's largest minority, yet the social pathologies of this group and of other ethnic groups are ignored by the media and the black tough-love entrepreneurs like Gates, Jr., Williams, Patterson, Michelle Bernard, CNN's Tara Wall, who works for Rev. Moon's far right *The Washington Times,* and President Obama, yet these people are promoted as those who place race in the background. As an example of *The Washington Times'* attitude toward Obama, on November 17, 2009, an opinion written by Wesley Pruden, editor emeritus, drew shock for its coarseness and hostility. Not only do Pruden and others desire to control the reproductive rights of American women, but whom they should date. "It's no fault of the president that he has no natural instinct or blood impulse for what the America of 'the 57 states' is about. He was sired by a Kenyan father, born to a mother attracted to men of the Third World and reared by grandparents in Hawaii, a paradise far from the American mainstream." (Don't expect Tara Wall, Brian DeBose, Walter Williams, Tom Sowell and other *Washington Times* black columnists and reporters to object to such distasteful comments.)

In the language of recovery, don't the objects of tough love get some positive behavior points or some positive reinforcement when they do something right? And if these commentators are truly beyond race why not extend their tough love to other ethnic communities. I once told Gates that some of the white men who sponsor him for his tough-love views have a worse record of treating women of their ethnic group than the brothers. He wasn't aware. Marty Peretz, then editor of *The New Republic,* where a surrogate was hired to call me a misogynist, said that black women were "culturally deficient." When FAIR asked Tabloid Tina Brown to condemn him the way that one of her surrogates did a hit job on Minister Louis Farrakhan, she refused. You won't find a discussion of tensions between Jewish women and Jewish men in *The New Republic,* which are so strained that Katha Politt of *The Nation* accused Jewish men of having "anti-Semitic attitudes" toward Jewish women. Maybe Charles

Blow should come up with a graph about this situation. David Simon, a television series. Steven Spielberg, a movie.

Though Gates, Jr., who views himself as the leader of the Black Intelligentsia (essentially people clustered around a few colleges and universities located in the Northeast), is pessimistic about Obama's election leading to a reduction of drug addiction among blacks, out here in California white suburban women do more dope than blacks and Latinos. Why no tough love for these women? The Gates piece, published at *TheRoot*, was congratulated by white subscribers for whom he had given their required superiority injection by commenting on the moral degeneracy of blacks, which, according to him, wouldn't improve even if you had a Clintonite black president in the White House. These underclass blacks are obviously incorrigible and will never drink white wine at the Harvard Club.

Professional critics of African Americans also viewed it ironic that blacks would vote for a black president yet vote for Proposition 8, the California initiative that opposed gay marriage. Latinos (sixty-one percent) and Asian Americans also voted for the proposition and the money that got the measure over came from the coffers of the Mormon Church. As a sign of how members of other ethnic groups are cashing in on the market of boosting white esteem by dissing blacks, the writer hired by the *San Francisco Chronicle* to comment on the black vote for Proposition 8 was a Latino. Predictably, *The New York Times*, that casts blacks as the key players in social pathologies including crime, anti-Semitism, homophobia, etc., ran an article blaming the success of Proposition 8, the referendum on gay marriage, on blacks, though most of the hate crimes against gays are perpetrated by white men—the group the media has seen as its target audience since the 1800s—two white journalists were hired to explain black attitudes toward gays to the *Times* readers. One was Benjamin Schwarz, who once wrote that black men in the South who were lynched probably deserved it, and Caitlin Flanagan. (Schwarz now writes for *The Atlantic Monthly*, which was among the first magazines to excerpt Scots Irish writer Charles Murray's *The Bell Curve*, which carries stereotypes aimed at his ethnic group over to blacks. The joke is that because of incest, Charles Murray's Scots Irish are feeble minded. This is why Vice President Cheney got into trouble for his remark, "I have Cheneys on each side of the family and I'm not even from West Virginia." He was talking about the incest stereotype applied to Charles Murray's people.) I guess we can't get Ms. Flanagan to write about how Irish Catholics voted. On the Sunday that their *Times* piece appeared, December 7, 2008, the BBC reported that the Vatican had opposed a measure that France and The Netherlands sponsored, a declaration that would de-criminalize homosexual relationships. Maybe Ms. Flanagan was too busy blaming homophobia on blacks and explaining black homophobia to the readers of the *Times* to notice this BBC report. The response of segments of the Catholic Church to Obama's election was bizarre. One headline read: "Vatican Cardinal calls Obama Apocalyptic." In the article, His Eminence James Francis Cardinal Stafford criticized President-elect Barack Obama as "aggressive, disruptive and apocalyptic."

"For the next few years," Stafford went on to say, "Gethsemane will not be marginal. We will know that garden," comparing America's future with Obama as president to "Jesus' agony in the garden." "On November 4, 2008, America suffered a cultural earthquake," said Cardinal Stafford, adding that Catholics must deal with the "hot, angry tears of betrayal" by beginning a new sentiment where one is "with Jesus, sick because of love."

At *The Daily Dish,* Bell Curve supporter Andrew Sullivan opined, "the notion that the recent election of Obama is a sign of the Apocalypse has, until now, been restricted to Protestant loonies." Though many members of the chattering class, as segregated an institution as Old Miss before integration, have commented that Barack Obama has gotten a free pass, or as David Gregory, Imus Alumni and new *Meet The Press* host, said on December 14, "a lot of latitude…," Obama was confronted with the dirtiest and most racist campaign in American history. Not only did MSNBC bring in its right-wing black clean-up crew including Tara Wall, DeBose, Larry Elder, Amy Holmes, Bush preacher, Rev. Eugene Rivers, and Jonathan Capehart, a black journalist whom *The Washington Post* considers safe, to criticize the candidate; Richard Prince, media watcher from the Maynard Institute, said that one powerful news agency, The Associated Press, supported McCain. No candidate in the past has been called "The Anti Christ," or "The Beast of the Apocalypse, 666." Yet, Howard Kurtz said that the press was one hundred percent behind Obama. One hundred percent? Appearing before a group of radio and television producers, Roger Ailes, president of Fox News, and one of the masterminds behind the notorious Willie Horton ad, made a joke: "It is true that Barack Obama is on the move. I don't know if it's true that President Bush called Musharraf and said: 'Why can't we catch this guy?'"

This remark explains why Fox continued to portray Obama as a terrorist.

Later, during the debate over health legislation, Fox News was responsible for spreading false information about the legislation. On October 20, 2009, indefatigable media watcher, Richard Prince, cited a Pew Poll.

> The Pew Research Center for the People & the Press, reporting on the health-care reform bills in Congress, reported in August that 'Among those who say they regularly get their news from Fox News, 45 percent say claims of death panels are true, while 30 percent say they are not true. By contrast, majorities among regular viewers of rival cable news channels MSNBC and CNN and nightly network news say they think it is false that health care legislation will create "death panels." There are no such "death panels" in the legislation.
>
> An NBC News/Wall Street Journal poll found that the same misinformation took hold among Fox News viewers about whether the health-care plan will cover illegal immigrants.

Richard Prince also cited Jacob Weisberg on Fox. "Weisberg argues in *Newsweek* that 'What matters is the way that Fox's model has invaded the bloodstream of the American media. By showing that ideologically distorted news can drive ratings,' Fox News Chairman Roger Ailes 'has provoked his rivals at CNN and MSNBC to develop a variety of populist and ideological takes on the news. In this way, Fox hasn't just corrupted its own coverage. Its example has made all of cable news unpleasant and unreliable.'" CNN wasn't much better. On Sunday, October 18, during a panel discussion, David Gergen, a Washington insider tried to explain why the public was against the public option. The next day, Monday, an ABC/Washington poll reported that fifty-seven percent of the public supported a public option.

The candidacy of this Celtic-African-American president drew the racist poisons from the American psyche and they crawled out like the slime that oozes from the innards of those victims in the Exorcist movies. Examples:

· A sign was posted on a tree in Vay, Idaho, with Obama's name and the offer of a "free public hanging."
· In North Carolina, racist graffiti targeting Obama was found in a tunnel near the North Carolina State University campus.
· In a Maine convenience store, an Associated Press reporter saw a sign inviting customers to join a betting pool on when Obama might fall victim to an assassin. The sign solicited one-dollar entries into "The Osama Obama Shotgun Pool," saying the money would go to the person picking the date closest to when Obama was attacked. "Let's hope we have a winner," said the sign. A law enforcement official who also spoke on condition of anonymity because he was not authorized to speak publicly said that during the campaign there was a spike in anti-Obama rhetoric on the Internet—"a lot of ranting and raving with no capability, credibility or specificity to it."
· In Denver, a group of men with guns and bulletproof vests made racist threats against Obama and sparked fears of an assassination plot during the Democratic National Convention in August 2008.
· Just before the election, two skinheads in Tennessee were charged with plotting to behead blacks across the country and assassinate Obama while wearing white top hats and tuxedos.
· In Milwaukee, police officials found a poster of Obama with a bullet going toward his head—discovered on a table in a police station.

One of the most popular white-supremacist Web sites got more than two thousand new members the day after the election, compared with ninety-one new members on Election Day, according to an AP count. The site, *stormfront.org*, was temporarily off-line November 5 because of the overwhelming amount of activity it received after Election Day. On Saturday, one Stormfront poster, identified as Dalderian Germanicus, of North Las Vegas, said, "I want the SOB laid out in a box to see how 'messiahs' come to rest. God has abandoned us, this country is doomed." The taunts and threats continue.

Despite these threats, pundits continue to complain that the media were giving Obama a free ride. Howard Kurtz, Lou Dobbs, Joe Scarborough, Tucker Carlson and other pundits kept up the mantra that Obama had caused the media to "swoon" over Obama, while giving Sarah Palin and John McCain a hard time. Studies from the Shorenstein Center, George Mason University and LexisNexis concluded otherwise. As late as Sunday, December 28, Kurtz was continuing to describe the media's attitude toward Barack Obama as "sympathetic," and none of his fellow panelists Jessica Yellin, Terence Smith, Bill Pressman and Amy Holmes challenged him. Ms. Holmes, a Zambia-born black woman whom the network bosses shuttle from panel to panel for the purpose of dissing the black underclass and Barack Obama, agreed. (Once in awhile she is handled by the fellows over at *The National Review* where she was brought on to diss Obama. She said of Obama's race speech, at their site, *National Review Online*: "My first reaction? Race speeches are rarely good, and this was no exception. For all of Obama's new talk of change, courage, politics you can believe in, I heard a whole lot of liberal boilerplate dressed up in euphemism and offering no fresh solutions.")

Studies by reputable organizations, whose goal is not that of drawing ratings by putting down blacks, differ from the conclusions about the media treatment of Obama. On July 27, 2008, James Rainey, writer for the *Los Angeles Times* wrote:

> Cable talking heads accuse broadcast networks of liberal bias—but a think tank finds that ABC, NBC and CBS were tougher on Barack Obama than on John McCain in recent weeks. Haters of the mainstream media reheated a bit of conventional wisdom last week.

> Barack Obama, they said, was getting a free ride from those insufferable liberals.

> During the evening news, the majority of statements from reporters and anchors on all three networks are neutral, the center found. And when network news people ventured opinions in recent weeks, 28 percent of the statements were positive for Obama and 72 percent negative.

I wrote last week that the networks should do more to better balance the airtime. But I also suggested that much of the attention to Obama was far from glowing.

But the center's director, Robert Lichter, who has won conservative hearts with several of his previous studies, told me the facts were the facts.

Another myth promoted by the media held that Hillary Clinton received less favorable treatment than Obama during the primaries. This claim by Mrs. Clinton and her followers led to the candidacy of Sarah Palin, whose choice was made cynically by the Republican Party. They wanted to woo disaffected Clinton voters who believed that Mrs. Clinton was robbed of the nomination when, in terms of delegate strength, she was done after Wisconsin. Her claim and that of her followers that she was the victim of unfavorable press coverage is disputed by a study from the Pew Research Center's Project for Excellence in Journalism issued on May 29, 2008:

> If campaigns for president are in part a battle for control of the master narrative about character, Democrat Barack Obama has not enjoyed a better ride in the press than rival Hillary Clinton, according to a new study of primary coverage by the Pew Research Center's Project for Excellence in Journalism and the Joan Shorenstein Center on Press, Politics and Public Policy at Harvard University.
>
> From January 1, just before the Iowa caucuses, through March 9, following the Texas and Ohio contests, the height of the primary season, the dominant personal narratives in the media about Obama and Clinton were almost identical in tone, and were both twice as positive as negative, according to the study, which examined the coverage of the candidates' character, history, leadership and appeal—apart from the electoral results and the tactics of their campaigns.
>
> The trajectory of the coverage, however, began to turn against Obama, and did so well before questions surfaced about his pastor Jeremiah Wright. Shortly after Clinton criticized the media for being soft on Obama during a debate, the narrative about him began to turn more skeptical—and indeed became more negative than the coverage of Clinton herself. What's more, an additional analysis of more general campaign topics suggests the Obama narrative became even more negative later in March, April and May.

Yet, with all of this evidence pointing to the rough media terrain that Obama had to navigate on the way to his election, as late as December 28, 2008, Howard Kurtz was complaining about the "sympathetic" treatment that the media accorded Obama. None of his guests—Terence Smith, Bill Pressman, and Jessica Yellin—challenged Kurtz. Amy Holmes agreed.

As if to put this reasoning to a test, on the same day *The Washington Post* and the Associated Press gave a sympathetic treatment to Chip Saltsman, a candidate for Chairman of the Republican National Committee who sent out a CD that included the song *Barack the Magic Negro*. He said that it was only meant to be satire.

For the media, Rev. Jeremiah Wright, a former Marine, was the epitome of hate. Imus Alumni Howard Kurtz, who has said that in private he and his friends agree with what Imus says, went completely bonkers against Rev. Wright on his *Reliable Sources*, December 13. He accused Rev. Wright of "fulminating. Of engaging in diatribes, rants, and hate filled speeches," the kind of criticism of black male intellectuals by whites that we've heard for over one hundred years, even James Baldwin, an elegant, French speaking jewel of a man was called "antagonistic," while Pope Benedict was treated by a fawning media as though he were truly an emissary of a god. While condemning Rev. Wright, Chris Matthews said of Pope Benedict: "I think this new Pope, just on a very cosmetic level, is amazing. He's 78 years old. I remembered him being talked about when we studied Vatican II back at the Holy Cross in the 60s. Ratzinger was a major figure. And here he is now radiant, looking strong, solid... what a leader he looks like." For them, Rev. Wright's offense was condemning the United States and enumerating atrocities committed by its government. Pope Benedict, when cardinal, tried to cover up one of the greatest scandals confronting the Catholic Church. The following story appeared on the site of *The Daily Kos*, April 19, 2005, at 03:43:27 p.m. PDT:

> [A] 69-page Latin document bearing the seal of Pope John XXIII was sent to every bishop in the world. The instructions outline a policy of "strictest" secrecy in dealing with allegations of sexual abuse and threatens those who speak out with excommunication.

They also call for the victim to take an oath of secrecy at the time of making a complaint to Church officials. It states that the instructions are to "be diligently stored in the secret archives of the Curia [Vatican] as strictly confidential. Nor is it to be published nor added to with any commentaries."

[...] bishops are instructed to pursue these cases "in the most secretive way... restrained by a perpetual silence... and everyone... is to observe the strictest secret which is commonly regarded as a secret of the Holy Office... under the penalty of excommunication."

Lawyers point to a letter the Vatican sent to bishops in May 2001 clearly stating the 1962 instruction was in force until then. The letter is signed by Cardinal Ratzinger, the most powerful man in Rome beside the Pope and who heads the Congregation for the Doctrine of the Faith—the office which ran the Inquisition in the Middle Ages.

What we do know from his letter is that as recently as 2001, he supported and encouraged the drawing of a curtain of secrecy over widespread sexual abuse by clergy.

During the media's all-pope-week, former altar boy Chris Matthews compared the values of Rev. Wright, the subject of a relentless vicious smear and media inquisition, unfavorably with those of Pope Benedict.

Apparently a minister saying "God Damn America" in a speech that the media quoted out of context—like an adolescent reading *Hustler*, they're only interested in the meaty parts—is more offensive than a pope, who, when cardinal, tried to cover up a scandal, which has resulted in thousands of victims suffering from post-traumatic stress.

Moreover, since the media slapped the killer label anti-Semite on some of Rev. Wright's comments, why, during a week in which Fox TV's Brit Hume described the Pope as a man of "beatific sweetness," was there no reference to Pope Benedict's drawing a complaint from the Anti-Defamation League for his revival of the Latin Mass, which calls for the conversion of the Jews. The Anti-Defamation League said the Pope's decision was "a body blow to Catholic-Jewish relations." *The Observer* quoted Abraham Foxman the national director in Rome.

We are extremely disappointed and deeply offended that nearly forty years after the Vatican rightly removed insulting anti-Jewish language from the Good Friday mass, it would now permit Catholics to utter such hurtful and insulting words by praying for Jews to be converted. It is the wrong decision at the wrong time. It appears the Vatican has chosen to satisfy a right-wing faction in the church that rejects change and reconciliation.

After the election of the president, Benedict was criticized by Jewish groups for un-excommunicating a bishop who had denied the Holocaust, and for proposing sainthood for Pope Pius XII. On December 21, 2009, AFP reported that the Wiesenthal Center was "shocked at Pius sainthood moves."

The founder of the Simon Wiesenthal Center voiced dismay and disappointment Monday at weekend Vatican moves to raise controversial wartime pope Pius XII to sainthood.

The Vatican sparked anger in Jewish communities worldwide with moves to nudge Pius—whose beatification process was launched in 1967—closer to sainthood, its ultimate honor.

The Catholic Church argues that Pius saved many Jews who were hidden away in religious institutions, and that his silence during the Holocaust—when millions of Jews were exterminated by Germany's Nazi regime—was born out of a wish to avoid aggravating their situation.

But others believe Pius's inaction when it mattered to the lives of so many was appallingly wrong.

"I'm sort of amazed," Rabbi Marvin Hier, founder and dean at the Simon Wiesenthal Center, a prominent Jewish human rights group, told AFP.

"It has become our business, because in my opinion, there would be a great distortion of history" were Pius XII to be elevated to sainthood, he said.

"Pius XII sat in stony silence" as the most egregious crimes against Jews took place. In 1941, when massacres began, "you'd expect to see a thick file" of cases in which he sought to intervene.

"But you do not," Hier noted. In addition, Pius's predecessor, Pius XI, wrote an encyclical about anti-Semitism. Yet instead of publishing it or drawing attention to it, Pius XII buried it, Hier noted.

"These were turbulent times. You had people who stood up to dictators. Pius (XII) did not," Hier stressed.

During this campaign, comedy shows like *Saturday Night Live* and *Bill Maher* and shows like *The View* did the job that the corporate media and its hirelings were too intimidated to do. The right's coming down hard on Chris Matthews and Keith Olbermann for their comments about the Republicans prompted NBC heads to travel to Minneapolis hat in hand and beg forgiveness from these Republican bullies. For going along to get along, Imus defender David Gregory was given the plum job as host of *Meet The Press*. Of Pope Benedict, the former Cardinal Ratzinger, Bill Maher said, "Whenever a cult leader sets himself up as God's infallible wing man here on Earth, lock away the kids," he laughed. "I'd like to tip off law enforcement to an even larger child-abusing religious cult," Maher said. "Its leader also has a compound, and this guy not only operates outside the bounds of the law, but he used to be a Nazi and he wears funny hats." By contrast, MSNBC's Norah O'Donnell and CNN's Kyra Phillips tee-heed all over themselves as they anticipated the Pope's plane landing in Washington. This is the Kyra Phillips who said that she was "outraged" by the way Michael Vick treated those pit bulls (and asked a black guest whether dog fighting was "cultural.") She cares more about the fate of pit bulls than the victims of child abuse. Jonathan Capehart, who like Juan Williams was brought on by the white men who run the media to diss Rev. Wright, said that he was "nervous" about what to call the Pope. "Your highness?" "Your holiness?"

CNN's Wolf Blitzer, one of those who worked the Wright story to death, could have questioned the pope about the pedophilia cover-up and the revival of the Latin Mass, but he said that he was so much in "awe" of the Pope that he was rendered speechless when he and other journalists were invited to question the Pope.

ABC's Cokie Roberts hitched a ride with the Bushes who were on the way to greeting the Pope. Mrs. Roberts complained during one session of ABC's *This Week With George Stephanopoulos* about Barack Obama's audacity to run for president during a year when it was possible for a woman to be elected. She was clearly annoyed.

While Barack Obama and Rev. Wright were twinned (ads also appeared linking him to O.J. Simpson and Kwame Kilpatrick), the associations of John McCain, who once called the media his base, were underplayed.

Washington Post columnist Dana Milbank wrote about McCain's appearance before the Associated Press: "The putative Republican

presidential nominee was given a box of doughnuts and a standing ovation. The likely Democratic nominee was likened to a terrorist." (An
AP questioner that day mistakenly referred to the Al Qaeda mastermind
as "Obama bin Laden." At one point, Stephanopoulos asked McCain
about his soliciting the support of Rev. Hagee who has made anti-Catholic
statements. McCain said that Rev. Hagee was good for Israel even though
his position is similar to that of the Latin Mass, that Jews must be
converted in order for the Rapture to occur. George Stephanopoulos
doesn't know this apparently and asked no follow-up question. Unlike
Obama, who distanced himself from the comments of Rev. Wright,
McCain said that he disagreed with Hagee's position, but still welcomed
his endorsement, which he solicited. Predictably, there was no ratings-
driven outrage resulting from McCain's reaffirming his embrace of
Rev. Hagee.

Meanwhile, Hillary Clinton became, in Pat Buchanan's words, "the
coal miner's daughter," in an effort to win the votes of beer drinkers,
hunters and bowlers. This hundred-million-dollar-plus populist, who
opposed women on welfare continuing their college education, joined
Senator McCain (who, with his hundred-million-dollar wife, owns eight
homes), and a bunch of rich columnists, David Brooks, William Kristol,
and confessed white supremacist George Will (FAIR), in criticizing
Obama for his remark about people in small towns (The headline on Lou
Dobbs' show read "Obama slams small towns") being bitter about government. Wall Street's Lou Dobbs said that the remark was "ignorant."

The media consensus was that Obama had insulted these god-fearing
salt-of-the-earth types with his comment about their being bitter. How
did the salt feel? Zogby Poll on April 17 reported that, "Pennsylvanians
by a two-to-one margin (sixty percent to twenty-nine percent) are more
likely to agree with supporters of Obama that voters in Pennsylvania are
bitter about their economic situation than with Clinton and critics of
Obama that he is an elitist who does not understand working people."
Yet, on April 28, big bucks reporter Andrea Mitchell, appearing on her
MSNBC show, said that Barack's remark constituted a "self-inflicted
wound." April 28 saw an all-day ignorant reply to a speech made by Rev.
Wright at the National Press Club where he was subjected to a third-

degree grilling by a woman who admitted that she hadn't read Wright's entire speech during which "controversial" remarks were made. Neither did the usual upscale entertainers posing as journalists. Though Rev. Wright said that his was not a "liberation theology" they kept referring to it as such. MSNBC's Dan Abrams sicced some members of the black right on Rev. Wright: Michelle Bernard, and Rev. Sun Moon's Tara Wall. Bush's preacher, Rev. Eugene Rivers, was also brought in. Just as MSNBC didn't check the connections of its military experts to defense contractors, apparently, Rivers' background hasn't been vetted. Joe Klein, who rose to power by dissing black culture, so much that FAIR dubbed him "a white militant," harshly questioned Wright's patriotism, as though Klein had a tiny flag waving from every orifice of his body. Tucker Carlson termed Obama's remarks about Wright "pathetic."

There's something deranged about a corporate media that would engage in character assassination against Rev. Wright for his views, yet praise a man who tried to cover up the destruction of thousands of lives. But the people who own the media have found that character assassination and driving a wedge between different groups is a moneymaker. One is reminded that the introduction of the 1830s penny press featured sensational reporting of the autopsy of a black woman whom P.T. Barnum claimed was George Washington's nurse. This was the O.J. story of the time. The modern media continues features that were perfected by the circus. Jonathan Klein told his token Latino commentator, right-wing Cuban Rick Sanchez, who wants New Orleans to become a Mexican-American city, that the issue of race was something that could make big bucks, according to *The New York Observer.*

When the primaries began to move west, the lead became something about the long-standing enmity between blacks and Latinos. It's certainly there. Strife between blacks and Latinos on the school playgrounds and in prisons. (In California's Central Valley there is conflict between Latinos and immigrants from South East Asia.) There are also tensions between Mexican immigrants and blacks, which is understandable since the Mexican media runs the kind of images of blacks that in the United States have been consigned to the Jim Crow museum at Ferris State University, except for the kind of materials that the Republican Party uses from time to time. But could Latino-black relations be more complex than a sensational cable news lead?

It took Gregory Rodriguez in *Time* and syndicated columnist Ruben Navarrette, Jr. to offer a perspective missing from cable. Navarrette pointed to the many instances where Latinos have supported a black candidate. Challenging some of the assumptions made by white commentators, who cited "a history of uneasy and competitive relations between blacks and Latinos in…Chicago, Los Angeles and New York," Rodriguez wrote that "each of those cities have, in the past, elected black mayors who captured the majority of the Latino vote."

Missing in most of these discussions was any reference to the African heritage of millions of Latinos, sometimes known as Hispanics, or indigenous people. If, using the standard established by slave traders, "one drop" of black blood makes you black, why aren't they considered black?

Writing about the most recent mayoral race in Oakland, whose main competitors were a black and a Latino, I said that race wouldn't be an issue because the Mexican-American candidate was darker than the black candidate. A month ago, when I was having dinner on the Lower East Side with a famous Puerto Rican poet and two Puerto Rican scholars, I repeated a joke that comedian Paul Mooney tells: Puerto Ricans and Cubans are "[Negroes] who can swim." He didn't say "Negroes."

They said that whites in Pennsylvania wouldn't vote for Obama because of his remarks about the white working class being bitter and clinging to guns, a line that was worked by the corporate media almost as much as the Rev. Wright film, which became sort of the Zapruder moment during the primary. Obama won Pennsylvania. They said that white women wouldn't vote for Obama because of the way he treated Hillary Clinton (whom he praised during debates and on the stump) yet Obama won the white women's votes. Their breaking ranks with Gloria Steinem shows that the elite elements in the feminist movement are not only out of touch with their followers but follow a double standard when judging white and black men, a tendency noted by feminist critic bell hooks. The low point in the primary came when these women supported Sarah Palin, one of the worst demagogues in American history and probably the tackiest.

In a novel, *Reckless Eyeballing,* that left me for literary road kill and caused at least one boycott of my appearance at Baton Rouge led by feminist Emily Toth (it fizzled when a professor challenged them; they hadn't read my books), I had a feminist character in my book defend Eva Braun on the grounds that she was a woman. I was reminded of this on November 18 when Tina Brown, the publisher of a zine called *The Daily Beast* and MSNBC's Mika Brzezinski carried on about how unfair the media treated Sarah Palin. Not to compare Sarah Palin with Eva Braun. Ms. Palin is more dangerous. Yet Ms. Brown and Mika Brzezinski succumbed to the hockey mom presentation of this rabble rouser by McCain campaign manager Rick Davis showing her cooking dinner with Bush One caddy, Matt Lauer and such. Mika agreed with Tina Brown. She said "it was pretty ugly it got really vicious—while images of Obama were overwhelmingly positive." Like when Sarah Palin told Gwen Ifill that she would select which questions she wanted to answer during her debate with Joe Biden? Was the media unfair to Mrs. Palin? While Rev. Jeremiah Wright was subjected to a massive form of character assassination the media made little notice of Mrs. Palin's ties to groups led by kooks. One of which was The Third Wave Movement. Here is how the publication *Enlightened Catholicism* described that movement.

> The Third Wave Movement is also known as the New Apostolic Reformation, Joel's Army, and The Manifest Sons Of God. Essentially this movement believes we have entered the end times. Joel's Army sees this as evidenced by the passing of Roe V Wade in 1973, and that those born after this year are part of that army. All these linked groups believe they have a Divine Mandate to clean up the world by taking over the "seven secular mountains," as explained in this quote from Mary Glazier. Mary Glazier is the leader of Palin's 'spiritual warfare group,' an admission Palin made when interviewed by *Focus On The Family*: "Glazier's sermon, which featured her comments on Palin, was given at a conference Opening the Gate of Heaven on Earth that also featured a number of speeches and sermons on the plans of leaders of the New Apostolic Reformation to take control of the seven 'kingdoms' of society through their 'Seven Mountains Strategy.'"

Mika said, "what I liked about her was that she wasn't guilty about being ambitious, being wired to work." She cast the Palin family as "truly a modern American family." Mika Brzezinski casted about for right-wing eyes when she concluded that the media were afraid to criticize Obama because he was black.

Her lowbrow appeal worked. She and "Morning Joe" have been hired to add a three-hour show on radio and she was the subject of a lengthy and flattering profile by Imus Howard Kurtz in *The Washington Post*.

But regardless of how Mrs. Palin became a pawn in the style of old South Carolina 2000 and Tennessee 2004 campaigns against black male candidates, which included race baiting, red baiting, and even reaching back to the nineteenth century by showing black men in the company of white women, it could have been worse. They could have nominated Bobby Jindal, the Louisiana Governor. This is a man who has such little regard for black life that he has failed to call for the prosecution of white vigilantes who massacred black men and women during the flooding of New Orleans. So sure of themselves that they are above the law, these vigilantes boasted about their killing spree on Dutch television. Blackwater, the off-the-shelf mercenary group, was down there killing people too. The Republican Party won't abandon its Southern Strategy. It will most likely continue with a brown or yellow face fronting for it. An Indo-American like Jindal. Or a Vietnamese American, a member of a recently arrived immigrant group that might not be aware of the gains that the Civil Rights Movement has made for all colored groups. Vietnamese Americans voted for McCain even though he participated in bombing raids over their country, and called Asians "Gooks."

CNN's Wolf Blitzer asked Sarah Palin was there a need for affirmative action following Obama's successful ascendancy to the presidency. Blitzer is convinced that affirmative action is a black giveaway program yet the Department of Labor reports that the typical recipient of affirmative action is a white woman.

The most accurate account of affirmative action and those who benefit that I have read came in an exchange between Professor Sumi Cho, a visiting professor at the University of Michigan and University of Iowa law schools, who currently serves on the Board of Directors for LatCrit. Professor Cho holds a JD and a PhD in Ethnic Studies from the University of California at Berkeley and Rashida Tlaib, the Advocacy Coordinator for ACCESS, the Arab Community Center for Economic and Social Services. Ms. Tlaib earned her Jurist Doctorate degree from Thomas Cooley Law School and a Bachelor's Degree in Political Science from Wayne State University. Both dismantled the myth of affirmative action as a black program and unveiled the media's circus-like propaganda effort to make money from white resentment, in their case, *Newsweek,* but they could have had in mind CNN, MSNBC, and talk shows that reach millions of people. Their conclusions:

> Contrary to popular belief, African Americans are not the sole, or even the primary, beneficiaries of affirmative action. Rather, a wide range of groups have benefited from these policies which promote equality by directing resources, outreach and other opportunities to targeted underrepresented communities.

> These groups include women, Native Americans, Arab Americans, Latino/as, Asian Americans, and African Americans. Of these groups, the United States Department of Labor found that **white women are the primary beneficiaries of affirmative action**.

> A broad range of minority groups have also benefited from these policies. Programs that direct resources, outreach and opportunities to people of color have been extraordinarily important in opening up American institutions to a wide variety of communities. Yet even the beneficiaries of affirmative action, like most Americans, may not realize that these programs are under an intense nationwide assault. Many may mistakenly assume that the admission of blacks into colleges is the principal focus of efforts to eliminate these policies. In fact, however, attacks on Affirmative Action programs have included everything from English as a Second Language programs to breast cancer screenings, from mentoring and after school programs to magnet schools, from programs that require Asian-owned businesses to be advised of possible government contracts to battered women shelters that create a safe space for victims of domestic violence and their children. Simply put, there are countless initiatives across the country that affirmatively use race and gender to address the unwarranted obstacles confronted by the beneficiaries of Affirmative Action. Because these vital programs are neither colorblind or gender blind, they are put at risk by attacks on affirmative action.

> What is the scope of these programs? And why do African Americans continue to be the subject of media focus when they are discussed?

Consider [a *Newsweek*] cover story. The story promises ten ways to think about whether affirmative action is still necessary. But how does the cover illustration lead us to think about these programs? For example, who does it suggest Affirmative Action is for? Who is left out of the picture? Is it about gender? Is it about all people of color? Is it about all classes of Americans, or just the privileged members of one marginalized group? What do you think about the person in the picture? Does he still 'need' affirmative action?

There are so many things wrong with this picture that we will address only the single most problematic element: this is an artistic rendering of affirmative action, wholly created by the editors of the magazine.

The person in the picture was not chosen because he attended University of Michigan, the focal point of the controversy. Nor was he chosen because he was a beneficiary of some other affirmative action program. He was chosen because the cover artist wanted to tell a specific story, apparently that affirmative action is for the benefit of privileged blacks. This is a paid model playing a character. The preppy clothes he is wearing are not his. Not even the glasses are his own—there is a credit for them on the inside cover. He is a black body on which someone draped a collared shirt, chinos, and a tie. Using the model in this way serves a very deliberate function: it makes us think that Affirmative Action is not about women, or all people of color, or people of all classes. In so doing, it triggers stereotypes in the viewer, stereotypes that most likely will lead readers to answer the question, "Do we still need affirmative action?" with a resounding "NO!"

This is the kind of propaganda with which the media circuses attack blacks daily, and black public intellectuals, the ones who are accorded air and publishing space, haven't found an answer. In fact some of them make money by joining in on the attack and have fallen prey to the myth that affirmative action is a black giveaway program that offends white working class men many of whom are alcoholics, drug addicts, divorcees, and domestic violence abusers yet are set up by the media as the gold standard for how men should behave toward women.

In the course of a lengthy article he provides us with why neo-liberals love Obama's Joshua generation so much. It's because "Obama allowed that black anger about past and present wrongs was counterproductive." I guess I'm part of the Moses generation because I get angry when I hear about the police emptying their weapons on an unarmed suspect and I'm glad that my fellow Moses, Al Sharpton, is around to protest these police actions.

I also get angry about suburban gun stores pouring weapons into inner city neighborhoods like mine and I am grateful to Jesse Jackson for his sit-in and arrest at a gun store located in the suburbs of Chicago, one that had been supplying guns to Chicago gangs, otherwise the problem would not have received notice from the local press. Some people smugly dismisses Jackson's career as one about "rhetoric of grievances and recompense." It was Jackson who demonstrated that an African American who did not talk down to foreigners, the practice of white ambassadors and members of consulates in many parts of the world, could be successful at diplomacy. I'm sure that the relatives of the dozens of hostages who were freed by foreign governments as a result of Jackson's efforts view his career as having to do more than with rhetoric and recompense. Those who dismiss Jackson might view their pitting of Obama against Jackson as a clash of generations, but I view it as a continuation of the old plantation sport called the *Pat Juber* in which rival white plantation owners would contrive a contest between two bucks who would engage in murderous combat. Both Ralph Ellison and Richard Wright have written about modern versions of this custom.

Appearing on *This Week with George Stephanopoulos*, May 30, 2008, Obama critic Paul Krugman said that many women felt that Senator Clinton had been treated unfairly, ignoring the poll conducted by Pew that concluded differently. He also reminded us that those Hispanic journalists who warned their white colleagues that they should be cautious when writing off Barack's efforts to win the Hispanic vote aren't the only points of view that are neglected by a segregated arrogant media. In her reply, his fellow panelist Donna Brazile, dissenting, had to remind him, "I'm a woman, too!"

Obama Scolds Black Fathers
Gets Bounce in Polls[*]

(Barack Obama was congratulated by white politicians and members of the media, some of whom were divorcees, adulterers and substance abusers, when he criticized black fathers for their lack of "personal responsibility." When Rev. Jesse Jackson correctly described this speech as one that talked down to black people, he was sacked by the media. A week after his Father's Day speech, Obama appeared before The Council of La Raza and said that he shared the values of the Hispanic community, which, in some categories, have more dire statistics than those of blacks.)

* A version of this essay was first published at Counterpunch.org, June 24, 2008.

It's obvious by now that Barack Obama is treating black Americans like one treats a demented uncle, brought out from his room to be ridiculed and scolded before company from time to time, the old Clinton Sister Souljah strategy borrowed from Clinton's first presidential campaign when he traveled the country criticizing the personal morality of blacks and wooing white voters by objecting to what he considered anti-white lyrics sung by rapper Sister Souljah. (Though former President Clinton denied that his campaigning for his wife included a racist appeal, a book published in January 2010, *Game Change*, by John Heilemann and Mark Halperin, quoted him as telling the late Senator Ted Kennedy: "a few years ago, this guy [Obama] would have been getting us coffee.")

As in Clinton's case, Obama's June 14 finger wagging at black men was a case of pandering to white conservative voters. This follows a pattern of using public perceptions of black men fanned by the media and Hollywood to win political favor. Bush One and his sleazy cohorts won votes by depicting black men as dangerous. After the Willie Horton ad, featuring a black rapist, was aired, support for Bush soared twenty percent among southern white males, according to Willie Brown, former San Francisco mayor. Obama, by depicting them as irresponsible, saw his poll numbers climb to a fifteen percent lead over McCain, according to a *Newsweek* poll. With his speech, he received a bounce in the polls that was denied to him after he gained the Democratic nomination. He also enjoyed the bounce in the polls from Pennsylvania and Ohio.

According to pundits, the reason he lost these states during the primary was because he couldn't bowl. His Father's Day speech was meant to show white conservative males that he wouldn't cater to "special interests" groups, blacks in this case. This was the consensus of those who appeared on MSNBC and other opinion venues of the segregated media on June 16, 2008, even the progressive ones. (Segregated? Not quite. The two percent of African Americans who support Bush all seem to have jobs as pundits, columnists and Op-Eders). Michael A. Cohen, writing in *The New York Times*, June 15, 2008, acknowledging Mr. Obama's Sister Souljah moment, wrote: "Indeed, just yesterday, Barack Obama had his own mini-'Souljah moment' as he decried the epidemic of fatherlessness and illegitimacy among black Americans. While it is a message that Mr. Obama has voiced before to other black audiences, speaking unpleasant truths about issues afflicting the black community may provide political benefit for a candidate whom some working-class white voters are suspicious of—just as it did for Clinton sixteen years ago. " (When is Cohen going to air "unpleasant truths about issues afflicting" his community?)

The talking heads also concluded that Obama's speech before a black congregation in which he scolded black men for being lousy fathers and missing in action from single-parent households and being boys, etc., was clearly aimed at those white male Reagan Democrats, who, apparently, in Obama's and the media's eyes, provide the gold standard for fatherhood, which fails to explain why there are millions of destitute white women, "displaced housewives" and their children whose poverty results from divorce, or why, according to one study, ninety percent of middle class white women have been battered, or have witnessed their mothers, sisters, or daughters being battered. A smug John Harwood of *The New York Times* said that Obama was telling black men to "shape up." As long as men of Mr. Harwood's class dominate the avenues of expression, who's going to tell white men to "shape up?" Judging from my reading, American men of all races, ethnic groups and classes need to shape up when it comes to the treatment of women.

Blaming black men exclusively for the abuses against women is a more profitable infotainment product. Hypocrisy is also involved. MSNBC host, Joe Scarborough, who welcomed Juan Williams' latest demagogic attack on blacks, printed in *The Wall Street Journal*, still hasn't addressed the mysterious circumstances surrounding the death of his staffer, Lori Klausutis, who was found dead on the floor of his office or why he had to resign abruptly from Congress (http://www. whoseflorida. com/lori_ klausutis. htm). And is Juan Williams, whose career has been marred by repeated sexual harassment complaints against him really one to criticize the personal morality of others? Is Bill Cosby?

According to the census, a woman's income on the average is reduced by seventy-three percent after divorce in a country in which fifty percent of marriages end in divorce. Moreover the *Times* revelation, shocking to some, that elderly whites are taking to cocaine and heroin, a genuine epidemic, hasn't drawn a response from the legions of columnists and commentators and book publishers who profit from any signs of social "dysfunction" among blacks. Nor have Harwood, George Will, David Brooks, Pat Buchanan, who are always scolding blacks for whatever, commented on the rising incarceration rates of white women. Apparently, Lindsay and Paris are not alone, nor are the Barbie bandits.

Don't expect Obama to bring up this rampant substance abuse before a white congregation. He had to just about whisper about the values of blue-collar whites, those who he said clung to guns and religion; he was exposed by a woman who recorded his comments, furtively. Even though the media, which rank ratings above facts, continue to criticize him for these remarks and have made them a campaign issue, sixty percent of Pennsylvanians, according to a Zogby poll April 17, agreed with him. (The media were also wrong to suggest that Hillary got the worst of it from the press during the primary. A Pew study from Harvard contradicts this.)

Predictably, Obama's verbal flagellation of black men, who don't have the media power with which to fight back, was cheered on the front page of *The New York Times*, which places a black face on every story about welfare, domestic violence and unmarried mothers, and uses Orlando Patterson to parrot these attitudes on the Op-Ed page, yet a study published by the *Times* showed a steep decline in the rate of births to unmarried black women over the decade while the rate among Hispanic women has increased, contradicting what Cohen described as an "epidemic of illegitimacy" among blacks. An indication that the Op-Ed editors at the *Times* are so willing to believe the folklore perpetrated by such writers as Cohen that they don't fact check a writer whose assumptions are at odds with the reports from the Centers for Disease Control and Prevention *that they published* on December 6, 2007, and at odds with their token black columnist, Bob Herbert, who said on June 20, 2008 that illegitimate births have "skyrocketed" over the decades.

Patterson, Williams and Herbert have to rough up the brothers and sisters from time to time in order to hew the editorial line set by their employers. This was the conclusion of a study (*The New York Times*, June 23, 2008) by Bob Sommer, who teaches public policy communications at Rutgers, and John R. Maycroft, a graduate student in public policy. They examined 366 opinion articles published in *The New York Times*, *The Wall Street Journal* and the *Star-Ledger*. They found that at each newspaper ninety to ninety-five percent of the published articles agreed with the editorial page stance on the issue at hand.

Moreover, why aren't Obama and other tough-lovers acquainted with a study cited by Michael Eric Dyson in *Time Magazine* on June 30, 2008? In his Viewpoint piece, "The Blame Game," in which he also takes on Obama's blame-the-victim speech, he refers to research by Boston College social psychologist that found "black fathers not living at home are more likely to keep in contact with their children than fathers of any ethnic or racial group."

I asked for a correction of both Herbert and Cohen's assertions, since the Centers for Disease Control and Prevention report indicated a higher rate per thousand births to unmarried Hispanic women, but only received an automatic reply from the Times. A June 11, 2009 report commissioned by The National Campaign to Prevent Teen and Unplanned Pregnancy and the National Council of La Raza found that "Latino teens have the highest rate of teen pregnancy and births among all racial/ethnic groups." Why don't the legion of politicians like Obama, writers like The Manhattan Institute's John McWhorter, Fox News's Juan Williams, Harvard's talented tenthers, all of whom scold blacks under the guise of tough love, love Hispanics, the country's largest minority group? No box office appeal? No publishing contracts? No votes from Reagan Democrats?

A 2007 report from the Centers for Disease Control and Prevention showed some alarming statistics. "Latino high school students use drugs and attempt suicide at higher rates than their black and white classmates." In addition "Latino students were more likely than either blacks or whites to… ride with a driver who had been drinking alcohol, or use cocaine, heroin or ecstasy. "

Other studies show that of the three hundred gangs located in Los Angeles, over sixty percent of their members are Latino. Most of the nation's drive-by shootings occur in Los Angeles. Over fifty percent of the nation's school dropouts are Hispanic.

One month after the 2007 report, I still hadn't read a single tough-love column about the conclusions. Not even from the handful of Hispanic commentators or syndicated columnists, who, like the colored mind doubles, are restricted about what they say lest they alienate the white viewers or readership by appearing to be angry. For example, I asked Jonathan Capehart, the genteel editorial writer for *The Washington Post*, whose assignment from MSNBC is to link Rev. Wright to Barack Obama, why he didn't explore the relationship of Senator Clinton and John McCain to pastors who've made outrageous statements? I mentioned McCain's buddy, the late Rev. Falwell and his remark that the Anti-Christ was a Jew. Capehart answered that this wasn't the topic.

While white commentators might range over a number of topics, the black commentators have to stick to their assignment lest they appear to be out of control or "angry." That's why the black commentator who spends the most time on camera at MSNBC and elsewhere is Michelle Bernard, president of the far-right Independent Women's Forum. She apparently puts the white audience at ease. People For The American Way provides some information about the Independent Women's Forum at their website:

* The Independent Women's Forum (IWF) is an anti-feminist women's organization founded to counter the influence of the National Organization for Women (NOW) and "radical feminists" on society.
* Frequent targets: Title IX funding, Affirmative Action, the Violence Against Women Act, full integration of women in the military, and those who oppose President Bush's controversial judicial nominees.
* Opposes the United Nation's Convention on the Elimination of all forms of Discrimination Against Women (CEDAW).
* IWF's credo/mission: "The Independent Women's Forum provides a voice for American women who believe in individual freedom

and personal responsibility. We have made that voice heard in the U. S. Supreme Court, among decision makers [sic] in Washington, and across America's airwaves. It is the voice of reasonable women with important ideas who embrace common sense over divisive ideology."

* IWF was organized in defense of Supreme Court nominee Clarence Thomas during his controversial nomination hearings.
* In the words of Media Transparency, "The Independent Women's Forum is neither Independent, nor a Forum. Not independent because it is largely funded by the conservative movement. Not a forum because it merely serves up women who mouth the conservative movement party line." Two other black MSNBC favorites are Ron Christie, former aide to Bush and Cheney and Joe Martin, Republican strategist.

Either Obama and the pundits don't love Hispanics or there's more money and political opportunity in exhorting blacks. Racist appeals played a role in the election of Richard Nixon, Ronald Reagan, both Bushes and even Clinton, but there is such euphoria among many African Americans about the possibility of a black presidency that his dumping of a bunch of lazy clichés on them will be forgiven. They will forgive him for throwing them under the bus as he did Rev. Wright, whose criticism of American foreign policy and remarks about the toxic attacks on the inner city were based upon facts. He provided his corporate media critics with a bibliography, but they apparently were too busy palling around with the people whom they cover to read it.

Blacks will overlook Obama's snubbing of the distinguished panel of black educators, politicians and intellectuals who appear on Tavis Smiley's annual *State of the Black Union*, and overlook the fact that he found the time to appear before the American Israel Public Affairs Committee where he made belligerent threats against Arab nations and even promised Israel an undivided Jerusalem, he got so carried away, which undercuts a notion, held by Maureen Dowd and Susan Faludi, that he is the feminine candidate. When it comes to seeking Jewish votes and putting down black men, in order to obtain votes from white male conservatives, he can become John Wayne.

Finally does anyone doubt that the hypocrisy exhibited by some leaders of the conservative movement in recent years doesn't trickle down to many of their white working class followers in both states, who are idealized like a Norman Rockwell by talking heads, like Hitler-apologist Pat Buchanan?

I had a glimpse of these talking heads' lifestyle last May when walking toward a New York City restaurant called The Bombay Palace located across the street from CBS. The street was lined with chauffeurs awaiting the talking heads, who pose as experts on the white working class.

And if many African Americans agree with John McWhorter that racist attacks on African Americans, including predatory mortgages, racial profiling, capricious traffic stops, racism in the criminal justice system, job and medical discrimination, outlaw drug experiments and the exoneration of police who murder unarmed blacks will end the day after the election of a black president, they're in for a big let down. Again.

McCain Gurgles in the Slime[*]

(While the Clintons tried to use the fear of black rule and painted Obama as the *Other* in their effort to break him, McCain's campaign used the tactics that had been used against blacks in the South, historically, that of presenting Obama as a threat to white women and children, an image that Mrs. Clinton's associates used in the infamous 3:00-am ad. So desperate was McCain that he enlisted the help of those who used robocalls to slander him as the father of a black child, the calls that got Bush elected. At first, he even employed the mastermind of the ad that associated Harold Ford with a white *Playboy* model. Later, he took the advice of Kristol the Younger and accepted Sarah Palin as his vice-presidential candidate, a choice that doomed his candidacy. This was the assessment of even those inside McCain's campaign in post-election interviews. A book entitled *Game Change*, published in early 2010 revealed her lack of qualifications. She didn't know about the Korean War and didn't comprehend why North and South were separated. She didn't know what the Fed did. She said it was Saddam Hussein who attacked the United States on 9/11. When asked to identify the enemy that her son would be fighting in Iraq she drew a blank. No wonder that PolitiFact at *The St. Petersburg Times* cast her comment associating the health care reform bill with "death panels" as "The Lie of the Year.")

---

[*] A version of this essay was first published at Counterpunch.org, August 11, 2008.

Unlike *The Zulu's Heart*, *The Girls and Daddy* (1909) constructs
a blackface caricature as an outright sexual predator,
a wanton threat to two angelic white girls.

Daniel Bernardi, writing about the films of D.W. Griffith in
The Birth Of Whiteness: Race And The Emergence Of U.S. Cinema.

McCain campaign manager, Rick Davis, in a television performance, which, if he were a woman, would be called strident, or a black man, angry, faced down a cowed Andrea Mitchell after she questioned him about a McCain ad that even offended *The New York Times'* gentle Bob Herbert. Herbert wrote:

> Now, from the hapless but increasingly venomous McCain campaign, comes the slimy Britney Spears and Paris Hilton ad. The two highly sexualized women (both notorious for displaying themselves to the paparazzi while not wearing underwear) are shown briefly and incongruously at the beginning of a commercial critical of Mr. Obama.

> The Republican National Committee targeted Harold Ford with a similarly disgusting ad in 2006 when Mr. Ford, then a congressman, was running a strong race for a U.S. Senate seat in Tennessee. The ad, which the committee described as a parody, showed a scantily clad woman whispering, "Harold, call me."

Herbert even located some dog-whistle meat in the ad. Phallic symbols like the leaning tower of Pisa. Davis for his part accused Obama of playing the race card, when he commented that he didn't look like the presidents whose faces appear on the currency. Of course, Hillary Clinton said something similar during the primary, yet nobody accused her of playing the gender card, but Davis and his associates weren't interested in consistency.

Their ad, which suggested a sexual connection between Obama and two blondes, was meant to do for McCain what the Willie Horton ad did for Bush One and what the Ford ad did for Senator Bob Corker. So clumsy and obvious and removed from contemporary culture was this ad that Paris Hilton replied with one that was superior and probably cost less.

That they would slime-ball Obama from the bottom at this stage of the campaign might be viewed as a sign of panic, no matter what cable reports claim about a tight race. His campaign must know something that the MSNBC and CNN infotainers and McCain enablers of the segregated media don't. This kind of Hail Mary pass, using the kind of sports metaphor that commentators on shows like *Morning Joe* use to convince their viewers of their familiarity with the working class, usually occurs in October a few weeks before the election. What Robert Crumb might call the When-The–Niggers-Take-Over-America ad. After the ad, cable ran panels which included the usual prattle, filler that takes place between ads, except this time, Rachel Maddow, the brightest of the on-air commentators, David Gergen and Ron Brownstein deciphered the racist codes of Davis's recent appeals, for example, that Obama was "presumptuous," while black on-camera puppets of the far right denied that this was the case. They all seemed to be employees of Rev. Sun Moon, one of whom was used to frame the discussion on Jonathan Klein's sinister attempt at gaining ratings, the sleazy infotainment spectacular, *Black In America*, replete with the sort of images of blacks CNN runs each day: criminals, addicts, sexual predators (especially when the victims are white women) and the stragglers of American society, only this time dignified with panels—a carnival of charismatics—who competed with each other for applause lines. Klein, America's Julius Streicher (Nazi propagandist), and Davis probably think that their values are superior to those of the families of Paris Hilton and Lindsay Lohan.

To respond to the Davis ads, MSNBC ran Joe Mitchell, a black regular and former Cheney speechwriter, all day. He was one of those who predictably discounted the racist features of the ad. I'm wondering where the MSNBC and CNN producers get these far-right black people. Does Karl Rove have a secret Maryland laboratory where if one could hurdle a barbed wired fence, one would find a windowless building where inside these black right-wingers are being created in tubes, ready for use by the networks as opinion stand-ins?

Maybe I shouldn't have been surprised that Congressman Harold Ford defended McCain's camp from charges of racism. He's the head of Clinton's post-race Democratic Leadership Council, an outfit that was formed to stop Jesse Jackson. The Democratic Leadership Council holds that whatever problems black Americans encounter are a result of their personal behavior. I think that my personal behavior is okay, yet when I show up at an exercise track in a white neighborhood, I get stalked regularly by the Berkeley police. (Progressive Berkeley is now the whitest tract in Contra Costa County.) It's a tract owned by the university where I'm a faculty member. What do the Upper West Side progressives say about class being the basic "contradiction" of the United States? To the police, blacks belong to the same class.

I'm sure that Congressman Harold Ford was aware that McCain meant to spring one of these skanky ads from the beginning of the campaign, the ad that exposed the other McCain, not the beatific-faced martyr laying on a prisoner-of-war cot, but the man who makes sick jokes about bombing Iran, finds humor in rape, and offers his wife as a contestant in a biker's beauty contest in which nearly nude women do awful things with bananas while gyrating their buttocks, which makes you wonder why some of the Clinton feminists are threatening to vote for the man or assent to his election by staying home? The Zogby poll says that Obama is losing the votes of younger white women. Maybe you got to treat them rough. In order to woo this faction, maybe Obama should invite Mrs. Clinton to join him in an Apache dance.

I'm sure that Ford knows that McCain's first hire was Terry Nelson, a former Bush-Cheney campaign operative, who gets to exhibit his weird fantasies before the public and get paid for it. McCain fired him in July of 2007 for "mismanagement of operations and excessive spending." Nelson was the man who designed the ad connecting Ford to a blonde *Playboy* girl. The notorious bimbo ad for which Rev. Jesse Jackson got him fired from Walmart. Thank god for Jesse Jackson. Maureen Dowd sounds silly when she sums up Rev. Jackson's career as that of exploiting "white guilt," on the basis of comments by Shelby Steele who gets paid by the far right for his recycling of the same two or three ideas: that blacks are prone to "victimization," and that they exploit white guilt, which he repeats endlessly like a windup toy. His ideal is an African American who allows injustices to happen to them without protest less they be accused of "victimization," a word that rich publishers insist be used in scores of Op-Eds that blame black men for all social problems so as to deflect attention from the excesses of the taxpayers' subsidized "Free Market" system. In the nineteenth century, Steele's ideal African American was known as "The Contented Slave." Like John McWhorter, who told a C-Span audience that whatever complaints blacks lodge about their treatment in American society stem from their "insecurity," Steele even accepts money from billionaire eugenics quacks.

If his associating Obama with two hot blondes were not enough, McCain's bottom feeders followed this one up with one of Obama grinning after the fading image of a vulnerable white man and a child, an ad that was supposed to have been based upon the form used by the show *America's Most Wanted.* They were reaching all the way back to the Middle Ages with that one. According to legend, St. Nick's assistant Zwarte Piet (Black Peter) stuffs white children into sacks and transports them across the border from the Netherlands into Spain.

They also did an ad in which Obama was linked to a movie made in 1956, starring Charlton Heston.

If I were to cast Obama in a movie, I would have him fighting through a crowd of flesh-eating zombies and the lead zombie would be labeled "the media."

How did I feel about the ads? Some years ago, a clique of white students tried to needle me by writing racially offensive stories. I told them that they could write all of the racist material that they desired as long as they made it fresh and original. That ended their efforts. The ringleader finally came to my office and confessed that I reminded him of his father.

BOOGIEMEN

How Lee Atwater Perfected
the GOP's Appeal to Racism*

(The founder of the dirty tactics that were used by Bush One in the infamous Willie Horton campaign was the late Lee Atwater. In 2008, filmmaker Stefan Forbes approached me to appear in a film about Atwater.)

* A version of this essay was first published at Counterpunch.org, October 24-26, 2008.

One of the founders of the neo-Confederate organization called the League of the South, which will probably renew its call for secession of the southern states if Barack Obama wins, was the late Grady McWhiney. In his book, *Cracker Culture, Celtic Ways of the Old* (University of Alabama, 1988), he traced "cracker" to the Gaelic word *craic*—still used in Ireland and anglicized in spelling to "crack"—and said it meant "entertaining conversation." (According to *The New York Times*, folk etymology had had it that cracker came from cracking or pounding corn, or using whips to drive cattle.) He was quoted in the *Irish Literary Supplement*.

> Celts and Southerners, in Dr. McWhiney's view, are pastoral groups with a taste for gambling, drinking, "raucous music," dancing, hunting, fishing and horse and dog racing. They are lazier than the English and Northerners and cling to an easily offended sense of honor, naturally linked to "a propensity to violence."… He resigned from the League of The South complaining that it had been taken over by "the dirty fingernail crowd."

I learned first hand about how the media buckled under when self-described crackers seized the Republican Party. The kind of people who even use hot sauce on ice cream. Who, like South Carolinian Lee Atwater, love black culture, especially the "raucous" music Rock and Roll, but have issues with its creators. (In this tradition, check out Sarah Palin's hands-in-the-air moves on the October 25, 2008 *Saturday Night Live*.)

During the administration of Bush One, I was invited to do commentaries on National Public Radio's *All Things Considered*. After the infamous Willie Horton ad ran, an ad that criticized a Massachusetts program that led to the furlough of a black rapist and murderer, Willie Horton, and an ad that some contend caused the defeat of Democratic nominee, Michael Dukakis, I wrote a commentary about how the ad would backfire on Bush One and on Lee Atwater. The commentary was rejected and that was the end of my career as a commentator on NPR. Atwater also employed tactics that were used earlier by Richard Nixon, one of his admirers, and are being used in the current campaign by Senator McCain. Painting one's opponent as unpatriotic (a socialist, even) and packaging his wealthy clients as ordinary Joes, like Bush One pretending to enjoy pork rinds and cowboy boots. Atwater's playing of the media is also a current strategy.

A number of news entertainers have repeated the McCain charge that the media are in the tank for Obama. Two academic studies and one by LexisNexis have disputed the media's supposed love of Obama. I watched three hours of *Morning Joe* on October 20, 2008. Much of the time was spent analyzing General Colin Powell's endorsement of Barack Obama and debating whether it was given because both were black.

Pat Buchanan, member of the media that's so cozy with Barack Obama, is on MSNBC all day championing the cause of Senator McCain. During this show he joined Tucker Carlson, Howard Kurtz, and others who believe that the media love Obama. An Obama representative was riddled with questions, while Rick Davis, McCain's man and Atwater impersonator, wasn't questioned at all. The male commentators expressed their having the hots for hot Sarah Palin without mentioning Troopergate. Even Lawrence O'Donnell was panting about the vice-presidential candidate's measurements.

William Ayers of the 1960s Weathermen was brought up without reference to the support for projects on which Ayers and Obama worked from the Annenberg family, a Republican family that supports McCain. None of the media has followed up on Obama's listing of Republicans and conservatives who served on the same board as Ayers and Obama. On October 24, 2008, Joe Scarborough and Mika Brzezinski chided *The New York Times* for suggesting that there were hints of racism in John McCain's campaign. I suppose they missed the ad coupling Barack Obama with Paris Hilton and Rudolph Giuliani's playing of the Willie Horton card.

Here's the script of a Giuliani's Robocall:

> Hi, this is Rudy Giuliani, and I'm calling for John McCain and the Republican National Committee because you need to know that Barack Obama opposes mandatory prison sentences for sex offenders, drug dealers, and murderers.

It's true, I read Obama's words myself. And recently, Congressional liberals introduced a bill to eliminate mandatory prison sentences for violent criminals—trying to give liberal judges the power to decide whether criminals are sent to jail or set free. With priorities like these, we just can't trust the inexperience and judgment of Barack Obama and his liberal allies.

(With this appeal, Giuliani was up to his old tricks as the racial divider, an appeal he would later use in the 2009 mayoral race in which he supported Mayor Bloomberg against a black candidate and an appeal for which he was chided by *Times* columnist, Bob Herbert. The media emboldened Giuliani by supporting the myth that the administration of black mayor David Dinkins was a failure during which crime was permitted to flourish. A belated revisionist assessment of Dinkins appeared in *The New York Times*. Also, ignoring the criticisms of the mayor's actions on 9/11 by firemen and those who lost loved ones during the attack, the corporate media crowned Giuliani, whose support among New Yorkers was forty percent prior to the catastrophe, "mayor of the world.")

Walter Isaacson, appearing on this typical all-white cable panel adjudicating what's racist and what's not, agreed with Mika and Joe about the *Times* charge against McCain.

This is the same Walter Isaacson who traveled to the headquarters of David Horowitz, an ideological thug, and begged forgiveness after Jack White called Horowitz a racist. Mika Brzezinski chimed in that it's hard to run against an African-American candidate, which probably explains Governor Tom Bradley and Senators Harvey Gantt and Harold Ford.

The fact that we hear more about Rev. Wright than the preacher who embraces John McCain, Rev. Hagee, is an example of how the right has intimidated the media. For the same reason, we hear more about Bill Ayers than about Sarah Palin's ties to an Alaska outfit that advocates secession, the Alaska Independence Party (AIP) whose founder, Joe Vogler, made comments that in comparison make those fulminations of Rev. Wright, a former Marine, seem tame. Rosa Brooks of *The Los Angeles Times* (September 4, 2008) writes of Sarah Palin's palling around with secessionists:

> Over the years, Palin has actively courted the Alaska Independence Party, or AIP, an organization that supports Alaskan secession from the U.S. To

be clear, we're not necessarily talking about friendly secession either: As the AIP's founder, Joe Vogler, told an interviewer in 1991: "The fires of hell are frozen glaciers compared to my hatred for the American government. ... And I won't be buried under their damn flag."

The Robocall being used by McCain's campaign was one of Atwater's tools. Slyly disparaging your candidate by asking a series of leading questions. When McCain's Robocalls imply that Obama and Ayers planned the bombing of the Pentagon, some of the recipients of these calls are so ignorant that they probably think of the 9/11 attack and not the 60s Weathermen activities that occurred when Obama was eight years old.

Predictably in the final weeks, code terms like "Welfare" and "Socialism" are being bellowed by McCain and Palin. These are the standard Atwater tricks. Slithering beneath McCain's speeches is the idea that Obama is going to take the hard earnings of people like tax dodger Joe the Plumber, and give it to lazy black people who, as whites have been told by the media for decades, receive all of the Welfare, when it would take a couple of hundred years for blacks to attain the kind of subsidies and government support that whites have received. If one refers to these appeals as racist, the little Goebbelses surrounding McCain's campaign would plead innocence, another leaf from the Atwater handbook. Only Rick Davis has expanded the technique by accusing the accusers of racism.

Among Atwater's clients was George Bush One. So powerful is the Bush family, two of whose presidential campaigns were managed by Lee Atwater, that they were able to crush the promotion of Kitty Kelley's devastating portrait of the Bushes, *The Family*, for which she received Pen Oakland's Censorship Award.

The Bush family has even been able to wuss Hollywood. In Oliver Stone's *W*, George W. Bush is portrayed as a clownish loveable and clumsy dope and reformed party boy who was misled by incompetent and sinister advisors into believing that Iraq harbored weapons of mass destruction, not someone who was bent on invading the country from the beginning of his presidency, WMDs or no WMDs.

Bush One is portrayed as a wise leader, a Solomon, despite his connection to the Iran-Contra scandal, his support of Central American death squads, the Willie Horton campaign and his invasion of Panama that cost three thousand Panamanian lives. Nothing is said in *W* about the slaughter in the desert of thousands of retreating Iraq soldiers on "The Highway of Death." Lee Atwater is barely identified in this film. In his attempt to be objective, Stone chickened out.

Stefan Forbes, a young filmmaker with little money used a small HD camera, the HYX-200, edited his film, *Boogie Man, The Lee Atwater Story*, on a Macbook Pro laptop, the kind of brilliant use of technology that will lead to the decline of Hollywood in the same way that cyberspace is undercutting the flaccid Jim Crow corporate media where Joe Barbies and Jane Bimbos are awarded the status of journalists, and they have the temerity to ridicule the vacuity of Sarah Palin. Filmmaker Stefan Forbes, an outsider, has done what corporate Hollywood has failed to do with his *Boogie Man, The Lee Atwater Story*.

Forbes's is the most courageous film about the use of Atwater's tactics by the Republican Party and his beyond-the-grave influence on the McCain campaign, the kind of campaign that Joseph Goebbels used against Germany's *Others*.

Last year a bubbling, bouncy young Stefan Forbes asked whether I would be interviewed for a documentary on Lee Atwater, the Republican idea man who raised the dirty tricks strategy to an art form. Forbes and his producer came out to the house and asked me a series of on-camera questions about Atwater, specifically his use of the fear of race mixing, the old strategy that ex-Confederate candidates for office used to stir up fears about blacks being elected to office, while these officers were doing some heavy race mixing with African women prisoners. I also gave my opinion about Atwater's exploitation of anxieties about black men and his love for black music. Indeed in Forbes's film, Atwater comes across as a "white negro," a term that appears during the Civil War when a Southern newspaper accused Jefferson Davis of treating Southern whites like "white negroes."

After the interview, Forbes and I exchanged information. I sent him some historical documents and he kept me informed about the progress of the film. Early this year, Forbes announced that his documentary, *Boogie Man, The Lee Atwater Story*, would be shown at the Los Angeles Film Festival. It received rave reviews.

Next I learned that it was screened at the Democratic Convention. Preparing for a trip east on September 19 for appearances at Yale, Colgate, The New School, New York University and a trip to Buffalo, New York, for my mother's book party, I learned that Stefan's film would be showing at the New Cinema in New York on East 12th Street.

I didn't know what to expect. Our guests at my movie debut were my daughter, Tennessee and her friend the famed poet from Puerto Rico, Linda Rodriquez-Guglielmoni; Carla and her friends Karin Bacon, whose business is creating events all over the world—she got to talk to Michael Jackson in Dubai—and Kate Hirson, a film editor who has worked with Clint Eastwood.

People exiting from the theater recognized me and asked what I thought of it. I told them that I hadn't seen it. I sat in a rear corner of the theater in case I had to crawl beneath my seat were my performance not up to par. The full house was riveted as Lee Atwater's life unraveled before us. Forbes's interviews with politicians and commentators were mixed with archival footage. But the way the archival footage was used was ingenious. Some of it seemed to do for Atwater what talk therapists do for those who use their services. Though surrounded by his fellow good old boys, even at home, some of the stills show him to be distant from the celebratory events following the success of those politicians whom he packaged. In some of the scenes he seems to be daydreaming. When a child, Atwater caused an accident in his home that killed his younger brother. His screams haunted Atwater all of his life.

Lee Atwater perfected the appeal to racist feelings among some white voters. For over a hundred years politicians ran against fears of a black uprising, from the ex-Confederate officers, who regained their power in Congress after the Civil War, through Tom Watson, a politician who began his career as a populist, through the colorful Southern demagogues of the twentieth century. Instead of using explicit language, Atwater suggested code terms. "Welfare." "Crime." "Busing." In his famous quip, Jesse Jackson said "The bus is us." In Clinton's time, African Americans were alluded to with terms like "personal responsibility," a code term used by Barack Obama who Sister Souljahed black fathers in his Father's Day speech.

After some interviews with Joe Conason, a chilly Mary Matalin, editor of a foul work called *Obama Nation*, Michael Dukakis, who was destroyed by Atwater, and Ed Rollins, whose comments are frank, surprising and remarkable, my face loomed above the audience. I commented on my reaction to the Horton ad and had a voice over during a scene of the Bush One inauguration, commenting on Bush One, whose family includes some dysfunctional members, speaking of "urban demoralization." It's been three weeks and Hollywood hasn't called. My fifteen minutes of fame lasted exactly fifteen minutes.

Boogie Man, The Lee Atwater Story is not only informative but entertaining. One wonders whether the tactics invented and developed by his dirty-tricks successors, including the sinister bunch packaging McCain, will succeed this time. (These guys make Atwater's campaign seem benign. In one ad they presented Barack Obama as a sexual threat to white children.)

My only criticism of the film is the lack of discussion about Roger Ailes's role in the nefarious Willie Horton ad and the relationship that Lee Atwater had with the late Ron Brown, Clinton's Secretary of Commerce. Ailes appears in one of the movie's stills in the company of Atwater. Ailes, president of Fox News, once told a *Time* reporter (August 22, 1988): "The only question is whether we depict Willie Horton with a knife in his hand or without it."

The final scenes are ghastly as well as pitiful. Atwater is shown suffering from the final stages of brain cancer. He sits slumped in a wheelchair with a head the size of a prized pumpkin as his former allies ignore him. We're informed that as death approached, Atwater was consulting religious leaders. These include Buddhists. Maybe Atwater was reincarnated as the Fox News Network.**

** *Boogie Man, The Lee Atwater Story*, was shown in thirty-five cities before election day. For more information go to www. boogiemanfilm.com.

Morning in Obamerica[*]

(I wrote a light satire for *CounterPunch* of my vision of what a post-race America would look like.)

---

* A version of this essay was first published at *Counterpunch.org*, November 5, 2008.

The wolf shall also dwell with the lamb,
and the leopard shall lie down with the kid;
and the calf and the young lion and the fatling together;
and a little child shall lead them.

Isaiah, 65:25

The great American satirist George Schuyler's prescient and comic work, *Black No More*, is about a scientist named Dr. Crookmore who comes up with a formula that turns blacks to whites (I wonder how Schuyler would treat the current profitable back-to-Africa DNA hokum). As a result of a country that is totally white, the civil rights organizations go out of business, and even the last hold out, the character, based upon the black nationalist Marcus Garvey, in the end, tries some of Dr. Crookmore's solutions. Would something like this happen were Barack Obama to become president? A country where there exist no social divisions and the issue of race has become defused.

The leader of the NAACP says that the work of the organization will continue even with an Obama victory. Why? Wouldn't it be better that the NAACP shut its doors, as cable's leading conservative intellectual, Tucker Carlson, has suggested? Auction off its assets and join the post-race fever? In his *The New Black Aesthetic* (1989), author Trey Ellis announced the arrival of a generation of African Americans who would place the issue of race in the background unlike we "curmudgeons" and "cranks," who came of age in the 1960s and who are still carrying on like those Japanese soldiers who weren't aware that World War II was over. "The New Black Intellectuals" was even praised by Robert Boynton in an essay that appeared in the *Atlantic Monthly* (March, 1995:53-69.)

To many, Martin Luther King's dream has been realized. He said:

I have a dream that one day every valley shall be exalted, every hill and mountain shall be made low, the rough places will be made plain, and the crooked places will be made straight, and the glory of the Lord shall be revealed, and all flesh shall see it together.

Obviously me and my over-sixty pals are still lingering in those crooked places and refusing to process the sunlight that is available to everybody else. People like us are going to have to adjust to this post-race America, which resembles a painting by Edward Hicks. A place where blacks have reached the Promised Land?

What does this Promised Land look like? This Obamerica? Shortly after Obama is sworn in, the police, instead of subjecting blacks and Hispanics to capricious traffic stops, will only stop them to offer free tickets to the Policemen's Ball. Throughout the country, they will address blacks and Hispanics as sir and ma'm. The overcrowding prison problem will end because all of the blacks and Hispanics who've been sent there as a result of prosecutorial and police misconduct—probably half—will be set free. And all of those police who have murdered unarmed blacks only to be acquitted by all-white juries will be retried. Blacks will have the freedom to shop in department stores without being watched.

In the media, all of the black, Hispanic, and Native-American and Asian-American journalists, who, according to the Maynard Institute's media watcher, Richard Prince, are being "shown the door," will be rehired. The progressive media will spend as much time on the torture of black suspects in Chicago, New York and Los Angeles as they do torture at Gitmo. Blacks will be liberated from the crime, entertainment and sports pages exclusively and appear in other sections. They will appear in the more cerebral sections as scientists, engineers and astronomers. Jonathan Klein and other cable producers will stop managing black opinion so that it doesn't alienate its white audience and voices other than those of black correspondents from Rev. Moon's church will be awarded air time. Global-warming denier Michelle Bernard will be replaced by Jill Nelson.

Jesse Jackson will be appointed lead editorial writer for *The Wall Street Journal*, and Al Sharpton will assume duties at *The National Review*. Rush Limbaugh will inaugurate a series called "Great African-American Inventors." Spike Lee will be invited to run Columbia Pictures and Amy Goodman will take over at NBC. The Newspaper Society of America will apologize for the lynchings and civil disturbances caused by an inflammatory media over the last one hundred or so years. A choked-up Rupert Murdoch will read the statement on behalf of his colleagues.

In an emotional press conference, John McWhorter, Ward Connerly and Shelby Steele will admit that they have been tools of the Eugenics Movement and donate all of the millions they have received from far-right organizations to scholarships for black and Hispanic students. Blacks will have as much access to a good education as those members of Al Qaeda and Saddam's government who studied in the United States. This will end the policy of you educate them, we fight them.

Gertrude Himmlefarb and Lynne Cheney will insist that the works by Hispanic, black and Native Americans be added to the cannon. Cornel West will co-host a show with Dr. Phil. *The New York Review of Books* will end its white-only policy and begin to resemble America. Philip Roth will admit that all of his novels are autobiographical. Several prominent Abstract Expressionists will confess that they can't draw.

All of the blacks and Hispanics who have been driven out of New York, Oakland, and San Francisco, as a result of the policies of ethnic cleansing, advocated by Jerry Brown, Giuliani and San Francisco's Newsom, will be invited to return. The banks that aimed toxic mortgage loans to blacks and Hispanics, who would have qualified for conventional loans had they been white, will halt the foreclosure process and renegotiate these loans. CEOs on Wall Street will forego bonuses and golden parachutes. Sales conferences will be held at Day's Inn. For Rent signs will go up on K Street. The American Enterprise will close its doors.

The right will stop using worn out phrases like "political correctness," and "victimization" and hire Sean "Puffy" Combs to provide them with some hip language.

An Obama administration will launch the Obama doctrine, which will advocate friendly aggression and soft diplomacy in Africa, Asia, the Middle East and other global spots where American forces are killing people. These trouble spots will be inundated with artists, writers, dancers and musicians, engineers, doctors and people who speak their languages.

American students will be required to learn an Asian and African language as well as a Western one. President Obama will call for an end to warfare by air so that these forces will at least look their victims in the eye before murdering them. No more drones. Missiles. Members of the Joint Chiefs of Staff will address him as Mr. President, both in private and in public. The White House, haunted by the ghosts of the Indian fighters and slave owners and KKK sympathizers like Woodrow Wilson, who once ruled from there, will be demolished and the first family will reside in a St. Louis condo as the country seeks a fresh start. Cindy McCain will sell her wardrobe and donate the proceeds to rebuilding New Orleans' Ninth Ward. Any one outfit that she wears on a given day would help to rebuild a block. John McCain will acknowledge the black members of his family whom he has snubbed up to now. Obama critic Governor Schwarzenegger will be among the new president's well-wishers. He will offer to improve President Obama's physique by sending him some steroids from his private stash. And, by the way, doesn't an effort to put some meat on somebody's bones begin at home?

A big step toward a green America would be to return the land that was stolen from Native Americans. (The Southwest will be returned to Mexico).

A Tale of Two Callahans
The Irish Black Thing*

(Dr. Nancy Mercado complains about the media confusing Mexican Americans with Puerto Ricans. Pakistani-American characters in Wajahat Ali's play, *The Domestic Crusaders*, complain about being confused with Afghani Americans. Many of us have a tendency to treat "whites" as one undifferentiated mass. I do it all the time. As a short cut it serves a purpose, though if one were to examine history, one would find that those whom we consider white are one or two generations away from being something else. When the Armenians entered California's Central Valley, they were classified as Asians. Because of my education by Bob Callahan, and Danny Cassidy and others, I was able to notice that with the exception of Lawrence O' Donnell, those Irish Americans who appear on shows like NBC's *Morning Joe*, Scarborough, Pat Buchanan, Peggy Noonan, represent the Irish right and that an Irish American of the left was as rare as a leftist African American or Hispanic American. I was one of those who spoke at Bob Callahan's memorial.)

* A version of this essay was first published at *Counterpunch.org*, April 7, 2008.

When the media probe the homicides resulting from gang wars taking place in my Oakland neighborhood, they call upon the two or three African Americans listed on their Rolodexes to comment. Most of them live in places like Cambridge, Massachusetts.

Similarly, those on cable, who are commenting about how the "white working class," or "Reagan Democrats" are going to vote in Pennsylvania are as distant from "the white working class" as those Harvard experts are distant from the lives of those who live in neighborhoods like mine.

From the way they behave as experts on the "blue collar workers," however, you'd think that they brown-bagged peanut butter and jelly sandwiches to work instead of dining in some of the most exclusive restaurants in New York and Washington, often with the people whom they cover. That they motor to work in used Chevys instead of being chauffeur-driven in network limousine services.

Columnist Maureen Dowd identified the ethnics who are referred to in euphemistic phrases. She said that they were members of her tribe, the Irish (*The New York Times*, March 19, 2008), who are opposing Barack Obama's steady march toward the Democratic nomination, ignoring the fact that hundreds of thousands of Irish Americans have probably already voted for the senator. As the late Dan Cassidy, author of CounterPunch Books' *How The Irish Invented Slang* emailed me:

> The [Rev]. Wright pseudo-flap sure isn't keeping mainstream Dem. Micks from endorsing Obama in slews, i.e. Bob Casey other day, Pat Leahy, Teddy Kennedy, Caroline Kennedy, Patrick K., etc. I was with a slew of writers from Bill Kennedy to Dan Barry at NYT, TJ English, Peter Quinn, Terry Golway, etc., & all are for Obama.

Although there are many progressive Irish Americans like Cassidy, the media profile of Irish America lies somewhere between shrill talk-show hosts, who yell and interrupt their guests, or snarling resentful Archie Bunker types, or Bernard McGuirk, whose comment about the

Rutgers basketball team led to Don Imus's firing, or a pugnacious Pat Buchanan, who believes that it was Grant who surrendered at Appomattox.

In the movies it's "Dirty Harry Callahan" who violates the constitutional rights of suspects. There seems to be no place for a Pat Goggins of the San Francisco United Irish Cultural Center, or authors Bob Callahan and Dan Cassidy, who have worked for decades to heal whatever divisions exist between African Americans and Irish Americans.

When a memorial was held for Bob Callahan in Berkeley, a few weeks ago, there were African Americans in attendance including Al Young, the poet laureate of California, and Joyce Carol Thomas, winner of a National Book Award. Callahan not only counted friends in the African-American community but Native-American and Hispanic communities as well. He's the one who put me in touch with the late Andy Hope, poet of the Tlingit tribe, a relationship that led to my partner, Carla Blank, and I being made honorary Klan members on September 26, 1998, during an all day potlatch held in Sitka, Alaska.

When I told a professor at an eastern college that my mother and grandmother claimed Irish ancestry, he laughed. Since the Irish were indentured servants working on the same plantations as African Americans, why should it be a surprise that hundreds of thousands of African Americans are members of the Celtic Diaspora as well as the African Diaspora? Gerry Adams, of Sinn Fein, cited this plantation experience when lecturing to students at the University of California at Berkeley.

He said that it was the plantation owners who created whiteness as a standard. They wanted to separate the two groups. Some of those Irish men who left Ireland during the potato famine married African-American women, and as Noel Ignatiev points out in his book, *How The Irish Became White*, Irish-American women married African-American men. He writes:

> In New York, the majority of cases of "mixed" matings involved Irish women. The same was true in Boston. A list of employees of the Narragansett and National Brick Company in 1850 includes a number described as of Irish nationality who are also listed as "mulattoes."

In the 1860s, Muhammad Ali's great great grandfather, Abe Grady, came from Ireland. If Alex Haley had done a *Roots* about tracing his father's ancestry it would have taken him twelve generations into Ireland. Isn't it odd that so-called Reagan Democrats—Maureen Dowd's Irish—would be opposed to Obama. His mother was Irish, a descendant of Falmouth Kearney, who arrived in New York in 1850, a fact never mentioned when the cable guys are exhibiting their expertise about bowling and beer guzzling.

As the late John Mahar of the Delancey Street Foundation said when introducing me at a dinner held by the Celtic Foundation, if one drop of black blood makes you black—a commercial definition created by those for whom human beings were assets like cattle—why doesn't one drop of Irish blood make you Irish?

The cotton planter's one-drop rule shows little change in racial definitions since the medieval notion that the child of a black and white relationship would be polka dot.

American scientists may be able to analyze the chemical composition of one of Saturn's moons, but when it comes to race, the national discussion is back in the Stone Age. Some of our leading public intellectuals sound like Fred Flintstones when discussing the issue. Callahan knew his way around this and other topics, because he did his homework. In the material distributed during his memorial service held at Anna's Jazz Island in Berkeley, Robert Owen Callahan was described as "Gifted with a silver tongue, rapid-fire synaptic flashes and a huge store of talk, he was unabashed in his enthusiasms, embracing the best of both the schlock and the sublime of American culture and with a characteristic Callahan zeal."

He had a gargantuan intellectual appetite. (He could eat, too!) He was a genius. He had a mind that roamed over a number of fields of interests, from ecology, archeology, anthropology, botany, the Native-American oral tradition to comics.

He edited *The New Smithsonian Book Of Comic Book Stories*. He wrote the narrative for the famous graphic novel, *The Dark Hotel*, illustrated by the great cartoonist, Spain Rodriguez. It was a cult classic. He was also a publisher.

I introduced Callahan to Zora Neale Hurston. He was responsible for republishing some of her books, including her masterpiece, *Tell My Horse*. At the time of his death, he was working with Joyce Carol Thomas on a graphic novel based upon Zora Neale Hurston's work. We both took tenuous steps into each other's world. When Callahan invited me to a dinner held by the Irish Cultural Center, I called him several times during the day to seek his assurance that I wouldn't be harmed. I was treated very well, and my presence was even announced from the stage. On the night of the Holmes-Cooney fight, Callahan, his son David and I went to the Oakland auditorium to watch it on the big screen. While David, who was a youngster at the time, mingled with the crowd, Callahan, seeing that he and David were the only whites in attendance, looked around and said, "I hope that Cooney loses."

While the Irish and blacks have clashed in street riots, there have also been instances where the blacks and Irish joined in rebellion. On the evening of March 5, 1770, Crispus Attucks, an African American was in the front lines of a group of thirty to sixty Americans who clashed with the British, resulting in the Boston Massacre. Behind Attucks were those described by John Adams, who represented the British soldiers in court, as "a motley rabble of saucy boys, negroes and mulattoes, Irish teagues and outlandish jack tars."

The result of this confrontation was the Boston Massacre. In 1741 a group consisting of Irish and blacks engaged in a "plot to burn New York and murder its inhabitants." The leader, a slave named Caesar, Peggy Kerry and a Catholic priest named John Ury were executed.

John F. Kennedy, in the minds of some, did more to advance the Civil Rights movement than any president in history, publicly as well as privately. When I visited the black employees at Lockheed Martin in February, I was informed that Kennedy threatened to withhold federal funds unless Lockheed integrated its lunchrooms. Maybe that's why, according to Abraham Bolden, author of *The Echo from Dealey Plaza*, some white Secret Service men called Kennedy "a nigger lover," and vowed never to take a bullet for the president. Both Callahan and I were Kennedy admirers; Callahan was co-author of *Who Shot JFK?*

We listened to each other and learned from each other. It was Callahan who selected some New York Irish-American intellectuals to lecture at the Studio Museum in Harlem.

Such inter-ethnic communication is far more useful than cable shows pitting one group against another in an effort to raise ratings. No one denies that a racial divide exists in the country; the media exacerbate it for money. That's been the American media's mission for over two hundred years. A number of those murderous riots during which the Irish and blacks clashed were inflamed by a yellow press.

Callahan taught me a lot about myself and about the history of white ethnics, something that my formal education neglected to cover. In the schoolbooks as well as in the media, we're either blacks or whites. The whites are always San Antonio, and blacks are always the Knicks.

Callahan was a white man who listened, though he would object to such a designation. Callahan, editor of *Callahan's Irish Quarterly*, and author of *The Big Book Of Irish-American Culture*, was most of all an Irish American.

We got along with Callahan because unlike many "whites," he never forgot where he came from. He never forgot his roots.

The Inaugural
And My Coffee Pot Search

(The relationship of blacks to Hollywood and the media is like that of mine to some of my neighbors. I pay for my garbage collection. For years a neighbor instead of paying for theirs dumped their garbage on top of mine. Blacks have to carry their garbage and everybody else's. One of the recent big moneymakers for CNN was a stunt called *Black In America*. This was a profit-making enterprise that drew large numbers of viewers of the sort who gawked at P.T. Barnum's fake black nurse's autopsy. I wrote a satire about an imaginary behind-the-scenes discussion between CNN president Jonathan Klein and Soledad O'Brien, the show's moderator. Though Mrs. O'Brien was the up front face for both *Black In America* and *Latino In America*, she relied on scripts that were created by whites, each one assigned to an aspect of black life. Black males were done by a blonde woman with predictable results.)

White in America

My overall grade for this documentary is incomplete and unsatisfactory. In fact, most of the recent endeavors by major networks on the subject of Latinos in America have failed. *Latino in America* is incomplete because it ignores major Latino socio-demographic dynamics. It's unsatisfactory because it perpetuates a negative stereotypical depiction of Latinos in the U.S. While our (Latino) community is indeed troubled by many of the challenges Ms. O'Brien explores, it is unacceptable to paint that as the exclusive image of Latinos. Frankly, I expected better from Ms. O'Brien.

Victor Paredes, *Advertising Age* (October 27, 2009)

CNN reporter Soledad O'Brien should have her sisterhood card revoked immediately and never returned! She has damaged, betrayed, and disrespected the entire black female community with her negative, short-sighted, half-assed, stereotypical, and repetitive "investigative reporting" on black women in America.

Her program *Black in America: The Black Woman And The Family* was a complete and total fraud! This program did not address the lives and experiences of black women in America at all! It was two hours of the same negative racist and sexist stereotypes that the majority of white America believes about black people, particularly black women.

Professor Tracey, *Aunt Jemima's Revenge*

Act 1

(*Office of Jon Klein, president of CNN. He is a middle-aged white man whose attire is 50s. Dark blue business suit, striped tie. His hair is grey and white and he wears black-rimmed glasses.*)

KLEIN: Yessir, I understand that the shareholders are putting pressure on you and you're merely the bearer of bad news, but we have tried to improve our ratings.

(*So loud and belligerent is the voice on the other end after his reply that KLEIN removes the phone a little distance from his ear and makes a painful expression.*)

KLEIN: Won't you give us some more time? (*Pause*) But sir, with all due respect, I would like to avoid more staff layoffs. Come up with some cost cutting measures? Yessir. Tell all of my friends at Time Warner.... Hell.... He hung up.

(*Outside, chants are heard: "Fire Lou Dobbs, Fire Lou Dobbs." Goes over and shuts the window.*)

KLEIN: How am I going to keep Lou from going to that three-ring circus at Fox? Wish we had their ratings though. (*Returns to seat behind his desk. Lays his head on the desk.*) If I don't come through, I'll end up doing weather in Boise.

(*SOLEDAD O'BRIEN, CNN's two-fer, three-fer and four-fer peeks in. Cheeky, a smile that nearly reaches her ears. Egg-shaped face. Dark shoulder length hair.*)

SOLEDAD: Jon, may I have a word?

(*KLEIN looks up.*)

KLEIN: Sure Soledad, how may I help you?

(*SHE enters the room.*)

SOLEDAD: The memo, Jon. Requesting that CNN women wear more mascara like those over at Fox and MSNBC. Jon. Those Fox women look like Raccoons! Jon. Jon, are you listening to me? What's wrong with you?

(*KLEIN shoves the "Business Day" section of* The New York Times, *October 27, 2009, toward SOLEDAD. Right column reads, "CNN Last in TV News On Cable." A hand goes to her mouth.*)

SOLEDAD: This is terrible. What are we going to do?

KLEIN: How about doing a *Black In America, 3* narrated by Michael Vick or Chris Brown or maybe we can get O.J. out on bail? Or what about Gabourey Sidibe, the star of *Precious*, you know, the three-hundred-fifty-pound black girl who plays an illiterate Harlem black girl who is impregnated by her father? Why she's trampling from magazine cover to magazine cover and showing up at awards ceremonies like a baby elephant. She was even honored at the Mill Valley Film Festival. The only black person within five miles of the site.

SOLEDAD: (*Thinking to herself*) What is it with some of these white men and their fetish for overweight black women? Have to ask Paul Mooney next time I see him.

(*Aloud to KLEIN*) Er—good idea Jon but I think that we can get a bigger share of the market if we did *White In America*. We've already done two *Black In America* shows where we traced the problems of blacks to their making excuses instead of institutional and structural racism and we did *Latino In America* in which we concentrated on mostly illegal immigration, desperation, poverty and crime, grafting ideas from *Cops* and *48 Hours,* which you used to produce, now maybe *White In America*. (*SOELDAD Paces up and down the room.*) The increase in the incarceration of white women, showing that Martha Stewart, Lindsay, Paris and the Barbie Bandits are not alone, the fact that California white women do more drugs than black and Latino teenagers, heroin overdoses and emergency room admissions on Long Island and the suburbs of Dallas, the thousands of rural white families destroyed by meth—not only poor people but upper class whites like Andre Agassi, hate crimes against blacks, gays and Hispanics committed by white male teenagers, Sam Roberts' report that while two-parent households are on the rise among blacks, those among whites are on the decline, the rash of kidnapping and murders by white male pedophiles, the cover-up of child abuse cases committed by male members of the orthodox community, reported by *The New York Times*...

KLEIN: OK. OK. I get the picture. Let me think about it.

(*SOLEDAD exits. KLEIN dials.*)

KLEIN: Yessir, about our conversation earlier. I think that I have a cost-cutting idea. Fire Soledad O'Brien.

(*Scene ends*)*

* * *

Seeing that Jonathan Klein made money from his *Black in America* side-show, NBC decided to do one. This time narrated by Al Roker, a black newsman. That way it won't seem so racist.

---

* This satire was first published at *Counterpunch.org*, on November 2, 2009.

Such projects are meant to draw advertisers and money by using the testimony or stories of individuals to defame all blacks as some used the Madoff scandal to raise classical stereotypes about Jews. These projects, according to *The New York Times*, provide the producers with a "gold mine of opportunity," the words used by the head of one studio who was fighting with another over who would receive the profits from the movie *Precious*, a story about a black Harlem illiterate girl impregnated by her father, one that will be used to cast collective blame on black men in the same manner as *The Color Purple*, which, the producers claim, is the model for this film and which provided men and women of other ethnic groups to use black men as substitutes for whatever resentment they might have for the men in their groups. Black men give them an opportunity to vent. Tradition dictates that they have to keep their abuse a secret. So much money is being made from books and television that present Nazi-like images of blacks that one of the black exploiters Richard Price is moving to Harlem, which is an improvement over his former strategy for making millions from such shoddy products as *The Wire*, that of making "brief forays into the ghetto."

Obviously there are huge profits in blaming black men for social pathologies so much so that maybe the fellas should get a cut for serving this purpose. Not only from profit-minded producers (I wrote the *Times* blog, which held a discussion about the film *Precious*, asking when we were going to get a movie about how men who are members of the ethnic groups to which the producers belong treat women; it wasn't printed), but even saintly Amy Goodman broadcast a commentary by a guy who does her annual year end summary, which supported the Cosby/Gates/McWhorter line that problems confronting African Americans are self-inflicted.

I'm reading a book about a newspaper tycoon who wants desperately to gain the approval of the old-money New York crowd. So one day reading the obituary pages he learns that the scion of an old family has died and his great apartment overlooking the Central Park Zoo is available and thinks that maybe if he buys this place (forty million), the old money folks will overlook the fact that he runs sleazy news products even sleazier than Tabloid Tina Brown's and that he tells fart jokes and drinks a lot and though his newspapers preach family values to blacks, he's working on his third wife who is forty years younger than he. In his seventies, he's dyed his hair like a punk rocker and moved to a bohemian section of town. His hot young wife looks at the apartment and finds out that the old-money folks haven't kept it up and that it needs repairs.

I was reminded of this story when watching the coverage of President Obama's inauguration. The corporate media have hundreds of millions of dollars at their disposal but like the old scion with the great apartment who wasn't interested in repairing his dwellings, they haven't found the need to repair their operation. They annoy us with the same kind of structure they've been using since the 1830s. One writer says that the newspapers should get a bailout. He wrote the essay in *The Nation* which, if it were a black magazine, might be called *White Nation*.

Like National Public Radio and Pacifica Network, the majority of the contributors to *The Nation* are white men as are the authors of the majority of books reviewed. So if *The Nation*, *The New York Times*, *The Washington Post* and other publications receive bailouts, so should black, Hispanic and Asian-American publications. These white ethnic publications have always been aimed at a white market with blacks, Hispanics, Native Americans treated as foreign news. Athletes, Criminals, Entertainers. Especially entertainers. Even the Nazis liked black entertainers. Some of the Nazi generals loved jazz. They'd make the gypsies perform for them before putting them to death.

The Showman And The Slave, by Benjamin Reiss, traces the influence of P.T. Barnum's use of stunts and hoaxes on the early mass media. Only the stunts and hoaxes have become more sophisticated. In comparison to Judith Miller's hoax about Saddam Hussein's fictional weapons of mass destruction, Barnum's fake mermaid was harmless. Of the early mass media, "The standard picture," Weiss writes, "… was one of whites watching in dismay as members of 'savage' races devoured the flesh of humans. Africans, after all, were widely assumed to be the most cannibalistic of races and this was a sign of their savagery, their moral inferiority to whites."

Well, stories about African cannibalism are rare except for the neo-con *New York Times Magazine* section, which prints one from time to time about that subject and the periodic *Times* stories about people in Burundi hunting down Albinos under the belief that their body parts possess magical powers (but ignoring the fact that the economic growth rate on the African continent is five percent higher than that of the United States, whose is zero percent).

Selling the black "moral inferiority to whites" product has gone high tech. This accounts for big moneymakers like *The Wire*, a number of Clint Eastwood movies (who's sort of like Hollywood's Lee Atwater; he loves black music) plays like *Spinning Into Butter*, and stunts like CNN's *Black In America*, where CNN's lead bimbo, Soledad O'Brien, interrogated a black man about why he didn't attend his daughter's birthday party.

If this woman believes that the absentee father is a peculiarly black phenomenon she should listen to the hundreds of white students I've talked to over the last thirty-five years. One student told me that the parents of him and his friends leave them with hundreds of dollars with which they buy drugs (and so unlike some poor kids they don't need to commit criminal acts to get the money). One memorable line from one of these students was about a father who was "a tourist in his own home." According to one study, seventy-five percent of white children at some point in their lives will live in single-parent households.

O'Brien, following the lead of her boss, Jonathan Klein, also believes that crack is used by Harlem parents, exclusively, this comment following a report indicating soaring use of cocaine and crack among white students while that among black youth has leveled off. This is one of the frequent hoaxes that the media creates at the expense of blacks, like the yarn about how black voters passed Proposition 8, the measure that denied same-sex marriage to gay and lesbian couples, or the one about how affirmative action benefited blacks, exclusively. Hollywood and the media have found huge profits in promoting negative stereotypes and hoaxes about black Americans.

(What the black critics of Moynihan missed at the time was that the majority of white women on welfare were probably Celtic, members of his tribe, but in a shameless act of self-promotion he figured rightly that he would be more successful joining the Nixon administration by dumping on blacks, the route to power and wealth used by a number of individuals and groups.) Remember the "crack baby epidemic," a rumor begun by Charles Krauthammer? A hoax.

Ronald Reagan's welfare queen? A hoax. Affirmative action as benefiting blacks, exclusively? A hoax. Widespread mayhem and rioting after hurricane Katrina and the murder and rape of a seven year old? A hoax perpetrated by CNN who eventually fired the black correspondent responsible for the rumor after he made up stories while assigned to cover the entire African continent. Widespread rioting reported in Oakland after the shooting of Oscar Grant, one of forty-seven unarmed black men shot by Oakland police in recent years, a hoax perpetrated by Jesse McKinley, *The New York Times*'s invisible West Coast correspondent. The list is long.

The man who could be called the founder of the American mass media, P.T. Barnum, was a slave owner and a master of the hoax. He made money from exhibiting a black woman, Joice Heth, who claimed that she, after Barnum gave her some shots of whiskey, was 161 and nursed George Washington. When she died her autopsy fascinated readers and gave them something about black life to gawk at. Barnum even charged admission to those who wanted to witness this grisly undertaking. It was the O.J. story of the time and like the contemporary media have made millions from O.J. (his trial saved CNN), the penny press and its readers just couldn't let this autopsy story go.

I began a novel about the O.J. phenomenon in 1994, and what I've noticed is that O.J. is dragged into stories that have little to do with the ex-football player and even President Obama was joined at the hip with O.J.

Barnum and James Gordon Bennett's *Herald*, among the first of the penny presses, which debuted in 1835, made cash from Joice Heth's story but I doubt whether they were as blatant about their aims as CNN's Jonathan Klein who, according to *The New York Observer*, told Rick Sanchez, their right-wing Hispanic token, that money could be made from the race issue. *Black In America*, which was meant to make whites feel superior and humiliate blacks by proxy, made so much money that P.T. Barnum's heir, Jonathan Klein, says he's going to do another one in July 2009. People, whose interpretation of movies like *The Crash* and David Simon's black products differ from mine, say, well, Ishmael, you have to agree that these products, no matter how ugly and cynical and racist, give black actors jobs. So did *The Birth of a Nation*. But at least the actors performing in these venues get paid. The black panelists who are brought on to dignify town halls like *Black In America*, produced on the cheap, do it for free. They do talk shows where commentators have to fill sometimes three hours at a time. This costs less than some real investigation or in-depth interviews. Whatever you might say about the BBC, you do get African leaders talking for themselves instead of a stateside classroom person posing as an expert.

The blacks on cable are either conservative or passive or both. Joe Watkins, a MSNBC regular, and Amy Holmes, a Zambia-born right-winger, even defended Cheney's use of torture.

Therefore, I was really taken aback when Carlos Watson, the kind of mellow fellow who won't get angry (while Scarborough and Buchanan can throw fits whenever they wish) challenged Joe Scarborough's comment that the Obama stimulus plan was "a stinking pile of garbage" and charged that he and Limbaugh had gotten the Republicans to vote against the package. (On October 29, 2009, it was reported that the stimulus had created three hundred eighty thousand jobs.) Scarborough went apoplectic on the guy. Yelling. Screaming. And so I turned on the *Morning Joe* at 6:30 a.m. (Oakland time) the day of the inaugural and, you guessed it, I found Mark Whitaker, Washington Bureau Chief and Senior Vice President, NBC News, and the first African-American top editor of a national newsmagazine use the sales pitch that dates back to the 1830s. He was asking two panelists and a Scarborough host whether Obama should go into the ghettoes and get the savages to behave better. He didn't say it that way. That's my putting words into his mouth. The moral-superiority-of-whites sales pitch has become subtler. He asked whether the new president should go into neighborhoods like mine and preach personal responsibility. We're like the unruly blacks who were always getting into trouble in the movie *Cadillac Records*. We need a white savior like Chess Records owner Leonard Chess to bail us out of our screwed up "dysfunctional" lives. The White Man's Burden.

The two panelists to whom he directed the question included a former general who tried to cover up the massacre of Vietnamese civilians (and who lent his name and reputation to an enterprise) and the invasion of a country that posed no threat to the United States. The invasion has resulted in the murder of thousands of civilians and army personnel. The other panelist was a convicted plagiarist. The host had to resign from Congress abruptly because of a scandal in his personal life. Surely persons that my inner-city neighbors should look up to for moral guidance!

Over the last year, while there have been purges, buyouts, firings, of distinguished African-American journalists, even the women at National Public Radio who were hired to replace black men, who made their target audience uncomfortable, the black right-wing sock puppets have been kept on. They can always be summoned to engage in a finger wagging session aimed at black America. President Obama found it necessary to use this tactic when he did his Father's Day speech in which he scolded black fathers for their wayfaring ways, and Jesse Jackson got into trouble for accusing him of "talking down to black people." Obama was congratulated by some himbos who got their jobs the way the bimbos got theirs. Many find them pleasant to look at, but none of them has the kind of intellectual curiosity that is required of great journalists. They're there to entertain. The women to reveal their knees. The kind of media people who thought the entrapment of Marion Barry was funny until Sam Donaldson let it slip that some of them were doing coke themselves.

Some of them are divorcees and have personal lives that are in shreds but there they were congratulating Obama for what they deemed his Sister Souljah moment. They also liked his race speech in which he sympathized with the resentment of Reagan Democrats for what the commentators said was their feeling that blacks were getting more of a lift from social programs than they. Considering that whites were receiving land subsidies when Indians were being driven from their lands and blacks were in chains, were receivers of the major benefits from federal housing programs (which discriminated against blacks), the FDR programs, the Great Society programs, federal highway subsidies, the G.I. Bill which relocated them from the cities to the suburbs, I'm wondering what on earth President Obama was talking about. What is the basis for this resentment?

Nevertheless, as the cameras roamed over the millions who turned out to watch Obama take his oath and deliver his speech one couldn't help being infused with excitement and pride.

I thought of the six hundred years of resistance and agitation that led to this moment, and when he was introduced as president-elect with trumpets blaring like in the Gladiator movies, and walked down the steps toward his seat, I was really moved. This was not only a triumph for the persistence of the African-American movement, but even the intellectuals who've commented on this election have failed to mention that Obama is also a member of the Irish Diaspora. And that one of his ancestors fled Ireland during Ireland's darkest period. A man who came to this country with few assets. For some reason, the guys on *Morning Joe*—Irish-American guys—can't bring themselves to mention that Obama's mother was an Irish American. Wonder why? Shouldn't Buchanan, Scarborough, Matthews and the rest be proud of a home girl made good?

I thought that the speech was wonkish as well as Kennedyesque. "Let the word go forth to friend and foe alike." But it was the kind of speech that the president of a country, whose economic system is a kind of welfare capitalism, had to make. As Kennedy said in a back channel exchange with Fidel Castro, he realized the oppression that Cubans suffered under Batista but he was the president of the United States, not a sociologist.

After Obama's speech, I went out to buy a coffee pot, maybe one that would make both espresso and coffee, my drugs. There was a long line at Macy's. Could Obama's speech have spurred a shopping spree? No. They were giving away perfumes and colognes. A salesperson asked me whether I wanted to buy some cologne. The Krup coffee maker I wanted had been sold out. The Mr. Coffee maker at Walmart was too plastic. Carla didn't even want to step into the place because of its labor policies. Once inside she walked about the place with her nose upturned. I did notice the tell-tale plastic odor of cheapness. I didn't see any clerks. I figured that they were in the basement hiding from the immigration authorities. I finally ended up on Fourth Street, one of Berkeley's white zones, like the ones that exist all over Obama's post-race America. The kind of place frequented by young whites. The kind of people who, as Warren Hinckle said, hang around ice cream parlors all day. They offered this

Krup coffee maker that looked like the ones they use in restaurants. Way over my budget. I finally settled on buying a larger version of the one we had at home. A Bodum, the kind of coffeemaker that they must have used in the Gold Rush days. With this machine it takes all morning to brew your coffee but the taste is superior to those of the other types.

When I returned home, I returned to channel surfing. On *Hard Ball* Chris Matthews was allowing Jeff Davis and Robert E. Lee fan Pat Buchanan to carry on his on-going vendetta against the president (among the predictions that he made that didn't come true, was that if Obama were nominated, the Republican Party would "rip him to pieces." They lost!). During the first month or so of Obama's administration Buchanan said that the troubled stock market was sending Obama a message. But on April 13, 2009, MSNBC financial reporter Erin Burnett announced that the stock market had had its best twenty-three-day rally since 1933. So protective of Buchanan, who is on camera for the purpose of selling white supremacy, the old 1830s media formula, that little mention was made of Buchanan's support of the Nazi prison guard John Demjanjuk, who was deported in May. It's not that Dan Abrams and the others who employ Buchanan are anti-Semites. Buchanan is a good salesman for racism, which is a big business. The rage he exhibited indicated that MSNBC's Buchanan was clearly bothered by the election of a black president. He wasn't the only one. That's probably why Justice Roberts flubbed the oath. He probably couldn't stand seeing a black man sworn in. Chris Wallace over at Rupert Murdoch's big tent said that the fumbled oath meant that Obama wasn't the president. While a clearly agitated Buchanan was carrying on, I had a vision of old Jeff Davis and Robert E. Lee looking up from hell and fulminating over this inauguration.

On April 12, Obama mojoed his critics again. Faced with his first foreign affairs crisis when some "pirates" off the coast of Somalia held an American captain, Newt Gingrich, who left Congress in disgrace, said that "this is an administration which keeps trying to find some kind of magical solution that doesn't involve effort, doesn't involve risk and doesn't involve making hard decisions... nobody has the will to do anything." A few hours later it was announced that under Obama's directions, the captain had been freed. On the morning shows, there was a consensus that this was a test for Obama. Yet the next morning Chuck Todd minimized Obama's role and gave credit to other agencies and individuals.

The *Morning Joe* show became, during the campaign and afterwards, an adjunct to Sarah Palin's campaign, yet because of a couple of token liberal and "progressive" programs, Imus Alumni Howard Kurtz was still describing MSNBC as pro-Obama on January 25, 2009.

Later Matthews dragged out this black preacher whom the right, without success, has been trying to install as a black leader since 2000 (but at least he doesn't wear red shoes like America's other favorite black preacher.) A Bush fan, his selling point for MSNBC is that he can always be relied upon to boost white moral superiority at the expense of blacks, the old journalistic shell game. This conniving tough-love entrepreneur and lard ball said that when Obama referred to putting away childish things during his address, he was addressing black people who were children and were like back seat drivers complaining all the time and not doing anything. Or, like the late Saul Bellow said, like teenagers begging Dad for the car keys.

My neighbors and I have been trying to rid our block of two criminal operations for four years. We succeeded in closing one but the other one is still in operation. An interracial gang (that's right, in California the gangs tend to be as mixed as those who riot) is making our lives miserable. Engaging in shootouts, littering up the streets and bursting our eardrums with this dreadful noise from boom cars. Noise that they consider music.

We've tried everything. We've alerted the police, zoning authorities, the health department—they're still operating. We're doing something. Oscar Grant was also doing something. He was a butcher's apprentice who was dragged off a train and murdered by a Bay Area Transit Policeman. The latest news of January 25, 2009, reports that he was beaten by the police before he was shot in the back by a policeman. A young black filmmaker, quoted in *The New York Times*, said that class has replaced race as the post-race paradigm. Apparently the police haven't read that memo. Oscar Grant had class. He was a family man with one child, and a butcher's apprentice with a job. It's not class, its one's black ass.

Over at CNN, Larry King brought in the kind of people who Jonathan Klein feels make whites comfortable to comment about the election: corporate Hip Hoppers, athletes and comedians. MSNBC thought it clever to solicit the views of a ten-year-old black who, in the old days of vaudeville, would be called a "pick." His white teacher was clearly miffed that President Obama didn't drop everything to give this journalist an interview.

(While great black journalists like Les Payne have lost their columns, CNN's Jonathan Klein gave a black comedian a news show.)

Amy Goodman's inaugural show had some excellent features. She invited a historian who provided some historical background about the building of the Capitol by African captives. I always thought that the figure atop the Capitol building was an Indian. The historian says that it was a slave and that originally the creator of the statue had to replace a cap that was made popular by the French as a symbol of liberty because Jeff Davis, a slaveowner, and a real character who tried to escape Union troops by getting up in drag, objected.

The show was marred by a weak poem by Alice Walker. She called it her inaugural poem. I'd call it Hallmark lite full of syrupy bland sentiments. The problem with Ms. Goodman and other white progressive feminists is that they are so desperate for the approval of black womanists, who smile at them when buying their books but secretly despise them, that they are responsible for promoting some of tritest of black literature none of which has the quality of Elizabeth Alexander's inaugural poem, which, for me, was the best of the four inaugural poems that I have heard. While Barack Obama reached back to the eighteenth century for a George Washington quote, Ms. Alexander went back to Anne Bradstreet, in a poem that combined the rhetoric of the Puritans with the concerns of the proletariat writers of the 1930s while using the literary devices of the modernists.

Hats off to C-Span and MTV for providing, in my opinion, the best of the inaugural coverage. C-Span let its cameras roam without being interrupted by pundits who are wrong most of the time or who are there to deliver asinine and saleable tough-love lectures to blacks. While MSNBC has right-wing black global-warming denier Michelle Bernard, certainly more evidence that MSNBC is favorable to Obama, CNN uses Tara Wall from Rev. Moon's paper. (Michelle Bernard asserts her right-wing leanings from time to time, interrupting her pasted on smile. She opposed the equal pay for women bill that Obama signed.) C-Span permitted one to snoop in on some interesting sights and sounds. Like when the Carters passed by the Clintons on the way to being introduced to the crowds. While they greeted the Bushes warmly they snubbed the Clintons. Maybe it's because they know the extent of the Clintons' vindictiveness, still sore at those who supported Obama. Maureen Dowd reported that they were responsible for derailing Caroline Kennedy's Senate bid as payback for her and her uncle supporting Obama. Instead of patronizing those whom they view as their target audience with comments about the inaugural from athletes and comedians, etc. C-Span had a first-rate African-American historian Daryl Scott, Chair of Howard University's history department, to act as its guide to the Inauguration.

The corporate media won't give the new president a break, regardless of what himbo and Imus lover Howard Kurtz said about the media being one hundred percent behind Obama, one of those media hoaxes that's been refuted by three studies. He wants to be beyond race but the TV producers won't let him. He may have a rainbow cabinet and a rainbow following, but those who control the opinion industry don't include a variety of colors. This not only applies to the corporate media but the progressive and liberal media as well. Their ridiculing the Republican Party as a white country club is a case of people living in glass houses. This media country club will pounce upon every Obama misstep.

Though millions of people of different backgrounds, races and ethnic groups all over the world applauded, they view him still as the black president. Some might find this limiting. When they interviewed Obamakins in the crowd of two million, they focused on the views of blacks, (but in studio he was evaluated by mostly white panels and the right-wing black help). They won't give the guy a break.

When he gave speeches that were soaring in oratory and rhetoric they said that he was trying to be a rock star or, as Mrs. Clinton said, all he has is a speech. Then when he delivers a sober low-key recitation—a list of the crises faced by Americans—Jeffrey Toobin, who got his job as TV commentator for his comment that blacks shouldn't be "patted on the head" because they supported the decision of the O.J. criminal trial, complained that the speech didn't include flights of oratory.

Other establishment elements are using his election to suggest that the fight for racial equality has been won. *The New Yorker* had a cartoon suggesting that blacks were "Free At Last." They had a portrait of Martin Luther King, Jr. above an angry Bush leaving town. The Bush administration had a higher percentage of black contributors than *The New Yorker, Rolling Stone, The Nation* and other hip publications that supported Obama. In October 2009, Eric Alterman of *The Nation* commented on the decline of white American power. Not to worry. Whites still have *The Nation* where, like Pacifica, ninety percent of the commentary is by white males and an equal percentage of books reviewed by white male authors.

That cartoon in *The New Yorker* reminded me of what the great Chester Himes once said. He said that if you made a black man a general in the army you could do anything you wanted with black enlistees.

If, as *The New Yorker* and other publications have announced, we've reached King's mountain top, I guess I'm a lousy mountain climber. I hear all of the shouting and cheering at the top as the Obamakins survey the Promised Land, but I'm down here struggling with these rocks. If I were a nineteenth-century cartoonist like Thomas Nast, I would label the rocks: discrimination against blacks and Hispanics by the mortgage industry; racial disparities in the health industry; racism in the criminal justice system, including prosecutorial and police misconduct; the flooding of the inner cities with illegal weapons.

And while the media are heralding the election of Barack Obama as signaling the advent of a new post-race period, their own profession has seen a virtual purge of minority journalists, eight hundred and forty lost their jobs during the year of his campaigning. Moreover, if the visuals they chose during inauguration are any indication, Barack Obama is the post-race president whom they won't allow to be post-race.

Since then, millionaires and billionaires who own the media have used their talking heads to pounce upon any of Obama's plans that are injurious to their interests. Already AOL news has shifted from presenting its daily black athlete in trouble to taking down Obama and while a first-rate writer and journalist like Amy Alexander is having trouble finding a place to place her copy, AOL employs the imported intellectual mercenary Dinesh D'Souza to write about black culture and politics which is like it would have been had Hollywood hired Strom Thurmond to write the screenplay for *The Martin Luther King Story*. MTV's Youth Ball demonstrated that if the corporate media doesn't repair its relying on the ancient carnie act, *The Wedge*, to raise ratings they will go the way of the Republican Party. Tennessee identified some of the MTV performers for an old school person like me. She and I get into it about which period is the best. I say the 1940s, she says now and maybe the 1960s. When I saw the enthusiasm of these young people, black, white, brown and yellow, helping to build houses, repair schools and "all fired up and ready to go," I, who have been critical of some of Obama's cynical political moves, after all he's a politician, thought that he might just bring it off his "Yes, We Can."

I was wrong about Obama's being elected. I thought that Clinton would win. I voted for Cynthia McKinney because her political views are more compatible with mine. (One of Obama's accomplishments was that up to now black men have been seen as evil; now maybe we're the lesser of two evils?)

But I wasn't ready for the Obama phenomenon that swept over the land like the legendary Big Wave that surfers talk about. I should have known that something different was happening when I heard a black man call into C-Span's *Washington Journal*. He said, "When I hear Obama speak, I feel like just getting up and doing something!"

Finally, one hopes that no harm will come to this young president. Already he has challenged the United States intelligence community. The last president who did that was JFK.

(The National Association of Black Journalists jointly sponsored poll of four hundred and sixty-two people attending the inauguration in Washington on Tuesday found that most said their primary source for news was cable television.)

HOW HENRY LOUIS GATES GOT ORDAINED AS THE NATION'S "LEADING BLACK INTELLECTUAL"

Post-Race Scholar Yells Racism*

---

* A version of this essay was first published at *Counterpunch.org*, July 27, 2009 after Henry Louis Gates, Jr.'s arrest by a policeman in front of his house in Cambridge, Massachusetts.

Now that Henry Louis Gates, Jr. has gotten a tiny taste of what "the underclass" undergo each day, do you think that he will go easier on them? Lighten up on the tough-love lectures? Even during his encounter with the police, he was given some slack. If a black man in an inner city neighborhood had hesitated to identify himself, or given the police some lip, the police would have called SWAT. When Oscar Grant, an apprentice butcher, talked back to a Bay Area Rapid Transit policeman in Oakland, he was shot!

Given the position that Gates has pronounced since the late eighties, if I had been the arresting officer and post-race spokesperson Gates accused me of racism, I would have given him a sample of his own medicine. I would have replied that "race is a social construct"—the line that he and his friends have been pushing over the last couple of decades.

After this experience, will Gates stop attributing the problems of those inner city dwellers to the behavior of "thirty-five-year-old grandmothers living in the projects?" (Gates says that when he became a tough lover he was following the example of his mentor, Nobel Laureate Wole Soyinka, as though his and Soyinka's situations were the same. As a result of Soyinka's criticisms of a Nigerian dictator, he was jailed and his life constantly threatened.)

Prior to the late eighties, Gates' tough-love exhortations were aimed at racism in the halls of academe, but then he signed on to downtown feminist reasoning that racism was a black male problem. Karen Durbin, who hired him to write for *The Village Voice*, takes credit for inventing him as a "public intellectual." He was then assigned by Rebecca Penny Sinkler, former editor of *The New York Times Book Review*, to do a snuff job on black male writers. In an extraordinary review, he seemed to conclude that black women writers were good, not because of their merit, but because black male writers were bad. This was a response to an article by Mel Watkins, a former *Book Review* editor, who on his way out warned of a growing trend that was exciting the publishers' cash registers. Books that I would describe as high Harlequin romances, melodramas in which saintly women were besieged by cruel black male oppressors, the kind of image of the brothers promoted by Confederate novelists Thomas Nelson Page and Thomas Dixon.

Gates dismissed a number of black writers as misogynists, including me, whom he smeared throughout the United States and Europe, but when Bill Clinton was caught exploiting a young woman, sexually, he told the *Times* that he would "go to the wall for this president." Feminists like Gloria Steinem defended the president as well, even though for years they'd been writing about women as victims of male chauvinists with power, the kind of guys who used to bankroll *Ms.* magazine. Houston Baker, Jr. criticizes Gates for defending the misogynist lyrics of Two Live Crew.

Not to say that portraits of black men should be uniformly positive—I've certainly introduced some creeps in my own work—but most of the white screenwriters, directors and producers who film this material—and the professors and critics who promote it—are silent about the abuses against women belonging to their own ethnic groups. Moreover, Alice Walker, Tina Turner and bell hooks have complained that in the hands of white scriptwriters, directors and producers, the black males become more sinister straw men than they appear in the original texts.

There are big bucks to be made in promoting this culture. Two studios are currently fighting over the rights to a movie called *Push* about a black father who impregnates his illiterate Harlem daughter. (The movie ended up being titled *Precious.)* A representative of one, according to the *Times*, said that the movie would provide both with "a gold mine of opportunity."

As an example of the double standard by which blacks and whites are treated in American society, at about the same time that the Gates article on black misogyny was printed, there appeared a piece about Jewish American writers. Very few women were mentioned.

Gates was also under pressure for making himself the head black feminist in the words of feminist Michele Wallace as a result of his profiting from black feminist studies sales because, as she put it in the *Voice*, he had unresolved issues with his late mother, who was, according to Gates, a black nationalist. The black feminists wanted in. As a result, Gates invited them to join his Norton Anthology project. The result was the *Norton Anthology of African American Literature*. One of the editors was the late feminist scholar Dr. Barbara Christian. She complained to me almost to the day that she died that she and the late Nellie Y. McKay, another editor, did all of the work while Gates took the credit. This seems to be Gates' pattern. Getting others to do his work. *Mother Jones* magazine accused him of exploiting those writers who helped to assemble his *Encarta Africana*, of running an academic sweatshop and even avoiding affirmative action goals by not hiring blacks. Julian Brookes of *Mother Jones* wrote:

> Henry Louis Gates, Jr. has never been shy about speaking up for affirmative action. Indeed, the prominent Harvard professor insists that he wouldn't be where he is today without it. Odd, then, that when it came to assembling a staff to compile an encyclopedia of black history, Gates hired a group that was almost exclusively white. Of the up to forty full-time writers and editors who worked to produce *Encarta Africana* only three were black. What's more, Gates and co-editor K. Anthony Appiah rejected several requests from white staffers to hire more black writers. Mother Jones turned to Gates for an explanation of this apparent inconsistency.

> *Did the staff members who expressed concern that the Africana team was too white have a point?* Gates responded:

> It's a disgusting notion that white people can't write on black history—some of the best scholars of Africa are white. People should feel free to criticize the quality of the encyclopedia, but I will not yield one millimeter [to people who criticize the makeup of the staff]. It's wrongheaded. Would I have liked there to be more African Americans in the pool? Sure. But we did the best we could given the time limits and budget.

While his alliance with feminists gave Gates' career a powerful boost, it was his Op-Ed for the *Times* blaming continued anti-Semitism on African Americans that brought the public intellectual uptown. It was then that Gates was ordained as the pre-eminent African-American scholar when, if one polled African-American scholars throughout the nation, Gates would not have ranked among the top twenty-five. It would have to be done by secret ballot given the power that Gates' sponsors have given him to make or break academic careers. As Quincy Troupe, editor of *Black Renaissance Noire* would say, Gates is among those leaders who were "given to us," not only by the white mainstream but also by white progressives. Amy Goodman carries on about Gates and Cornel West like the old Bobby Soxers used to swoon over Sinatra. In July 2009, Rachel Maddow called Gates "the nation's leading black intellectual." Who pray tell is the nation's leading white intellectual, Rachel? How come we can only have one? Some would argue that Gates hasn't written a first rate scholarly work since 1989.

CNN gave Gates' accusation against blacks as anti-Semites a worldwide audience and so when I traveled to Israel for the first time in the year 2000, Israeli intellectuals asked me why American blacks hated Jews so. In print, I challenged Gates' libeling of blacks as a group in my book, *Another Day at the Front*, because at the time of his Op-Ed, the Anti-Defamation League issued a report that showed the decline of anti-Semitism among black Americans. I cited this report to Gates. He said that the *Times* promised that there would be a follow up Op-Ed about racism among American Jews. It never appeared. Barry Glassner was correct when he wrote in his *The Culture of Fear* that the whole Gates-generated black-Jewish feud was hyped.

Under Tina Brown's editorship at *The New Yorker*, Gates was hired to do hatchet jobs on Minister Louis Farrakhan and the late playwright August Wilson.

The piece on Wilson appeared after a debate between theater critic and founder of the American Repertory Theater in Cambridge, Massachusetts, Robert Brustein, and Wilson about Wilson's proposal for a black nationalist theater. Gates took Brustein's side of the argument. Shortly afterward, Brustein and Gates were awarded a million dollar grant from the Ford Foundation for the purpose of holding theatrical Talented Tenth dinner parties at Harvard at a time when regional black theater was heading toward extinction. Tina Brown, a one-time Gates sponsor, is a post-racer like Gates. Like Andrew Sullivan, a Charles Murray supporter, she gets away with the most fatuous comments as a result of Americans being enthralled by a London accent. On the Bill Maher show, she said that issues of race were passé because the country has elected a black president. This woman lives in a city from which blacks and Latinos have been ethnically cleansed as a result of the policies of Mayor Giuliani, a man who gets his talking points from The Manhattan Institute. Thousands of black and Hispanic New Yorkers have been stopped and frisked without a peep from Gates and his Harvard circle of post-racers such as Orlando Patterson.

Even the Bush administration admitted to the existence of racial profiling, yet Gates says that only after his arrest did he understand the extent of racial profiling, a problem for over two hundred years. Why wasn't "the nation's leading black intellectual" aware of the problem? His exact words following his arrest were: "What it made me realize was how vulnerable all black men are, how vulnerable are all poor people to capricious forces like a rogue policemen." Amazing! Shouldn't "the nation's leading black intellectual" be aware of writer Charles Chesnutt who wrote about racial profiling in 1905?

The Village Voice recently exposed the brutality meted out to black and Hispanic prisoners at New York's Rikers Island and medical experiments that have damaged black children living in the city. Yet Maureen Dowd agrees with Tina Brown, her fellow New Yorker, that because the president and his attorney general are black, in terms of racism, it's mission accomplished. Makes you understand how the German citizens of Munich could go about their business while people were being gassed a few miles away. You can almost forgive Marie Antoinette. She was a young woman in her thirties with not a single facelift operation.

What is it with this post-race Harvard elite? I got to see Dick Gregory and Mort Sahl perform in San Francisco the other night, the last of the great sixties comedians. During his routine, Gregory said that he's sending his grandkids to black historical colleges because, even though he lives near Harvard and can afford to send them there, he wouldn't "send his dog to Harvard." Maybe he is on to something.

When Queer Power became the vogue, Gates latched on to that movement, too. In an introduction to an anthology of gay writings, Gates argued that gays face more discrimination than blacks, which is disputed even by Charles Blow, *The New York Times*' statistician, who like Harvard's Patterson and Gates, makes tough love to blacks exclusively. Recently, he reported that the typical target of a hate crime is black, but failed to identify the typical perpetrator of a hate crime as a young white male.

Moreover, what's the percentage of gays on death row? The percentage of blacks? Which group is more likely to be redlined by banks, a practice that has cost blacks billions of dollars in equity? Would Cambridge police have given two white gays the problems that they gave Gates? Why no discussion of charges of gay racism made by Marlon Riggs, Barbara Smith and Audre Lorde? How many unarmed white gays have been murdered by the police? How many blacks? Undoubtedly, there are pockets of homophobia among blacks but not as much as that among other ethnic communities that I could cite. The best thing for blacks would be for gays to get married and blacks should help in this effort, otherwise all of the oxygen on the left will continue to be soaked up by this issue.

For white gays and lesbians to compare their struggle to that of the Civil Rights movement is like Gates comparing his situation with that of Wole Soyinka's. Moreover, Barbara Smith says that when she tried to join the Gay Millennial March on Washington, the leaders told her to get lost. They said they were intent upon convincing white heterosexual America that "we're just like you."

Will the pre-late-80s Gates be resurrected as a result of what MSNBC and CNN commentator Toure calls Gates' wake up call? (This is the same Toure, a brilliant fiction writer, who just about wrote a post-race manifesto for *The New York Times Book Review*, during which he dismissed an older generation of black activists as a bunch of "Jesses".)

Will Gates let up on what Kofi Natambu the young editor of *The Panopticon Review* calls his "opportunism?" Will he re-think remarks like the one he made after the election of his friend, the tough-love President Barack Obama? Gates said that he doubted that the election would end black substance abuse and unmarried motherhood?

Is it possible that things are more complicated than tough-love sound bites designed to solicit more patronage? Will he reconsider the post-race neo-con line of his blog, *TheRoot.com*, bankrolled by *The Washington Post*? Will he invite writers Carl Dix and Askia Toure, who represent other African-American constituencies, as much as he prints the views of far-right Manhattan Institute spokesperson and racial profiling denier, John McWhorter.

Will he continue to advertise shoddy blame-the-victim and black pathology sideshows like CNN's *Black In America*, and *The Wire*? (Predictably CNN's Anderson Cooper turned Gates' controversy into a carnival act. The story was followed by one about Michael Jackson's doctors. CNN is making so much money and raising its ratings so rapidly from black pathology stories that it's beginning to give Black Entertainment Network a run for its money, so to speak.)

Predictably, the segregated media—the spare all-whites jury dominating the conversation about race as usual—gave the Cambridge cop the benefit of the doubt and the police unions backed him up. The police unions always back up their fellow officers even when they shoot unarmed black suspects in the back or, in the case of Papa Charlie James, an elderly San Francisco black man, while he was laying in bed. They back each other up and "testilie" all of the time.

Will Gates listen to his critics from whom he has been protected by powerful moneyed forces, which have given him the ability to make or break academic careers, preside over the decision-making of patronage and grant-awarding institutions? Houston A. Baker, Jr.'s *Betrayal: How Black Intellectuals Have Abandoned The Ideals Of The Civil Rights Era* offers mild criticisms of Gates, West and other black public intellectuals, who, according to him, are "embraced by virtue of their race-transcendent ideology." His book went from the warehouse to the remainder shelves. *The Village Voice* promised two installments of courageous muckraking pieces about Gates written by novelist, playwright and poet Thulani Davis; Part Two never appeared. Letters challenging Gates by one of Gates' main critics at Harvard, Dr. Martin Kilson, have been censored. Kilson refers to Gates as "the master of the intellectual dodge." And even when Professor Melissa Harris-Lacewell at *The Nation*'s blog defied the 24-hour news cycle that has depicted Gates, a black nationalist critic, as an overnight black nationalist—she calls him "apolitical"—she had to pull her punches. As an intellectual, she has more depth than all of the white mainstream and white progressive media's selected "leaders of black intellection," among whom are post-modernist preachers who can spew rhetoric faster than the speed of light.

It remains to be seen whether Gates, who calls himself an intellectual entrepreneur, will now use his "wake up call" to lead a movement that

will challenge racial disparities in the criminal justice system. A system
that is rotten to the core, where whites commit the overwhelming majority of the crimes, while blacks and Hispanics do the time. A prison system where torture and rape are regular occurrences and where in some
states the conditions are worse than at Gitmo. California prisons hospi-
tals are so bad that they have been declared unconstitutional and a form
of torture, over the objections of Attorney General Jerry Brown and
Arnold Schwarzenegger, who leased his face to the rich and was on television the other day talking about how rough they have it. A man who
is channeling his hero the late Kurt Waldheim's attitudes toward the poor
and disabled.

Gates can help lead the fight so that there will be mutual respect
between law enforcement and minorities instead of their calling us nig-
gers all the time and being Marvin Gaye's "trigger happy" policemen.
Not all of them but quite a few. Or Gates can coast along. Continue to
maintain that black personal behavior, like not turning off the TV at
night, is at the root of the barriers facing millions of black Americans.
Will he return to the intellectual rigor espoused by his hero W.E.B.
DuBois or will he continue to act as a sort of black intellectual Charles
Van Doren? An entertainer. (An insider at PBS told me that the network
is demanding that Gates back up his claims about the ancestry of celebrities with more solid proofs.)

Gates has discussed doing a documentary about racial profiling. I
invite him to cover a meeting residents of my Oakland ghetto neighborhood have with the police each month. (Most of our problems incidentally are caused by the offspring of two family households. Suburban gun
dealers who arm gang leaders. The gang leader on our block isn't black!
An absentee landlord who owns a house where crack operations take
place.) He can bring Bill Cosby with him. He'll find that the problems of
inner citizens are more complex than "thirty-five-year-old grandmothers
living in the projects" and rappers not pulling up their pants and that
racism remains in the words of the great novelist John A. Williams, "an
inexorable force."

Finally, in his 2002 Jefferson lecture, delivered at the Library of
Congress, Henry Louis Gates, Jr., during remarks about the eighteenth-

century poet Phillis Wheatley in which he excoriated the attitudes of her critics in the Black Arts movement, one more time, ended his lecture with: "We can finally say: Welcome home, Phillis; welcome home."

If Gates ceases his role as just another tough lover and an "intellectual entrepreneur," and takes a role in ending racial traffic and retail profiling, and police home invasions, issues that have lingered since even before Chesnutt's time, we can say, "Welcome home, Skip; welcome home."

WHY THE MEDIA AND ITS "GENERAL PUBLIC"
BOUGHT SGT. CROWLEY'S LIE

Let's All Have a Beer*

* A version of this essay was first published *at Counterpunch.org*, August 6, 2009

It's not surprising that some whites, who monopolize the means of expression both electronically and in print, mainstream and progressive, would automatically take Sgt. James M. Crowley's word against Henry Louis Gates, Jr.'s even though Crowley's account of the Gates arrest has been disputed by both Gates and Lucia Whalen, the woman who called 911.

They also disapprove of President Obama calling the action "stupid." According to a CNN poll, fifty-nine percent of blacks believe that Officer Crowley acted stupidly; twenty-nine percent of whites.

Whalen said nothing about "two black men with back packs," during her 911 call as noted by *The New York Times*, the day after two of its reporters embraced Crowley's version of the incident. She never used the word black. Crowley's invisible "two black men with back packs" came from the same part of the American imagination as Susan Smith's black man wearing a knitted cap, Bonnie Smith's invisible car-jacking black men and Charles Stuart's invisible black-male murderers. The same place as Barack Obama's invisible Kenyan birth certificate, a hoax accepted by the Gothic South where the uniform of its homegrown terrorist movement is that of Casper the Friendly Ghost.

Even twelve-year-old Christopher Pittman got into the act. After blowing his grandparents to Kingdom Come with a shotgun, young Pittman blamed the murders on an invisible over-six-feet-tall black man.

Now that there are fears of black and brown uprisings, fears stoked by Rupert Murdoch and CNN's Jonathan Klein, for ratings, the country is revisiting Cotton Mather, the real founding father, who wrote a book about his personal hallucinations called *The Wonders of the Invisible World Being an Account of the Trials of Several Witches Lately Executed in New England*. His Salem Woods were full of invisible black men. He was one of those nuts who sparked the witch hysteria, which has become the Obama hysteria, inflamed by Klein and Murdoch who go after eyeballs like vampires go after an exposed neck.

Birthers, the creator of Obama as the Joker, tea baggers and assorted anti-Obama nuts are always welcomed at birther-loving CNN, MSNBC and Fox. I don't know what all of this is leading up to, but I hope that members of President Obama's Secret Service detail have been rigorously screened. Abraham Bolden, author of *The Echo from Dealey Plaza*, writes about the racist attitudes of the men who "guarded" JFK. One of them said that he'd never take a bullet for a "nigger lover."

One of those who is under the post-race spell is Stuart Taylor, senior columnist for *National Journal*. Appearing on the August 3 edition of the *Washington Journal*, Taylor said that the Gates arrest had nothing to do with race. When a black caller from Michigan accused Crowley of lying, Taylor said that "there was no proof of a significant misstatement" by Officer Crowley. He argued that we've entered a post-race period because of Obama's election and that "there was not a single example of discrimination against Obama in his entire life," even though Obama says that he experienced racial profiling while serving in the Illinois Legislature. Taylor also denied the existence of racial profiling saying that "a lot of white people get treated worse by the police" than blacks.

Taylor also said that whites don't do crack, when studies I've read indicate that whites consume most of the crack; they just don't get sentenced for its possession and sale. "Crack penalties appear to hit minorities harder," was the headline of a *Los Angeles Times* story published in May 1995.

> Despite evidence that large numbers of whites use and sell crack cocaine, federal law enforcement in Southern California has waged its war against crack almost exclusively in minority neighborhoods, exposing black and Latino offenders to the toughest drug penalties in the nation.
>
> Not a single white, records show, has been convicted of a crack cocaine offense in federal courts serving Los Angeles and six Southern California counties since Congress enacted stiff mandatory sentences for crack dealers in 1986.

Yet Taylor attributed the obstacles facing black Americans to their personal behavior, which has been Skip Gates' line up to now. Like "poor work habits," which makes you wonder how over eighty percent of blacks manage to hold down jobs; given Stuart's error-filled interview, who is he to complain about poor work habits?

Taylor's main point was that "racial preferences pervade American society" when a number of studies, including one from the Department of Labor, describe affirmative action as benefiting white women the most. Taylor was interviewed by a white woman, Libby Casey, who neglected to point this out.

He said that a disproportionate number of blacks are incarcerated because they commit most of the crimes, another lie. They just get arrested more often. Seventy-five percent of blacks and Hispanics wouldn't be in jail if they were white, and lies coming from Taylor and his colleague at the *National Journal*, Ron Brownstein, contribute to the climate that sends them there. Brownstein and Taylor make a living by ratcheting up white resentment against blacks, a job so easy that you can do it from the beach. All that is required is a laptop.

Bill Cosby is providing these opportunists with ammunition through his poor command of the facts. I love the guy, and will never forget the time when he flew me up to Harrah's and provided me with accommodations that included a chef, and introduced me to Ray Charles, but his tough-love lectures are shaky.

Instead of lecturing "thirty-five-year-old grandmothers living in the projects," wealthy black Americans like Bill Cosby and Henry Louis Gates, Jr., who view the "underclass" from first class seats, should establish a black version of the Anti-Defamation League that would challenge the 24/7 false reporting about minorities, who don't have the media power to fight back.

I'd make a contribution and I know a number of people who'd do the same. For its part, the Anti-Defamation League exposes anti-Semites who are racists as well, some of them armed with deadly weapons.

Letters to the editor, like the one that NAACP president Julian Bond wrote to *The New York Times*, reminding them that affirmative action is preferential toward white women, don't seem to have an impact. Bond disputed the paper's recent right-wing hire, Op-Ed writer Ross Douthat, who, like a reporter for the *Times*, believes that affirmative action is primarily "race conscious."

Stuart Taylor's responses lacked the facts, yet he warned Gates that "he should be careful about what he says."

The fact that men of Taylor's background and prejudices dominate the discussion of race in the United States is just another bill that blacks have to pay, and you'd think that the media—both mainstream and progressive—would host white writers who weren't so much in denial about race. Writers like Leo Litwack, David Zirin, James Lowen, Russell Banks, Tim Wise and Dalton Conley, and Jack Foley, an Irish American who is not trying to impress WASPs by playing Handel on the harpsichord.

With his lies, Sgt. Crowley not only made fools of Stuart Taylor, *Huffington Post* commentators Robin Wells and Frank Serpico, who accepted his false report, but most depressing, Greg Palast, a leader in the fight against the caging of voters. Moreover, Crowley, who, after the beer summit, seemed grateful that things didn't have to get "physical" with Gates, a fifty-eight-year-old man who walks with a cane.

The American media have sided with the police most of the time, even when the police led the invasions of black neighborhoods where the inhabitants were massacred, or when they simply stood by and watched—something that the Cambridge and Boston police didn't learn in school, nor did the whites, the media's "general public," who, when polled, took Crowley's word over Gates'. The Newseum in Washington, DC should have a hall of shame, which would display the headlines of newspapers whose inflammatory reporting led to race riots: Tulsa, Oklahoma, 1921; New Orleans, 1900; etc.

Showman Lou Dobbs praised Sgt. Leon Lashley, the black policeman who backed Crowley as some kind of martyr to political correctness, without mentioning that the officer said that he would have handled the situation differently. Can you blame the guy? He has to work with people like Justin Barrett, the Boston cop who called Gates "a banana eating jungle bunny" and threatened that if Gates had given him some "belligerent non-compliance" he would have "sprayed him in the face with OC [pepper spray]." Officer Barrett is suing the city of Boston because in the view of him and his lawyer, he was fired, unjustly, by Boston's mayor. His suit lists the damage that the mayor has caused him "…Pain and suffering; mental anguish; emotional distress; post-traumatic stress; sleeplessness; indignities and embarrassment; degradation; injury to reputation; and restriction on his personal freedom."

His lawyer Peter Marano said that Barrett didn't mean to characterize Gates as a "banana eating jungle monkey," but only meant to characterize Gates' behavior.

Appearing on the *Larry King Show*, however, Barrett said that he didn't know what made him say that, a statement which just about pleads for a new branch of psychiatry, or at least of an exorcism. His pathetic attempt at wit is the kind of thing that black policemen have had to deal with for decades: racist graffiti posted on bulletin boards, on emails, overheard on police radios, pasted on their lockers.

Lou Dobbs wasn't the only commentator cherry-picking the information from the Gates-Crowley encounter. Ed Schultz, a progressive, didn't even mention Ms. Whalen's disputing of Officer Crowley's report. He supported the media line that both Gates and Crowley overreacted, with Gates doing the most overreacting.

The typical response by the talking heads—even the token progressives—took Sgt. Crowley's word over that of a black professor and a white woman. In a show of ethnic solidarity with Crowley, the *Morning Joe* show's Mike Barnicle said that the next time Gates needed a policeman, he should call the Harvard lounge, a remark that drew round-the-clock thigh slapping and yuks from his colleagues. In other words, blacks, Hispanics and Native Americans should accept any action from the police even when it violates their rights, because they, the taxpayers who pay their salaries, might need them in the future.

Chris Matthews, another member of MSNBC's Irish-American mafia, nominated Crowley for governor of Massachusetts after Crowley's arrogant and unremarkable press conference. (If a poll were conducted in Ireland, Gates' version of events would probably prevail over Crowley's.)

An on-camera left-wing Irish American is as rare as a left-wing African American or Hispanic. *Salon*'s Joan Walsh won't do. She agreed with the Albany jury that acquitted the police who murdered Amadou Diallo, who didn't have a PhD. Like Maureen Dowd, Joan Walsh has cops in her family. If CNN and MSNBC were interested in recruiting some left-wing

Irish commentators they might contact the newspaper *Irish Echo*, which they ought to read. Of course if Celtic-African-American President Obama showed signs of solidarity with the brothers and sisters, like that shown toward Crowley by Scarborough, Matthews, Barnicle and Joe Queenan, appearing on the *Bill Mahar Show*, he'd be dismissed as an angry black chauvinist. Black and brown cable faces are also drawn from the political right. The lone progressive CNN Hispanic contributor is often outnumbered three to one. The leader of CNN's Hispanic right is Cuban American Rick Sanchez, who ran down a homeless man named Jeffrey Smuzinick after imbibing "a few cocktails" at a Dolphins game. One of the few Hispanic syndicated columnists is Ruben Navarrete, Jr. whose assignment, like the three at CNN, is to take it to the brothers and sisters from time to time. (Leslie Sanchez, a Republican spokesperson, appears on both MSNBC and CNN.) For example, Navarrete, accepting Crowley's account, blamed the whole incident on Gates' not being deferential to the cop. Maybe Gates should have said something like "Bossman police, Iz sorry for bein' in my own house," followed by an offer to shine his shoes. I reminded Navarrete that Crowley lied. He answered with a sarcastic note. Navarrete is the writer who said that he was okay with *The New York Post* cartoon in which President Obama was depicted as a dead chimp slain by the police. Even Rupert Murdoch, the closest media owner we're likely to get to Goebbels, apologized for that one. The black face at *Time* is Ramesh Ponnuru, perhaps a reward for his taking the flak at *The National Review* when Asian-American groups protested a cartoon, which they found offensive. Ramesh Ponnuru defended the cartoon. One of the editors at the time told the protestors that he would not "kowtow" to their demands.

Gates might have raised his voice, he might have yelled, but there was no evidence that he was "belligerent," in the words of blogger and yoga instructor Robin Wells or "cantankerous," the word used by sportscaster Stephen A. Smith, who also blamed the incident on Gates. Why would Ms. Wells take the word of Officer Crowley over that of her colleague in the sisterhood, Lucia Whalen? Does Arianna Huffington agree with Ms. Wells?

The fact that black commentators also accepted the officer's testimony shows the compromises that some blacks have to make in order to keep their jobs in an industry owned by the white right. Oh, sure, the reporters might be liberal, but they don't run Clear Channel, Fox, CNN, MSNBC and McClatchy.

Before integration, black newspapers were so powerful and independent that J. Edgar Hoover wanted to charge them with sedition according to *A Question of Sedition* by Patrick Washburn. He was overruled by Franklin Roosevelt's Attorney General Francis Biddle. Black journalism was weakened when some of the more talented journalists got jobs with mainstream newspapers where they have no power. While Pat Buchanan and Joe Scarborough can go apoplectic any time they feel like it, the few blacks on camera have to keep their cool so as not to appear angry.

Even so, Eugene Washington, who speaks in almost a whisper, just about called Crowley a liar when he said that he didn't believe that Gates made a slur about the officer's mother.

Knowing Gates, I don't either, but then Washington caught himself by adding that he doesn't know whether a white Harvard professor would have received the same treatment. He called that hypothetical. Hypothetical? Like the theory of gravity? Even tough-lover Bob Herbert, who, like some other token black writers, got angry over the way Gates was treated (Herbert had received a Talented Tenth award from Gates). Herbert blames society's failings on rap music and says awful things about Michael Jackson, whose contributions to charities were in the millions, but his opinion isn't shared by the *Times*' sales department, which devotes whole sections to Jackson and the rappers in an effort to woo younger readers. He should go to the *Times*' advertising department and threaten to quit if they don't cut it out.

MSNBC's Jonathan Capehart, a real mousey fellow, said that Gates had grown up in a Jim Crow era and that accounted for his losing his cool, again swallowing Crowley's account of the encounter. Capehart said that he's never had an unpleasant experience with the police. He said that Gates' response was generational, a rumor started by a white *New York Times Magazine* writer who wrote about a divide between Jesse Jackson's and Barack Obama's generation on racial issues, even though Obama has been a victim of racial profiling. The writer knows as much about black history and culture as one of the scrub jays in my backyard. Well, a lot of people from Capehart's generation have had ugly encounters with the police, some of them lethal.

On the phone the other day, Toni Morrison's son, Harold, a Princeton architect, who was responding to my *CounterPunch* piece, told me about his encounter. The police, in the front yard of his home, beat up Adam Kennedy, son of the great playwright, Adrienne Kennedy. His mother and he wrote a play about the beating called *Sleep Deprivation Chamber.*

I was struck by a cop and called a nigger—in the presence of black cops—after he overheard me telling a friend that he was taking a bribe. He charged me with disorderly conduct and came to my cell that night at the Tombs. Unlike the maniac I'd encountered earlier that day he said in a very calm voice that if I pled guilty, I'd only have to spend the weekend at Rikers Island, a New York prison. I told him no deal, and got a lawyer and wondered how poor and Hispanic and black men without resources respond to such great bargains. The judge dismissed the charges.

Like Sgt. Crowley, the officer lied on his police report and most black men would agree with journalist Jack White that the police lie all the time.

There is no evidence that Gates "over-reacted" in the words of President Obama, and Colin Powell, a man who was part of an administration guilty of perhaps one of the most colossal over-reactions in history. To his credit, Tim Wise, author of *White Like Me: Reflections on Race from a Privileged Son*, was one of the first commentators to comment on the discrepancies in Crowley's report.

The dynamic young black intellectual, Joseph Anderson, actually looked up the criteria for disorderly conduct under Massachusetts law. He wrote to me:

> … merely verbally disputing, protesting, even being rude to and/or yelling at a cop is NOT "Disorderly Conduct," and that's specifically why those charges were later dropped (not merely because of bad PR by the Cambridge Police Department). I'm no supporter of Gates (he used to deny that racial profiling or targeting happened to other blacks), but once Gates provided information (his Harvard ID and his driver's license) that he indeed lived at that address, the cop should have left!

Moreover, there is no ranting or raving by Gates on the police tape. Not only did Crowley lie, but he flouted the law; yet the majority of whites who were polled, support Crowley over Gates and Obama.

In 1792, Captain Kimber of the slave ship *Recovery* was charged with murdering two African women after subjecting them to horrendous torture and sexual humiliation. The judge's charge to the jury led to his acquittal. The account appears in *Lose Your Mother: A Journey Along The Atlantic Slave Route* by Saidiya Hartman.

> [The Judge] advised the jury, when deciding the matter of the captain's guilt, to take in consideration the particular circumstances of the high seas, where all life is violence. This consideration makes a very great difference between the actions done upon sea and actions upon land… You have to judge ferocious men, who have few but strong ideas, peculiar to their own employment, hardened by danger, fearless by habit. The preservation of ships and lives depends often upon some act of severity, to command instant obedience to discipline and supreme command. These scenes of violence present a picture of human nature not very amiable, but are frequently justifiable, and absolutely requisite; as without which no commerce, no navigation, no defence (*sic*) of the kingdom can be maintained or exist.

The "high seas" have become "the urban jungle" full of "high risk" inhabitants or, as many of Sgt. Lashley's colleagues would put it, "banana eating jungle bunnies" who require control no matter how severe are the measures used to accomplish this. This was the reasoning of the suburban jury that acquitted "The Riders," a group of Oakland police who were accused of routinely beating and framing poor black drug dealers in West Oakland. They were acquitted by a suburban jury. According to the *San Francisco Chronicle*, "in four months of heated deliberations, they hurled insults at each other and even discussed 'Dirty Harry'—the rogue cop who believed the ends justify the means." And sounding like the judge whose charge to the jury led to the acquittal of the slave-ship captain, the mostly white jury "got bogged down in a series of long—and often contentious—debates over the law and the ethical conflicts of front-line cops in tough neighborhoods." The black juror, an alternate for a jury that except for an Asian American was white, was shocked.

"This blows me away," said alternate No. 1, an Oakland resident. "I can't believe this. They are so guilty. The evidence was overwhelming."

She said that the jury could not empathize with the alleged victims or believe that police would abuse their authority.

"Most black people know that police can lie to make an arrest," she said, fighting back tears. "But I think the people on this jury don't believe it's possible for police to lie. They just don't get it."

One of the policemen involved in the Riders case fled to Mexico and the city of Oakland had to pay ten million dollars to their victims, enough to have provided Oakland schools with much-needed equipment. Like the slave-captain's judge, most whites believe that such is the state of the inner city that the laws governing police conduct that apply elsewhere don't apply here. This attitude is supported by television cop shows, a format that has been adopted by both CNN and MSNBC. Notice the number of Hollywood movies in which the hero is a cop whose use of force is so excessive that he's ordered to turn in his badge by a superior, who is usually played by a black actor.

After the three beers at the White House, Officer Crowley appeared at a triumphant news conference like he owned the place and was immediately adopted as a new media star by cable. Move over Mark Fuhrman and Lt. Col. North! Maybe they'll make Crowley Sarah Palin's running mate. Crowley, thanking white men with guns throughout the nation for their support, had humiliated a young black president, which is how it's done in other countries where the civilian leader has to yield to the gun totters; the kind of governments that Obama criticized on his trip to Africa and Hillary Clinton is now accusing of corruption. Hillary Clinton!

The black professor has been carrying on like Ronald Reagan's speechwriter for a number of years. He acted as the leader of a band of exceptional black people, a "dream team." Then Skip Gates found out during his encounter with a lying policeman that it's not a matter of class, it's your black ass that gets you in trouble with the police. When Gates taught at Duke he got some racial profiling insurance by going to the police station and identifying himself as a Duke professor so that he wouldn't be subjected to the kind of police treatment accorded those less fortunate blacks. He was further humiliated when, after the beer-fest meeting, he had to come up with a statement which, though very eloquent and fancy, was similar to Rodney King's "Can't we all get along?"

In his statement, Gates bonded with a man, who tried to justify his arrest with a false police report, which damaged both Gates' and Lucia Whalen's reputations. Gates called him a nice guy in *The New York Times* and said that the two might attend sports events together and have dinner. He even offered to get the officer's kids into Harvard. Maybe the officer who killed a black man in Oakland the other night should send in her children's application to Gates. Is Gates a candidate for the Stockholm Syndrome?

But Obama and Gates aren't the only ones who are the targets of contempt from armed men. Such is the power that the white majority has granted the police that the California Corrections industry even turned Governor Schwarzenegger into a "girlie man." After contract negotiations, they bragged that for every nickel offered by the state, they got a dime.

An editorial in the *San Francisco Chronicle* shows how costly it is for those who choose revenge over rehabilitation: "For decades, the corrections budget has swallowed more and more of the state's general fund, starving priorities like higher education. But the political ramifications of looking 'soft on crime' cowed legislators and governors alike. So we built prison after prison and stuffed them all to overcapacity."

Now Arnold is going along with a plan to build a showcase state-of-the-art Death Row that will cost the taxpayers three hundred and fifty-six million dollars with a thirty-five million dollar cost overrun.

These California suburbanites are the people who gave us the Three Strikes Law after the tragic murder of a suburban white girl, Polly Klaas, a law that is one of the reasons for California becoming a failed state. As *The Wall Street Journal* put it, writing about white suburbanites, "those who have the least to fear from crime are driving the issue." *The Wall Street Journal* attributed their fear to watching images of blacks on TV. Maybe CNN's *Black In America*.

Three beers aren't going to do it. The only result will be a reality show about the event that will accrue more profits to Gates, the intellectual entrepreneur, perhaps co-hosted by his new pal, Sgt. Crowley, cable's latest matinee idol. Already they've gotten an invitation from Rabbi Abraham Cooper, associate dean of the Simon Wiesenthal Center and the Museum of Tolerance, to do a tag-team lecture. This is a road show that's certain to entertain the media, one of whose best-selling products is the "racial divide." I've heard through the grapevine that PBS is offering Gates millions of dollars to do a racial profiling special. Given PBS's politics, maybe a musical comedy which would end with blacks and police locking arms in a chorus line singing the show's hit song, *We Both Over Reacted*.

Racial profiling will continue and the attitude of most whites will continue to be: we don't care what you do with blacks and Hispanics and Native Americans; just keep them out of our hair.

A better solution would be the one practiced by citizens of my North Oakland district, black, white, Asian and Hispanic. For over twenty years we've met with the police on a regular basis, without suds being consumed. Maybe some cake and potato chips. Sometimes we raise our voices at them, without being hauled out of Oakland's Santa Fe School, where we meet, handcuffed and charged with disorderly conduct. But recently, when the police cracked down on a criminal operation that endangered the lives of residents of my block, I led the applause.

One of those who didn't share in our victory was Sgt. Daniel Sakai. He was trying to help us with our main problem: a recalcitrant absentee landlord (from a two-family household, Bill) who has put our neighbors' lives in jeopardy by allowing her abandoned property to be used by criminals, criminals who engaged in a full-scale shootout on our block one morning. She refuses to even put up a No Trespassing sign.

Sgt. Sakai was white. Some of our neighbors went to City Hall and signed the book to mourn his death. He was among four policemen who were murdered during an incident when the mean-spirited fear-inspired policies of three strikes, traffic profiling and the National Rifle Association collided.

Black Oakland Mayor Ron Dellums and Congressperson Barbara Lee showed up to join in the mourning during a televised funeral. As part of a calculated public insult, which offended Oakland's black leaders, Mayor Dellums was not permitted to speak.

Let's all have a beer.

Obama Souljahs On,
Africa This Time

Both the president's July 2009 Ghana speech, which absolved Europeans of the blame for the problems on the African continent, and the blame-the-victim NAACP speech have sparked a rise of anger among off-camera black intellectuals. The kind whose presence is missing from such MSM faux "Black" blogs, *TheRoot*, and NBC's *Griot*, and AOL's *Black Voices*. (Predictably AOL was among the corporate media that highlighted the "tough love" portions of Obama's speech. Like the other tough-lovers, Obama ignored the recent stories about gains that black students have made in closing the intelligence gap in the South and in New York. Obama feigned outrage about the media emphasizing the tough-love parts, but he, Rahm Emanuel and Axelrod knew the deal.)

Despite the monopoly that shareholder-driven market opinion might have over the public opinion, which includes the farcical sight of all-white panels discussing race, there is a movement on the Internet to make some space for nonwhites. A number of black intellectuals are using this space to challenge the mass delusion of a post-race America.

I asked three black intellectuals of the kind who wouldn't pass a cable producer's interview for an on-camera appearance their reactions to Obama's Ghana speech and his NAACP speech. Prof. Pierre-Damien Mvuyekure is Professor of English and African-American literature at the University of Iowa. He said: "Regarding Obama's comments, he seemed to rehash the words of another Kenyan, Prime Minister Raila Odinga. In his commencement address at the University of Buffalo Law School, Odinga said, 'We cannot continue to blame colonialism for Africa's problems' and added, 'I believe very strongly that it is because of poor leadership that Africa lags behind in development'"—I Googled it and *AllAfrica.com* came up. "While to some extent this may be true, we cannot ignore neo-colonialism whereby the former colonial masters and the United States continue to underdevelop Africa through the International Monetary Fund and the World Bank."

Pierre-Damien continued:

Yes, the French were arming the Rwandan Army, while the U.S. and Great Britain were arming the Rwandan Patriotic Front through Uganda. Last week, Rwanda gave medals to the Prime Minister of Ethiopia, President Yoweri Museveni, and the late Mwalimu Julius Nyerere of Tanzania, for their efforts in "liberating" Rwanda.

At the beginning of the 1990 war, Paul Kagame was training at Fort Leavenworth in Kansas as a Ugandan officer! Then he left to take over the war when three of his colleagues died within two weeks of the beginning of the war. Gerard Prunier's new book *Africa's World War: Congo, The Rwandan Genocide, and the Making of a Continental Catastrophe* documents some of this.

Justin Desmangles is the host for *New Day Jazz* broadcast over KDVS in Davis, California. He said:

He's lying, and he knows it. To think that this man has the wherewithal to stand on the very ground where Nkrumah was murdered at the behest of United States' interests. Even the choice of Ghana was a cynical ploy to further coerce leverage for AFRICOM, a plan initiated by Bush in 2007, to find a home. It is currently based, without irony, in Germany. Massive oil discoveries were recently made off Ghana's coast as well.

Not unlike his infamous Father's Day speech of last year, Obama was signaling, and signifying, elsewhere. In this case to the very centers of capital that were founded and solidified by colonialism in Africa! These remain to this very day, no matter what anybody would like to say, the paymasters for the various military, paramilitary, terrorist and so called counter terrorist groups throughout the continent.

The United States government, vis. the Pentagon, the State Department, etc. are fully intent on fighting a proxy war with China over the resources in Africa. The very resources that without which the economy of the West would come to screeching halt. Coltan, the essential ingredient in the manufacture of IT, Sony Play Stations, laptops, cell phones of all varieties etc. is known to be the source of the conflict in Northeastern Congo's Inure Forest. Can you imagine what would happen if the expedition of this precious mineral were slowed down or halted? Stocks, as you know, are traded on projected earnings. The height of the "dot com boom" was the period when, according to the UN and countless NGOs, that close to seven million people died there.

We didn't hear any outcry about that. Bob Herbert, whose column last week on Michael Jackson was unforgivable, seems to think it's all about rape. I guess that'll put him in solid with Eve Ensler and her crowd. Which brings us back to AFRICOM. Bush was laying down the groundwork for Obama to make that speech. He's following up on errands. Obama, however, can do this as propagandist foil in a way they could not. That aside, Bush had laid out a plan for war in Africa just prior to the formation of AFRICOM before its creation in 2007. As larger and larger oil discoveries were being made there in 2003, 2004, and 2005, organizations like the Council on Foreign Relations and Hoover Institute began publishing policy papers and research identifying the continent as the emerging front in the "war on terror." This is the true context for Obama's speech and the guide for its content as well. Obama's speech was even covered in the *Times* with the headline that it was "Tough Love"!

This kind of "personal responsibility" line is perfectly in tune with the recent attempts, sometimes successful, to shame and humiliate African leaders by dragging them in front of the ICC, such as Charles Taylor, or in lieu of that, falsely suggesting that they should be, as in Bashir of Sudan.

About Obama's NAACP speech Kofi Natambu wrote:

To constantly single out one general national community for what is frankly a rather theatrical and self-serving series of public performances and admonitions that too often treats us as a bunch of errant, mischievous children in dire need of Daddy's spankings is not only deeply insulting but an affront to what the president's relationship to us—and all other American citizens!— should actually be. That relationship is or should be that of a committed politician and public servant engaging and paying attention to its citizenry. After all, Obama is not a preacher/minister/pastor/rabbi and we are not his flock! And thank God/Allah/Buddha for that! The last thing the black community needs at this point in our history is yet still another arrogant preacher and/or fundamentalist and overly self-righteous church telling us what to do!

Obama chided black folks in his "Rev. Wright speech"; Obama chided black folks in his NAACP speech; Obama chided blacks in his Africa speech; he even chided Arabs/Muslims in his Cairo speech. When is Obama going to chide white people about anything? How about white people going out and getting a legitimate job, instead of turning to dangerous and even potentially explosive meth labs for income? How about working-class white people not blaming all their problems on Latino immigrants? How about white people raising their teenage sons not to go out and shoot up random innocent victims (often targeting girls) at the school for whatever reasons their sons do? How about white males being man enough to not go back and shoot up innocent victims at the workplace just because they lost their job and/or their marriage, but going out to look for another job (they tell us black people that any job is better than no job, right? Even flipping burgers at McDonalds, or sweeping floors, or doing menial yard work—no matter your age)?

So, it's Obama who regularly chides/chastises only black or brown people for all their stereotypical faults, before—and for—the white world's television cameras. It's Obama who told black Americans that, "We must respect the verdict," when the trial judge [a potentially risky jury trial, if I recall offhand, was opted out of by the cops] exonerated the New York City cops in the Sean Bell case, cop's hail of fifty bullets, legalized murder case. And it's Obama who publicly turned 180 degrees on his old friend Skip Gates, just as he turned his back on his old friend Jeremiah Wright (for something Wright said in church when Obama wasn't even in church and wasn't even going to that church at the time—or when Obama was a kid?) So, if these are "teachable moments," as Obama said, then what are they supposed to teach us about Obama or any, "finally, honest national discussion" about race—like the Clintons turned both their backs on their "old family friend" Lani Guinier (even in the face of right-right-wing racist and sexist slurs!) when she wanted to have an honest national discussion about race (instead Bill turned to his phony racism commission), especially in the nation's universities. So—once again—we know we will never get an "honest national discussion" about anything in the mainstream American media and especially not on television (not even on PBS or NPR), and certainly not from even the nation's first officially or ostensibly black/African/biracial (whatever he actually calls himself) American president. My total wrap on Gates' and Obama's initial comments about the Gates arrest incident: they both said (at least from what I caught on the news) all the right things for all the wrong reasons.

No publishers are rushing to publish manuscripts by the young writers Justin Desmangles and Kofi Natambu. They are engaged in noble guerilla warfare against a propaganda machine that has billions of dollars at its disposal. NBC is worth thirty-eight billion alone. News Corp which sponsors Fox News includes right-wing individuals on its board with ties to multinational corporations, according to San Francisco's *Bay Guardian* newspaper:

> Occupying other seats at News Corp's board table is an assortment of professors, attorneys, public-relations experts, and businessmen with their fingers in a variety of banks and multinational corporations. Among the more familiar names are Phillip Morris, Ford Motor Co., Hewlett Packard, Goldman Sachs, HSBC North America, and JP Morgan Chase. Lesser known are the investment banking firms that have stakes in the petroleum industry, utilities, mining companies, and real estate.

> While the connections between corporate interests and the country's leading conservative propagandist are extensive and obvious, there's a stark contrast between the message delivered by Fox News and the interests of its parent company.

Pierre-Damien, also a radio host, Justin Desmangles and Kofi Natambu are waging an uphill battle by using limited equipment against the corporate Behemoth that smothers dissenting opinion, but this is an improvement over the situation in the past when blacks, Latinos and others were subjected to an electronic mugging with no means with which to fight back. Others have chosen the stage to combat the media's smearing of unpopular groups. In the fall of 2009, I was also able to witness the collaboration between other young people of different ethnic backgrounds, in their effort to challenge the way unpopular and misunderstood groups are portrayed by the media.

To Cries of Kill Him

(AOL September 30, 2009. "White supremacists and neo-Nazis have committed violence against African Americans around the country and fomented hate online for years. But in recent weeks, anti-Obama speech and behavior hinting at or advocating violence has surfaced at so-called town hall meetings and demonstrations against Obama's health-care plan and other policies. The same has happened at forums frequented by fringe groups, including 'birthers,' who dispute Obama's U.S. citizenship.

In August, the Secret Service investigated a man who displayed a sign reading 'Death to Obama' and 'Death to Michelle and her two stupid kids' outside a town hall meeting in Maryland. And in New Hampshire, a man brought a holstered gun and stood across the street from a presidential town hall with his weapon on full display, according to ABC News. And just last month, a North Carolina man pleaded guilty to threatening the president after he called 911 twice from his trailer just south of the Virginia border, saying he was going to assassinate the president, the AP reported.")

The election of Barack Obama was a cause for celebration in November but by September 2009 there was real worry in the country about whether the president would live out his term. *The Boston Globe* pointed to the media's role in creating the atmosphere in which the assassination of the president might be committed by a deranged individual or as in the case of JFK and MLK, a conspiracy.

September 2009 was typical. A poll conducted by a "juvenile," appearing on Facebook, asked whether Obama should be killed. A writer for *Newsmax.com*, a site with connections with the Republican Party, called for a military coup against the president. *Newsmax* also distributed Sarah Palin's *Going Rogue*, a book that received almost round-the-clock coverage by the media beginning on November 15. On John King's *State of the Union*, from CNN where the ex-vice-presidential candidate, Sarah Palin, was treated as a serious candidate for president come 2012, Barack Obama was ridiculed for bowing before the Emperor of Japan, with William Bennett leading the panel's condemnation, without mentioning that President Eisenhower had bowed before General De Gaulle and that Richard Nixon had shown the same expression before Emperor Hirohito, who was the Emperor of Japan when Japan was regarded as an enemy nation! During the week film and photos surfaced showing George Bush Two holding hands with Saudi princes. Why didn't John King mention these other bows when moderating a discussion about Obama's bow before the Emperor of Japan? I run a zine that sometimes might receive one thousand hits in a day if we're lucky. It's managed by my youngest daughter. I sometimes fantasize about how formidable an outfit I would have were I to own the same kind of resources as the mainstream media. I would ask a member of my large staff—no intern could do the job— before going on to lead a discussion about Obama's bowing before the Japanese Emperor, hey go and find whether any other president has bowed before a head of state or royalty and while you're at it get me a cup of coffee at Starbucks. Was King lazy or was he instructed to treat Obama's bowing as entertainment? I watched John King asking a panel about Barack Obama while waiting for a plane at the airport in Minneapolis.

Some white hunters of the sort who journey into Minnesota during deer season were also watching. I could tell what they were thinking. Even though the majority of the public, sixty-seven percent, including the majority of Republicans saw nothing wrong with the president's bowing, the media carried the controversy into the last week of November.

Other shows also took up Obama's bowing while treating Sarah Palin as a serious person. Mike Malloy was right when he said that while only nine percent of the public said that they'd vote for Palin, if she ran for president, she has a powerful constituency: the media. Malloy said that Palin's appeal was her "hot ass" (Air America, November 19) and Jessica Yellin, one of King's panelists called her a sex pot. And as if to prove their descriptions, Palin appeared on the cover of *Newsweek* as a sort of *Playboy* centerfold model with clothes. This cheesy flesh shot caused outrage among her followers who would be at a loss if you were to ask them to spell one of their buzzwords like "Constitution," yet she posed for the photo. None of the cable networks, who reduced the president's historic trip to China and Japan to a photo to prove that he wasn't as manly as five-deferment and two-DUI Cheney, reported the career of Sarah Palin's ghost writer. *Gawker* did:

> Lynn Vincent, the woman who is writing a book called *Going Rogue* "by" Sarah Palin, sure can pick her co-writers. She's written books before with a general who kills "demons" for God and a guy who finds interracial dating "revolting." As Charles Johnson—whose ongoing reformation from Muslim-hating wacko to right-wing apostate continues to puzzle and delight us—points out, Palin's ghostwriter's previous work includes *Donkey Cons*, a thoughtful investigative look at the Democratic Party's criminality that blows the lid off that "killer and traitor Aaron Burr." Vincent's co-writer on *Donkey Cons* was Robert Stacy McCain, a former *Washington Times* editor who writes things like this:
>
> "[T]he media now force interracial images into the public mind and a number of perfectly rational people react to these images with an altogether nat-

ural revulsion. The white person who does not mind transacting business with a black bank clerk may.yet be averse to accepting the clerk as his sister-in-law, and THIS IS NOT RACISM, no matter what Madison Avenue, Hollywood and Washington tell us."

That was from a private email McCain once wrote that a recipient posted online, so in his defense, McCain (no relation to Palin's running mate) wouldn't write something like that in public. In public, he says things like slaves and whites in the Old South had "cordial and affectionate relations," and is a member of the League of the South, which wants to secede from the Union (again!), and writes for a web site called *VDare*, which proudly publishes the work of "rational and civil… white nationalists" who "unashamedly work for their people."

While playing down Federal Reserve Ben Bernanke's claim, issued during the week, that Obama and his team had helped the country to avoid depression, cable continued to cover a candidate whose dangerous rhetoric continues to ramp up death threats against the president.

On November 16, 2009, *The Christian Science Monitor* reported an escalation of threats against the president's life:

There's a new slogan making its way onto car bumpers and across the Internet. It reads simply: "Pray for Obama: Psalm 109:8"

A nice sentiment? Maybe not. The psalm reads: "Let his days be few; and let another take his office."

Presidential criticism through witty slogans is nothing new. Bumper stickers, t-shirts, and hats with "1/20/09" commemorated President Bush's last day in office.

But the verse immediately following the psalm referenced is a bit more ominous: "Let his children be fatherless, and his wife a widow."

By the beginning of winter, it was obvious that the media had become a sort of white power government in exile ready to pounce upon any of the young black president's missteps. Not only predictable outlets like Fox News, which Obama's advisor David Axelrod, on Sunday, October 18, 2009, defined as less a news organization than an arm of the Republican Party, but from "progressive" outlets like Pacifica, which had begun to view gay marriage as the civil rights issue of this period, thereby accepting the post-race thinking that racism was no longer an issue in American life and when blacks suggested that it was, they were playing "the race card," or making excuses which was the line promoted by entertainment sideshows like CNN's *Black in America*, or *Saving Our Children*. So powerful was the media that the titular head of the Republican Party was not a politician but a talk show host with a history of drug abuse and making outlandish and racially tinged remarks about the president.

It's appropriate that the party of family values, which reached it's height of power with the election of a man who contributed to the conception of a child while unmarried, and whose 2008 vice-presidential candidate was part of a family immersed in a tangle of social pathologies, be headed by a talk show host who, in the past, has had a drug problem. During this period it was revealed that Ayn Rand the Goddess of right-wing American politics was a crank addict. Lordy be!

None of this seems to matter to media financed by multinationals that curb any discussion of the hypocrisy of those who perform on behalf of its message. David Brock says that his homosexuality didn't matter to the Republican homophobes as long as he used his brilliance to promote their talking points.

While Obama is the nation's first rainbow president, put in high office by a coalition of white, black, Latino, Asian, and Native-American men and women, the opposition is no longer a political one but a sort of multinational-owned electronic government-in-exile which dictates the actions of the conservative and right-wing politicians, who cower before it. First they challenged the stimulus bill, the aim of which was to keep public servants like the police, firemen and teachers on the job.

(On October 30, 2009, it was announced that the stimulus had created and maintained more that six hundred and forty thousand jobs, 110,000 in California alone. On August 10, 2009, Paul Krugman, who had been media-appointed prime minster of a government-in-exile headed by Rush Limbaugh, wrote in *The New York Times*, "So it seems that we aren't going to have a second Great Depression after all. What saved us? The answer, basically, is Big Government.")

When Joe Scarborough and Mika Brzezinski of the *Morning Joe* challenged a wonkish recital by Sen. Jack Reid about the bill and were rebuffed; they brought in a back-up commentator, Jack Welch, the former owner of General Electric to provide an open-ended rebuttal to Reid. I needn't remind anyone that MSNBC is owned by General Electric. (As of this writing, they're trying to sell it.) Welch is the industry captain who noticed while visiting India that labor there was cheaper than United States labor.

First there was chatter about Obama's bad beginning. Neo-con David Frum said that it was "disastrous." Over at CNN Wolf Blitzer was even suggesting that the Obama administration might be over before it began. Paul Krugman was brought on to trash Obama's economic policies. (This is the Clinton supporter who said in February 2008 that Obama's followers were members of a venomous cult of personality.) The cover of *Newsweek* had a photo of Krugman above the caption, "Obama is wrong." By October of 2009, Krugman was defending Obama's economic policies from the judgments of George Will and Peggy Noonan who became famous by coining the phrase "a thousand points of light." Pat Buchanan who migrates from panel to panel on MSNBC to deliver comments that are proven wrong said that if Obama were nominated the Republican Party would rip him to pieces. When the market displayed a slump during the early days of the administration, he said that the market was sending Obama a message. Watching this hand-wringing over the Obama administration which was marked as doomed even before it had begun, one was reminded that not only did media moguls like Rupert Murdoch, who donated $25,000 to right-wing sock puppet Ward Connerley's anti-affirmative action drive, own the media but finance the think tanks from which the media draw some of their commentators and so, the morning after the stimulus bill passed, representatives from *The Wall Street Journal* and the right-wing Cato Institute spent three hours trashing the stimulus package while rehearsed right-wing callers accused Obama of promoting socialism.

Like a mob trampling over one another as the doors open for an Xmas sale, it was a consensus among outlets as diverse as *The Daily Beast* and Fox News that the first week of February 2009, was "Obama's Bad Week." How did the public feel about what the media described as Obama's bad week? The polls gave him high ratings. Gallup was sixty-nine percent,

CBS, seventy-nine percent, CNN, six out of ten gave him high ratings, McClatchy Ipsos sixty-nine percent. Of course these approval ratings will fluctuate, but it was clear during this week who or where was the source of Obama's opposition. While he might head the executive branch of government, his wealthy enemies, whose profits he wishes to diminish, and who represent a tiny fraction of public opinion, are able to magnify that tiny fraction through their ownership of the American media. At the same time Howard Kurtz and others will deny that this is happening. They will continue to claim that the media are being seduced by Obama. So now we have a situation where the media decide the outcome of elections—McCain said that they were his constituency—decide the outcome of trials before the accused has set a foot inside of a courtroom, and behave as a sort of government in exile. Something has changed in American politics when a pill-popping talk show host has become the head of a family-values political party. But in comparison to some of the fulmination rising from the margins, which was given tacit approval from the Republican Party, Limbaugh's entertaining rants about the president were mild and of course given attention from the ratings-hungry media those voices from the fringes were given round the clock treatment by cable. Much of the hatred was fueled by Sarah Palin whose speeches inspired shouts of "kill him," and "nigger" from her crowds. By the fall of 2009, a writer for *Newsmax* was wondering aloud about a military coup and *The Boston Globe*, in a chilling report asked whether the Secret Service was capable of protecting the president and his family.

Under the headline: "Obama Risks a Domestic Military Intervention," John L. Perry wrote:

> Imagine a bloodless coup to restore and defend the Constitution through an interim administration that would do the serious business of governing and defending the nation. Skilled, military-trained, nation-builders would replace accountability-challenged, radical-left commissars. Having bonded with his twin teleprompters, the president would be detailed for ceremonial speech-making.

A poll of New Jersey voters revealed that twelve percent believed that Obama was the anti-Christ, and a large percentage of Republicans still maintained that he was born in Kenya.

As usual, the corporate media was designing an America that was markedly different from the one that was reflected by the polls. Appearing on *Morning Joe*, a reporter from *Rolling Stone*, who unmasked the influence upon the town halls of the insurance companies, which spent three hundred and eighty million dollars in their effort to derail the health plan's public option, was challenged by Pat Buchanan, who still maintains that his boss Richard Nixon was wronged, and Canadian-born millionaire, Mort Zukerman. Buchanan and Zukerman insisted that the corporate-manipulated town hall meetings and the 9/12 Washington demonstrations organized by tea baggers were genuine and reflected the mood of the country, which was anti big government. However, Max Blumenthal, a *Nation* contributor, interviewed some of the marchers. He discovered that they were ignorant of the issues and many didn't know why they were there.

Zukerman, who has been very critical of Obama, turned up later on Lou Dobbs' show on CNN to criticize Obama for his attempt to have the Olympic Games in Chicago. His black employee, Errol Louis of *The Daily News*, who survived the purge of black reporters that occurred when Zukerman took over, agreed with his boss. Amazingly, Lewis poses as a progressive on Air America affiliate WWRL 1600.

So insistent on Obama's failure, the staff at Murdoch's *The Weekly Standard* erupted into cheers when it was announced that the Olympics would not be held in the United States. *The Weekly Standard* had been recently purchased by a Christian fundamentalist billionaire named Phil Anschutz who makes his money in oil and real estate. When Obama received the Nobel Peace prize, NPR, in the midst of firing some of its black personnel, brought on a *Weekly Standard* contributor to denounce the Nobel Prize committee for awarding Obama the prize, lending credence to Kofi Natambu's lack of confidence in NPR. So dire was the firing of blacks at NPR, which receives public funds, that the National Association of Black Journalists sent a letter. If Obama or members of his family are harmed, the same media that encouraged and in the case of Fox News, helped to organize the tea-baggers, will argue that with his policies he brought it on himself. As I predicted when asked to comment on his election by *The Oakland Tribune*, Obama is a centrist and to the right on some issues, but the infotainment media have cast him as a radical, a socialist, a Marxist, and a Muslim who was born in Kenya. The majority, forty-seven economists, polled by *The Wall Street Journal*, agreed that a recovery is underway and even Paul Krugman, who had been appointed the president's rival, appearing on *This Week* in October gave the president some faint praise, and while doing so revealed his fellow panelists' ignorance about the subject of economics. They were Peggy Noonan and George Will. On October 13, 2009, *The Oakland Tribune* reported a survey conducted by the National Association for Business Economics that "Eighty percent of economists believe that the recession is over and an expansion had begun, but they expect the recovery will be slow as worries over unemployment and high federal debt persist." By October 30, Barack Obama and his team had saved the country from a depression yet so pathological is white supremacy that the threats against his life have increased by four hundred percent. If any harm comes to him, the same media that are creating an atmosphere where such a deed is possible will blame the president. They'll give him some of the tough love that he and his fellow Harvard elite deal to blacks. They'll say that because of his Marxist leanings, he brought it on himself.

Blaming the victim is nothing new in American history. Francis Parkman, who has been called the greatest of American historians, blamed the seizure of Indian lands and the extermination of some Indian tribes on the Indians. He said "the Indians melted away, not because civilization destroyed them, but because their own ferocity and intractable indolence made it impossible that they should exist in its presence." Sound familiar? The cynical minds who serve the shareholders of NBC, CNN and Fox have used this explanation to make big bucks with little investment on their part, only the Indians have become blacks and Latinos. Noticing that CNN got high ratings from its blame-the-victim stunt, *Black In America*, MSNBC teamed Bill Cosby up with Michelle Bernard, a hired black mouth for the far right, who, following the neo-con line, and prompted by her funders, says that personal responsibility is a problem peculiar to black men. She's also a global-warming denier, and believes that we should go easy on the rich because after all they are creating all of the wealth, according to her. She is one of those who are spreading lies about Obama's health proposals. Bernard, president and CEO of the far-right funded Independent Women's Forum, has written:

> More American women are going to die of breast cancer if you and I surrender to President Obama's nationalized healthcare onslaught.

According to the site *SmackDown*:

> The Independent Women's Forum is the organization that has been running a malicious ad that focuses on scaring breast cancer victims into rejecting any of President Obama's reform initiatives. The Independent Women's Forum shares its premises and resources with Americans for Prosperity. Americans for Prosperity is the organization that created Patients First and Patients United Now, groups that have been critical to disrupting the health care debate in an effort to sidetrack the entire process.

She is a black Tokyo Rose making broadcasts on behalf of the enemy, without even using big band swing music as part of her appeal. That Cosby would enter into an alliance with this woman is another example of how the once-brilliant and trail-blazing comedian is spending his twilight years as a sad clown.

MSNBC's version of *Black In America* was something called *About Our Children*, an entertainment which featured some lines from Cosby aimed at getting laughs from the audience. He revived his Jello act in a discussion with some children. The Latino community was also represented by a comedian, Paul Rodriguez, who got on not only to entertain, but because he opposes bilingual education. Cosby and Rodriguez couldn't probe too deeply into the causes of American poverty because the entertainment was sponsored by one of the largest criminal operations in the country, the Bank of America. Also Wells Fargo, which is being sued by the city of Baltimore for aiming toxic loans at black neighborhoods. As *The Washington Independent* noted, "lawsuits over racial discrimination in sub prime lending are winding their way through the court system. Some of the allegations are nothing short of shocking; in one suit recently classified as a class action case, Wells Fargo is accused of using loan software with discounts on rates and fees in white communities, but forbidding loan officers in minority communities from access to it." Wells Fargo received billions of dollars in taxpayers' bailout and in October of 2009, announced a three billion dollar profit, yet the crime that the corporate-owned media concentrate on is street crime. Wonder why? Host Tavis Smiley is under attack for aiding Wells Fargo in peddling these loans that have cost black homeowners billions in lost equity.

Now, Cosby lends his name to this operation by appearing on a show that is sponsored by Wells Fargo. If Bernard accused Wells Fargo and Bank of America both, technically, individuals, of lacking personal responsibility her face would disappear from the tube forever. Obviously, Michelle Bernard, who, following her backers' script, is trying to blame black men for the country's social ills, isn't too choosey about who sponsors her, but Cosby ought to know better. Cosby wrote *CounterPunch* expressing annoyance with me after I wrote that he and Professor Henry Louis Gates, Jr. were viewing the underclass from first class.

I live in the ghetto and I can assure you that the rich Negroes who get on television don't know the half of it. Many of them are professors who live all of their lives in college towns and when they travel, it's usually to visit another college town.

I invited Bill Cosby to come to Oakland and sit in on one of our neighborhood meetings. We finally got a period of peace on our block because one of the gang members who were terrorizing our neighbors for at least four years was murdered around the corner and his brother seriously wounded.

They were Asian Americans, but I doubt whether CNN or MSNBC will do *South Asian in America*, a show devoted to the social pathologies of this growing community. Asian Americans must be cast as the model minority.

The purpose of this, according to the great Chinese-American writer, Frank Chin, is to embarrass blacks. But a toxic house, a criminal operation still flourishes in the neighborhood because of the power of a landlord, an absentee landlord, who has defied the city's attempt to shut down her property. The police tell us that because of the power of landlords who rent their property or allow their abandoned property to fester with criminal operations, they are helpless to do anything about the problem. Skip and Coz. These landlords who are aiding and abetting criminal operations in neighborhoods like mine are probably from two-parent households and won't be covered by The Discovery Channel's upcoming smear of the city. An entertainment all about Oakland's gang violence without acknowledging that under Ron Dellums, a black mayor and a new black police chief, crime is down.

The Cosby-Bernard show included a "town hall," a cheap way to get ratings; a device which relies on panelists and audience members competing with each other over who can come up with the best applause lines. These verbal shootouts are guaranteed to raise the revenue of CNN and MSNBC, but I doubt whether the panelists get paid. They do it for free like in the old plantation days. It's all about entertainment. Advertising to promote CNN's second *Black In America*, Soledad O'Brien, in a carnival tone, like one of the guys whose job it is to stand outside of strip clubs on North Beach in San Francisco, attempting to lure tourists to sex shows, promised the viewers, "You won't be able to tear yourself away from this one."

On the morning of September 14, I was watching CNN's *Headline News* version of attracting ratings near the AA gate at JFK airport in New York. In succession there were stories about Serena Williams' tantrum at the US Open, Kanye West going off on Taylor Swift at an awards ceremony, and your obligatory black sexual predator, the usual sideshow manner by which blacks are shown on the tube. It's fitting that white pundits and other writers consult comedians like Bill Cosby and Chris Rock for their insights about black culture because, traditionally, the media have treated blacks as comic relief. Hollywood, which in November presented blacks with yet another neo-Nazi incest film called *Precious*, has been in this business for over one hundred years. You would think that white American novelists and playwrights would oppose the current atmosphere that has raised fears that President Obama will meet the same fate as JFK, the details of whose murder are still being held a secret by the CIA. Instead, novelists like Tom Wolfe and Philip Roth promote images of blacks in their works that are no different from those promoted against minority men in Nazi Germany's media and worse than that from Glenn Beck and Rush Limbaugh. Both Saul Bellow and Philip Roth have depicted black men as flashers, which was the common manner by which Jewish men in the Nazi press were shown.

David Mamet lent his name to a repellent racist movie called *Edmund*, in which two black sexual predators appear (the sexual predator being the typical manner by which the Nazi publications like *Der Angriff* portrayed minority males). His predators, one is a pimp, the other a rapist, are even worse than the ones served up by D.W. Griffith. (Whether Mamet knows it, in the late Andrew MacDonald's *The Turner Diaries*, the ultra-right's bible and the book that inspired Timothy McVeigh of the Oklahoma Federal building, Jewish men are the pimps, black men are the rapists. Another reader was Richard Poplawski, who murdered three Pittsburgh policemen last April 4, 2008.)

While cable uses Bill Cosby and Paul Rodriguez to comment on black and Hispanic issues, comedian Chris Rock is Mamet's guide to black America and he quoted Chris Rock in his vapid self-serving *Times'* Op-Ed, an advertisement for his forthcoming play called *Race*. I've never seen an Op-Ed in the *Times* written by the great living black playwrights like Adrienne Kennedy, Amiri Baraka and Ed Bullins. In his Op-Ed, Mamet quoted Chris Rock's comment on Rev. Jeremiah Wright. He said "You cannot find a seventy-year-old black man who does not hate the whites." If Rock said that, he is ignorant and is susceptible to the cartoonish view of Rev. Jeremiah Wright offered by the media. Do you think that Rev. Wright hated the white members of his congregation? Of Rock's silly observation, Mamet wrote, "This made sense to me."

It only made sense to Mamet because he wanted it to make sense. Even given the hard time that whites have been giving the Jews since ancient times, does Mamet believe that all Jewish seventy-year-old men hate Gentiles? Or is it just seventy-year-old black men who hate whites, uniformly? Who all think the same way?

Mamet also wrote "Most contemporary debate on race is nothing but sanctimony—efforts at exploitation and efforts at restitution seeking, equally, to enlarge and prolong dissent and rancor."

Mamet doesn't know anything about most contemporary debates on race, because the hundreds of black intellectuals, scholars, writers, poets, etc. who know something about the topic are kept off stage by a media that has a thing about cerebral blacks and offers only those who serve the interests of the media owners like Ms. Bernard, Larry Elder, Joe

Watkins, Amy Holmes, Bob Christie and John McWhorter, a puppet for The Manhattan Institute, which supports eugenics "research." Such is the power of the Institute, which gets money from places like Chase Manhattan Bank, that on Sunday, September 20, the Associated Press gave McWhorter the lead in an article about President Carter's accusation that some of the vitriol aimed at President Obama is based upon race, another way that the far right manipulates public discussions affecting blacks through puppets like McWhorter and Bernard.

Does Mamet read *Panopticon Review*, or *Black Renaissance Noire*, or *The Black Agenda* or *The Final Call* or even *Ebony* and *Essence*, *TheRoot*, *Black Scholar* or *The Amsterdam News*? Has he ever heard of bell hooks, Michele Wallace, Adolph Reed, Jr., Gerald Early, Darryl Pinckney, Cecil Brown, Sonia Sanchez, J.J. Phillips, Bob Steptoe, Katherine Takara, Jill Nelson, Elizabeth Nunez, Thulani Davis, Quincy Troupe, Eugene Redmond, Adrienne Kennedy, Herb Boyd, Ed Bullins, Jerry Ward, Houston Baker, Jr., Ethelbert Miller, Askia Toure, Askia Muhammad, Keith Gilyard, Bernard Bell, Greg Tate, Justin Desmangles, Tricia Rose, Clyde Taylor, Kalamu ya Salaam, Joyce Joyce, Eugene Redmond, Reginald Martin, Al Young, etc.?

And as an example of how ignorance reaches the highest segments of American intellectual life in a racist society, Mamet has fallen for the media hoax that affirmative action is a black program; when, for Rabbi Michael Lerner, quoted in *Time* and the late Seymour Lipset, quoted in a book called, *The Broken Alliance: The Turbulent Times Between Blacks and Jews in America* by Jonathan Kaufman, it benefits Jewish women the most. Kaufman writes: "...he predicted that the great beneficiaries of affirmative action would be Jewish women. In fact, Lipset turned out to be right." (Pg.224) My view is that the purpose of Mamet's Op-Ed was an attempt to do a pre-emptive strike on black critics who will probably find his play *Race* as racist as the piece of dreck to which he lent his name, *Edmund*, which, as it turned out, closed soon after it opened.

Langston Hughes complained that most of the plays written about black life during the 1930s were written by whites.

Nothing has changed. Richard Price has made so much money creating blackface dialogue that he is moving to Harlem. Jimmy Carter doesn't have to undergo an identity makeover like Price in order to know about blacks, nor does he have to make "brief forays into the ghetto," which is how Price says that he gathered his material, like someone on a safari. Carter is a Southerner.

After Jimmy Carter made an accurate assessment of the racist response to the election of a black president, all-day cable shows featuring mostly all-white panels weighed in on the former president's remarks. Predictably, many dismissed him as a doddering fool. Except for Roland Martin, most of the black faces had to tone down their comments. Only Larry Elder, of the black right was allowed to get livid over Carter's remarks. Later, they jumped on Nancy Pelosi for telling it like it is. She said that the current atmosphere of political pornography drummed up by people like Glenn Beck's boss Rupert Murdoch and his Beelzebub, Willie Horton master-mind Roger Ailes, reminded her of the hateful atmosphere that led to the assassinations of Harvey Milk and George Moscone, a liberal who was on his way to becoming governor of California. The others were too timid to call a viral white supremacy that has infected thousands of birthers, deathers, tea baggers and armed miscellaneous crazies, as a result of Barack Obama's election, for what it is. A public mental health crisis. The fact that many educated whites in the media deny Carter's claim might be seen as part of the crisis. Talking about inmates running the asylum. George Wills, appearing on *This Week*, said that those who saw racism in the nutty 9/12 demonstrations were guilty of "liberal McCarthyism." Will once said, following the line promoted by McWhorter's Manhattan Institute, that blacks were intellectually inferior to whites. (As usual, Irish Americans were represented on this panel by a right-winger. This time, Peggy Noonan, a woman with, as a bluesman might say, ice water for blood. She doesn't seem to mind that forty-five thousand people will die each year from lack of health care, according to a Harvard study. She's against big government. Without big government, millions of Irish Americans would never have entered the middle class.)

Despite the ugly racist mood of the crowd that came to Washington on September 12, 2009, some of them displaying signs that depicted Obama as a communist, a witch doctor with a bone in his nose, designed by Fox news expert Dr. David McKalip, or as someone who belongs in a zoo, as a monkey or as someone who should be killed, David Brooks said that the demonstration had nothing to do with race, yet they're always criticizing Iranians for ignoring facts. Here's a man who gets quoted as though he is Solomon. He wasn't the only one. A steady stream of white politicians, pundits and their African-American tokens like Zambia-born Amy Holmes denied that race had anything to do with the ugly display against President Obama during the Fox and insurance industry sponsored 9/12 march on Washington. Neo-con David Brooks doesn't understand why many blacks won't assimilate, a process that has worked for him. His mentor is the late Irving Kristol who rose to power by scapegoating blacks for all of the country's social ills and associating them with welfare, the Great Society programs, and affirmative action when the largest group to receive the advantages of these programs have been whites.

Kristol became a consultant for the Bradley Foundation, one of those think tanks that finances quack studies about black inferiority. He even got all cozy with backwoods Christian fundamentalists, even though they believe that the Jews must convert before Jesus comes down from out of the sky. His friend Norman Podhoretz also used this formula to make it. Criticizing black family values. A hypocrite. According to Theodore Solotaroff, Podhoretz's colleague at *Commentary*, Podhoretz was a real party animal: "He was no longer the spokesman of our sober, mature look, whose wistful suggestion for acting up was a midnight plunge in the Plaza Hotel fountain. No, that Norman was history. In the past year or two he had teamed up with Norman Mailer, the lead rebel, iconoclast and sensualist of the New York scene. The result was a hard-drinking, sexually liberated Norman who didn't seem to spend many evenings at home." Solotaroff says that Podhoretz's wife Midge Decter, a woman who has spent years making a career of criticizing unmarried black mothers, made a pass at him. Like Michelle Bernard chastising black males instead of some of the corporate malefactors who sponsor her shows, the neo-con operation founded by Podhoretz and others served the purpose of redirecting attention from the criminal behavior of corporations, the money behind the neo-cons, to the bad habits of the so-called black underclass. The corporate-owned media use the same strategy.

The news media spent a week running footage showing a black student beating up a white student on a school bus, but three recent cases where white thugs murdered Hispanics and got off were virtually ignored. During the same period the police, and the media, which always take their side, accused some black and Hispanic youth of a gang rape. Later it was discovered that the rape victim had lied and that the police had jumped the gun, which is typical of how the police treat black and brown suspects. In the same week a white man suspected of killing an Asian-American woman at Yale was permitted to go home and after he was arrested the media showed pictures of him behaving like an altar boy and brought on friends of his who vouched for his character.

Howard Kurtz, a so called media critic, and an Imus Alumni, who has had it in for Obama ever since he announced his candidacy, spent Sunday, September 20 on Serena and Kanye for laughs, but hasn't commented about the media silence regarding the pharmaceutical giant Pfizer "which agreed to pay 2.3 billion dollars to settle civil and criminal allegations that it had illegally marketed its painkiller Bextra, which has been withdrawn." It was the largest health care fraud settlement and the largest criminal fine of any kind ever. So restrictive is the latitude accorded David Gregory by his corporate bosses that when Senator Joseph Lieberman appeared on *Meet The Press*, November 22, he failed to point out that Lieberman, who was on the show to oppose the health bill, receives millions from the insurance industry.

Nor did he utter a word about Bank of America, another criminal operation and sponsor of Bill Cosby and Michelle Bernard's entertainment, "that covered up 3.6 billion dollars paid out in bonuses when it purchased Merrill Lynch." Unbridled capitalism and their media hirelings make chumps of millions of whites by entertaining them with the antics of O.J., Serena, Kanye West and Chris Brown, (the sole U.S. domestic abuser), and Michael Vick so as to divert attention from their crimes. Big business ought to put O.J. and them on salary. MSNBC's criticism of Obama's mild health reforms makes sense when you realize that General Electric, which owns NBC, sells health insurance and Joe Scarborough, one of Obama's harshest critics, is just another salesman to them. During the same period that corporate criminality was unveiled, the media jumped on ACORN, the Association of Community Organizations of Reform Now, an organization that serves the poor and registers black and Hispanic voters to the consternation of the Republican Party and its media allies. ACORN warned of the foreclosure crisis.

I listened to some ignorant poor and middle class whites call *The Washington Journal* to complain about ACORN, a few of whose workers were entrapped by a conservative sting operation. The employees who fell for this sting should have been fired for falling for the idea that a conservative nerd was a pimp. In the case of the woman, I would also have been duped. She carried on like someone who had been turning tricks for years, bringing to her role the kind of zeal we've come to expect from wingnuts. (I guess that Ann Coulter wasn't available). The fact that ACORN lost over fifty million dollars as result of her performance makes her the most expensive play-acting whore in history.

These whites complain about big government but toady for big business that treats them like dirt. Poisons their food, overmedicates their children, hypnotizes them with the Bernay's principle so that they buy things that they don't need, and sends their jobs abroad. Instead of fighting those who view them as serfs, they travel all the way to Washington from places like South Carolina to call Barack Obama a monkey. (If South Carolina secedes again, which it's always threatening to do, would the country fight another war to persuade a state that still thinks of itself as Scotland to return to the fold? I don't think so.) The *Times*' ombudsman wrote a piece about how the liberal news media and his own newspaper were tardy in picking up on the ACORN scandal, which was uncovered by the vast right-wing media conspiracy, which was on ACORN like a bloodhound.**

I'd like to see the ombudsman report on why the media both liberal and conservative almost hid another of Bank of America's scandals. In December 2008, a federal jury in Manhattan found Bank of America liable in a securities fraud trial that centered on the sales of asset-backed securities and involved some of the biggest names on Wall Street.

** ACORN was found to have broken no laws by a congressional report issued in December 2009.

In a verdict delivered late Thursday after nearly six weeks of trial, the jury ordered Bank of America to pay more than 141 million dollars to a dozen institutional plaintiffs, including the American International Group, Allstate, Société Générale, Travelers, Bank Leumi, Bayerische Landesbank and the International Finance Corporation. The money includes interest that Bank of America, the nation's largest bank, is obligated by law to pay on the 101 million dollar award, which did not include punitive damages.

On September 29, 2009, the *San Francisco Chronicle* reported that Bank of America suspended its work with the ACORN group. Bank of America and ACORN had been working together on mortgage foreclosure issues. Bank of America severed ties with the group after GOP Reps. Spencer Bachus of Alabama, Darrell Issa of California and Lamar Smith of Texas sent a letter to fourteen banks requesting disclosure to the House Financial Services Committee of all financial arrangements with ACORN and its subsidiaries or affiliates.

"The Republicans are trying to intimidate banks that have stepped up to help stop the foreclosure crisis," said ACORN chief executive Bertha Lewis. "These same Republicans ignored ACORN's warnings about predatory lending and the foreclosure crisis, then gave Wall Street free rein and are now obstructing efforts to help families." You can't make this stuff up, the stuff that Republicans make up. In this land of white supremacists make believe, where Ayn Rand, the crank addict, is a goddess and Sarah Palin is the Moose Queen, fifty percent of Republicans believe that ACORN stole the election for Obama!

Yet, while I was sitting in the airport watching a newswoman dressed like a hooker by the sinister men who pay her bills, I wasn't feeling as cranky as sometimes. As a matter of fact, I was optimistic for once. During the previous two weeks, I had just witnessed two young people, one of whom is my daughter, demonstrate that books and theater—the arts—are still effective means by which those who are excluded from the airwaves can respond to those who monopolize the airwaves and who wish to distract from the excesses and greed of their class by pitting group against group and race against race and parading people like Michael Vick, Chris Brown, Whitney Houston and O.J. before the cameras, your old Puritan ducking stools with lenses.

While the news media define blacks with a series of hoaxes and stunts, their representations of Muslims are reminiscent of the early nineteenth-century Barbary Pirates days.

So where does one find the point of view of those who are being discussed? How do they view themselves? Blacks, Latinos and others don't have a Fairness Doctrine that would enable them to counter the 24/7 demagoguery aimed at raising anger (ratings) against their groups and even hate crimes.

Playwright Wajahat Ali, a Pakistani-American playwright, with his play *The Domestic Crusaders*, offered audiences at the Nuyorican Poets Cafe a view of a Pakistani Muslim American family that challenges those by a media that portray Muslim men as terrorists and Muslim women as courtesans. One could witness the joy and relief of members of the South East Asian audience grown weary of such portrayals. They are attending sold-out performances and rewarding the playwright, director, Carla Blank, the actors and crew with standing ovations. With a tiny budget of no more than thirty thousand dollars we got to view South Asian life not from a hack television and/or Hollywood script writer or an interlocutor like David Mamet but from a brilliant writer whose play *The Domestic Crusaders* scores a direct hit on not only on the stereotypes accorded to Muslims by the media, but challenges the points of view of those tokens chosen to interpret Muslim life for "the mainstream." Fareed Zakaria (who encouraged the Bush administration to attack Iraq) might be an expert on the Middle East for the men who own the media, but when some lines from the play described him as such, this audience made up mostly of young intellectual Southeast Asians, laughed. The play drew standing-room-only crowds and received standing ovations wherever it was performed on the West Coast. The same thing is happening at The Nuyorican where the play ran through October 11. Was the play's appeal limited to an ethnic audience? Not hardly. Actress Vinnie Burrows the great African-American diva loved it. She said that it reminded her of Lorraine Hansberry's *A Raisin in the Sun,* one of the dramas that inspired Ali, along with O'Neill's play about an Irish-American family, *A Long Day's Journey Into Night* as well as Arthur Miller's *Death of a Salesman.* Two black men, one of whom saw the play in the West and a Nuyorican

audience member said that the family on the stage could be their families. The play was produced by two African Americans, Rome Neal and
myself, directed by a Jewish American, Carla Blank, and performed at
the landmark Puerto Rican theater. In addition, two members of
American literature's royal families are part of a crew filming the pro-
duction for a forthcoming documentary. The documentary producer is
Ford Morrison, Toni's son, and James Baldwin's nephew, Tejan Karefa-
Smart, is operating First Camera. The director is a young black woman
named Taneisha Berg. Watching these young people, South East Asian,
Hispanic, black and a young white scenic artist, Rusty Zimmerman, col-
laborate on this project was refreshing. In the 1960s, Manhattan was black
and white. The black artists and intellectuals weren't speaking to whites
and the whites were always scrambling around to include a token black
on their guest lists.

During her book tour of the East, Tennessee Reed did not reach the
thousands that Wajahat reached with his challenge to age-old myths
about Muslims, ones not only encouraged by the media but by academia.
The play was covered by Al Jazeera, MSNBC, *The New York Times* and
The Today Show and *The Wall Street Journal*. (The only dissenter was *The
Village Voice*'s neo-con critic, Alexis Soloski, who objected to lines that
criticized the Bush Administration.) *CounterPunch* contributor, Wajahat
Ali, has been at it longer and the effort he made to get his play done east
of the Rockies took a lot of energy and resources. He doesn't sleep and
while writing plays he has to support himself part time as a lawyer.

Nevertheless Tennessee's East Coast bookstore appearances drew a
lot of fans and one bookstore appearance was broadcast at a later date by
C-Span. Those who showed up for her readings were startled by
Tennessee's inside look at how learning-disabled and black students are
treated by American education. For example, I noticed some jaw drop-
ping among some jaded New Yorkers when Tennessee recounted how
the Oakland public school system and the University of California at
Berkeley introduce students to African civilization by using Tarzan movies and how Reconstruction is taught from the point-of-view of *Gone
With The Wind*. Heads also turned when she reported that some white
teachers and professors award white students higher grades than blacks

and Hispanics even though the quality of their work might be the same, or, in the case of whites, inferior to that of blacks and Hispanics. They seemed startled by stories about how some teachers humiliate learning-disabled students in front of their classmates. This information comes on the heels of a report that learning disabled are those who are most likely to receive punishment in the nation's schools. Cuban, Puerto Rican and Peruvian-American students accorded her enthusiastic applause at Miami Dade College when it was reported that when she ran for Oakland school board she was the only candidate who insisted that black and Hispanic students receive the same treatment as those white students living in the affluent areas of Oakland. As a result of her visit to Miami she was invited to the Miami Book Fair and in October, she returned to New York to address The Girls' Club and students at Brooklyn's Boricua College. Her appearance prompted this poignant response from a young listener. Though her composition skills are flawed, her sentiment origin-ates in the heart, and her paying attention to a young writer who shares her background and experience demonstrates once again that young people are inspired by such literature, which is still ignored, by the edu-cation establishment except for one or two tokens. The establishment's idea of education is to convert students to the ways of the white man. Zoe's letter:

> Howdy, this is Zoe coming to you from Girl's Club. Today was really cool, as always. Yesterday Reene said that an author was coming to the club to talk about her book. I honestly didn't care to attend and listen to a writer because I'm not much a reader. Actually I rarely read for fun. I tend to read only if it's for school. But surprisingly I had a really good time and now this experi-ence has changed my perspective on a lot of things. so who's this author that blessed me with her presence? Tennessee Reed is her name and she is the author of her intriguing book entitled *Spell Alburquerque: Memoir of a "Difficult" Student*. While discussing her work of art, Ms. Reed was so lay back and relexed and it felt as if i was just talking to my friend. So what makes Ms. Reed and her book so special? Well at an early age she was diagnosed with serval language-based learning disorders. Thus one would believe that the odds are against her. how can an individual with so many disorders write an interesting book? Ms. Reed stated "it took a lot of support." Her mother, Carla Blank, and her father and publisher, Ishmael Reed, were Ms. Reed's

rock. Like any caring parents, "they did their homework" as Ms. Reed likes to say, about to how care and support their comely child. School was difficult for Ms. Reed nevertheless she made it through gradschool and even fought an educational system that often defined her disabilities as "laziness or stupidity". with all the negative things in her life, she still did what she loves to do. this leaves me with my final words: if you put your heart and mind to it, despite all odds, you can do ANYTHING. signing off"

Posted by Zoe on November 7th, 2009 under Girlville.

Bill Cosby has been very critical of young people and in my letter replying to him I said that he was acting like an old koot. I'm one too. In fact the title of my new novel is *Koots*, which my agent says that American publishers won't touch because one or two of the characters present scientific evidence to support the acquittal of O.J. Simpson in the criminal trial.

But even I who have been called a "sourpuss" by one blogger felt good about what I had seen during my three-week visit to the East. A cooperation between young people of different backgrounds, working together to challenge those slanders pushed by the media and in Mamet's case, by film and mainstream theater as well. I was feeling all gooey. Like what's that line about lighting one little candle? These young people in Wajahat's crew and Tennessee did much to shine a light on bigotry and ignorance and Bill Cosby should see this show and use his power to insist that it get a wider audience. I was impressed by the energy of those kids, South Asian, black and white, joining forces to invite an audience into the home of a South-Asian-American household, of a family beset by issues that we all have experienced. And a young writer who overcame a teacher's diagnosis that she would never learn to read or write through a present from Beat poet Ted Joans who found her a Scholastic Records 45 rpm of Arthur Rubenstein's orchestral composition to "Three Billy Goats' Gruff" in a flea market. She had a book with almost the same text, so she figured out how to read along. That was the breakthrough. She knows that the kind of caring support system that was available to her, tutors, understanding teachers, is denied millions of the nation's children, who are dumped into special education classes, misdiagnosed, and misunderstood. I remember all of the days that Tennessee came home in tears over the way she was treated by teachers and classmates who dismissed her as lazy, slow and difficult. This lazy, slow and difficult student had produced three books by the time she reached college, after we were told that her learning disability was so severe that she would never read nor write. Her book, *Spell Alburquerque*, published by AK Press, positions her to advocate for students like her.

And so as I sat there in the airport watching a woman present black Americans like one would present a carnival act I wasn't fuming as usual. The airport was teeming with armed soldiers. Because, as I was to learn later, President Obama was about to visit New York.

Observing those soldiers, I thought that the tea-bagger nut who threatened to return to Washington, armed, would have a hard time getting next to the president.

The pilot said that we'd have to taxi out to a remote part of the airport because the airport had been shut down because the president's plane was arriving. Shortly afterward, I saw out of the right window, Air Force One land. I regretted that my stepfather didn't live to see this. He was the kind of black man who doesn't show up on television or isn't discussed by Michelle Bernard. Like millions of black men, Bennie S. Reed reported to the same job, Chevrolet plant in Buffalo, New York, for over thirty years. He swallowed his pride as the permanent affirmative action, which is awarded to white males, permitted those who were less qualified than he to become foremen. Toward the end of his working days, they finally offered him the job. "Give it to my sons," he said, referring to my half brothers who followed him into the automobile industry. He would have been impressed by JFK being shut down because a black man was coming to town. I can see him now. Flashing that great grin of his.

Obama, Tiger, Vick, MJ, etc.
Is There Any Cure for Negro Mania?

*We may congratulate ourselves that this cruel war is nearing its end.
It has cost a vast amount of treasure and blood. It has indeed been
a trying hour for the Republic; but I see in the near future a crisis
approaching that unnerves me and causes me to tremble for the safety
of my country. As a result of the war, corporations have been enthroned
and an era of corruption in high places will follow, and the money
power of the country will endeavor to prolong its reign by working
upon the prejudices of the people until all wealth is aggregated
in a few hands and the Republic is destroyed. I feel at this moment
more anxiety for the safety of my country than ever before, even
in the midst of war. God grant that my suspicions may prove groundless.*

This passage appears in a letter from Lincoln to
(Col.) William F. Elkins, November 21, 1864

*We're also in the midst of a media feeding frenzy
not seen since the height of O.J. Simpson mania."*

The Washington Post

When you say "Barack Obama," Howard Kurtz thinks Tiger Woods.

December 23, 2009 10:55 am ET
by Jamison Foser

At the end of 2009, the Jim Crow media, progressive as well as mainstream, graded African Americans and vied with each other over which African-American male celebrity symbolized the tawdry aspects of the year or even the decade. As usual the highest grade given to African Americans was a D.

Typical were two episodes of media critic Howard Kurtz's program, *Reliable Sources*, carried on Jonathan Klein's CNN. White men and women were invited to evaluate the presidency of Barack Obama on Sunday, December 20 and 27, 2009. The composition of the panels reflected the segregated media at the end of the decade. April, 2009, The American Society of News Editors reported: "In this decade, there has been a net increase of Latino, Asian and Native-American journalists and a net decline of black journalists," meaning that the space for the points of view of black journalists was closing. I wrote about the decline of serious black fiction in *The Wall Street Journal*, a trend also noticed by Jabari Asim, editor of *The Crisis Magazine*, writing in *Publisher's Weekly*, and so when Senator Harry Reid was reported in the book *Game Change* by John Heilemann and Mark Halperin to have made a remark about Barack Obama that for some contained a tint of racism, since race is seen as a moneymaking issue for the media and their advertisers, the discussion of Senator Reid's remark was dominated by white opinion makers, much of the discussion ignorant, not only to blacks, but to a worldwide audience, for whom Hip Hop is a link between them and black Americans. He said in so many words that light-skinned people have an advantage over black-skinned people, which is true all over the hemisphere, as evidenced by the billion-dollar business in skin bleach.

Certainly, some immigrants view possessing light skin as a key to success according to *The New York Times* on January 28, 2007:

Light-skinned immigrants in the United States make more money on average than those with darker complexions, and the chief reason appears to be discrimination, a researcher says.

The scholar, Joni Hersch, a professor of law and economics at Vanderbilt University, looked at a government survey of 2,084 legal immigrants to the United States from around the world and found that those with the lightest skin earned an average of 8 percent to 15 percent more than similar immigrants with much darker skin.

"On average," Dr. Hersch said, "being one shade lighter has about the same effect as having an additional year of education."

Senator Reid indicated that for some white people "ebonics" or "the Negro dialect" is a source of ridicule unless they can make millions imitating "ebonics" in rock, rock and roll songs, novels, movies and television. He also used the term "negro," which thousands of blacks and black institutions still use. One of the reasons that the word "black" became popular is because, according to *Headlines and Deadlines: A Manual for Copy Editors* by R.E. Garst and Theodore M. Bernstein, newspapers found "black" easier to set than "African American." Senator Reid's comment was fodder for news entertainment for weeks, a kind of racial "Jeopardy," game shows and "town halls" that are cheap to produce and which distract from the real issues of race in American society like the apartheid criminal justice system, disparities in the healthcare industry, and red-lining.

During the final days of December 2009, Deborah Howell, former ombudswoman for *The Washington Post*, died. Her comment that the *Post*'s Op-Ed page was "too white and too male," could have been said of the rest of the media, even those headed by feminists, like *The Nation* magazine. A Christmas party photo reprinted by media hawk, Richard Prince, showed only one black staff member at the "progressive" *Huffington Post*, headed by the telegenic feminist and Obama critic, Arianna Huffington.

Despite the conclusion of several media studies that I cited in this book, Howard Kurtz, Imus buddy and supporter of National Public Radio's notorious black pathology show, *Ghetto 101*, continued to embrace the myth that the press coverage of Barack Obama had sent the presidency into the "stratosphere" only for him to "fall to earth." What "strato-sphere?" During the campaign it was noted that The Associated Press was in the pocket of Senator John McCain, and given the negative analy-sis of Obama's administration made by Ben Feller of that agency, printed in early January, they still were.

The coverage from the campaign through the first year of the admin-istration hadn't changed at Fox News either. For these and other media organizations, Obama's position was always terrestrial, including his position at MSNBC, which, regardless of the presence of two progres-sives, Rachel Maddow and Keith Olbermann, allows conservatives like Joe Scarborough, and hard core white nationalist, Pat Buchanan, and Mika Brzezinski and their guests to denigrate the president for three hours at a time some mornings.

The idea that Obama had fallen from on high to earth was endorsed by the panelists, which included Bill Press, the media's idea of a "progres-sive." This is the Bill Press, who, according to Lydia Chavez in her book *The Color Bind: California's Campaign to End Affirmative Action* opposed Affirmative Action in California. After an exchange about Proposition 209, the proposition that ended Affirmative Action, with a representative from the NAACP, Press told her, "you're nothing," accord-ing to the book.

Appearing on the December 27 program, Chris Stirewalt, a reporter for *The Washington Examiner*, said that in the conflict between the White House and Fox News, it was the White House "that got burned," an opin-ion that was contradicted in a report from *Media Matters*.

He also joined the parade of white commentators who used scandals involving black celebrities to symbolize the end of an era or a decade. His nomination was Michael Jackson who, for him, "symbolized a decayed, corrupted society," not the Army Corps of Engineers, whose negligence was cited by a judge during 2009 as being responsible for the flooding in the aftermath of Katrina, which caused widespread suffering, displace-ment, billions of dollars in property damage and the near extinction of the fabulous city of New Orleans. Not the large banks, and investment firms, whose crimes were tucked away on the business pages, or the drug companies who settled class action suits which held them responsible for putting toxic dangerous products on the market. Their profits exceeded the cost of the class action suits, so that poisoning people becomes just the cost of doing business. No, for this man, it was MJ, a performer who gave millions to charities located all over the world.

The rest of Kurtz's all-white media jury agreed with Stirewalt about Jackson, even though Jackson had been acquitted in a case where a child, who lied under oath in a previous case, was found to have been manipulated by his mother, who, in 2006, was convicted of welfare fraud, a story ignored by the media. The 2006 case was based upon a 1993 charge brought against Jackson by another child manipulated by a parent, whose mental problems were apparent to anybody who studied the case. In 2009, the year of Jackson's death, the parent committed suicide, another story ignored by the media.

Barack Obama gave his administration a B plus, a grade that some might consider modest, since it was the consensus among economists that his administration had saved the country from a depression. I'd give him an A minus because I understand the shackles placed upon him and his administration in a country where the most powerful weapons and the money are in the hands of whites. Though African-American celebrities and organizations might criticize him for ignoring the deepening depression now being experienced by African-American communities, where in some cities, the unemployment rate is at thirty-five percent, as a result of banks denying blacks access to capital, the decline of manufacturing jobs, as a result of the Bush-Clinton policies, and the swindling of black homeowners by criminal banks, whose crimes are ignored by a mainstream and progressive media that have gone bonkers over MJ, Tiger, Michael Vick, Chris Brown and O.J., whose case has led to mass hysteria, were Obama to behave like a black president, his doing so would expose him to more racist attacks than the ones he is now experiencing; it would cripple his administration. Though Obama sometimes reminds one of Martin Luther King, Jr. and Malcolm X, he might resemble Booker T. Washington more than the other two. Wearing the mask. Scolding African officials for their corruption, following a meeting during which he was able to increase the commitment to Africa by five billion dollars. When he answers critics who question his commitment to black employment by suggesting that economic recovery for all will lead to black employment, he sounds like Booker T. Washington.

I am disturbed by the collateral damage that is occurring in Afghanistan, but I am convinced that were Al Qaeda to get a hold of Pakistan's nuclear weapons there would be massive casualties. This is a group that wishes to restrict the rights of women by using the most extreme measures and whose leader has made racist comments about blacks living in Africa, calling African women "prostitutes" according to Chinweizu, who, along with other important African intellectuals, is alarmed by the spreading influence of Islam on the continent. This is an anti-Art group that destroyed thousands of years of Buddhist art.

What is the attitude toward blacks held by Al Qaeda? They bombed the embassy in Kenya, causing hundreds of African casualties and really didn't care about anybody's race when they bombed the World Trade Center. If Umar Farouk Abdulmutallab had succeeded in blowing up a plane over Detroit there might have been a large number of African-American casualties, yet I'm aware that it was the disease of white supremacy, rampant among Western nations, that led to the creation of groups like Al Qaeda in the first place. How many more people will have to be humiliated, racially profiled, and murdered for the maintenance of white supremacy?

Obama as president has made another contribution. His presence as the leader of the executive department has smoked out the virulent racism that has been covered by euphemism and code words like "busing," "political correctness," "welfare" and "crime." All one has to do is to read the vicious blogs about the president's family, the tea party signs, witness the joker who called Mr. Obama a liar during his address to Congress. He has ripped the mask off of "conservatism" and found the contorted ugly face of racism behind it. Even those who felt the sunrays of post-racism have been chilled by the president being likened to a witch doctor and a chimp (by Aussies at *The New York Post* who are referred to in a similar manner by the British) and his children being referred to as whores. When they refer to an African-American pioneer it's Jackie Robinson (but ignore the part where he used to beat up white officers who called him a "nigger"), but in comparison to the achievement of President

Obama, who, according to one historian, might be the most powerful black person in history, regardless of the limitations placed upon his presidency by the Jim Crow media, and a Republican Party, whose members believe that cooperating with Obama might get them called "nigger lovers" back home, Robinson's integrating baseball seems modest.

My giving Obama an A minus isn't the grade awarded Obama by the media where Obama received a low or failing grade even though at the end of the year, holiday retail sales were up, stocks were healthy and unemployment had not exceeded ten percent, some of the banks that had received bailouts were repaying billions of dollars to the government and GM, which, in 2009, was on the verge of collapse, predicted profits in 2010. Yet, the white nationalist pundits both on the left and right continued to mock him.

The week before, Matthew Continetti, appearing on Howard Kurtz's *Reliable Sources*, December 20, gave Barack Obama a C. Mr. Continetti is the author of *The Persecution of Sarah Palin*. He's employed by *The Weekly Standard*, a publication that was recently purchased by a wealthy Christian fundamentalist. One panel member was media juror Diane Dimond, a sleazy tabloid wag, a Michael Jackson stalker and pal of Jackson's persecutor and prosecutor, District Attorney "Mad Dog" Sneddon. During the show, Dimond, one of the most repugnant of tabloid personalities, who had rented a boat to go out and snoop about Tiger Woods' dwellings, lectured the viewers about personal morality.

Years from now, when the corporate media is stored away in a print and electronic museum, mercifully, media historians will mark a phase of its final period as being dominated by tabloid types like Dimond. I believe that this began when respectable journalists began appearing with reporters from *The National Enquirer* during the O.J. trial. This tabloid infection has even influenced the progressive media with places like progressive Air America getting as down and dirty as the supermarket tabloids. Bill Press, Keith Olbermann, Ed Schultz and other progressives devoted considerable amount of time to Michael Jackson and Tiger.

On the day that personnel from Blackwater, the off-the-shelf corporate warriors employed by the government, were acquitted for killing seventeen Iraqi citizens, progressive Ed Schultz was commenting on Tiger Woods' relationship with a porn star.

He spent a program on December 27 on Tiger, and two callers complained about Tiger's being rude to their children. He failed to mention Tiger Woods' contributions to charity. The *Orange County Register* was one of the few sites that noted his contributions.

> Say what you will about Tiger Woods and his latest antics. The golf star's OC-based nonprofit foundations raised more than $50 million and spent more than $40 million last year, and got high marks from charity watchdogs.

His contribution to charity was also ignored by sports writer David Zirin of *The Nation*, who criticized the athlete for not being activist enough.

On *Reliable Sources*, Kurtz linked Obama to Chris Brown, a black singer who was the subject of months of media scorn for assaulting his girlfriend.

About the host of *Reliable Sources*, Howard Kurtz, Jamison Foser of *Media Matters* wrote that "Kurtz just couldn't get Tiger off his mind," and as if to validate Foser's opinion, Kurtz came back to Tiger for a third program aired on Sunday, January 10, which turned into a feast of hypocrisy. Kurtz and David Brody of Pat Robertson's Christian Broadcasting Network defended Brit Hume's comment that Tiger Woods had a better chance at redemption from Christianity than from Buddhism. Brody saw nothing wrong with Hume's statement, because "Jesus is the god of creation." Brody said that Hume's remark was problematical since it dissed other religions. Hume went to Fox's Bill O'Reilly to defend his comments about Tiger's converting to Christianity, which raises the question, how is that band of god-fearing Christians at Fox News behaving? *DemocraticUnderground.com* reports:

> To be sure, in promoting the rumor of a Hume-Kendall tryst, Schur had help from reality. Hume's wife of thirteen years, Kim Schiller Hume, headed the Washington bureau until recently; a report in the *New York Daily News* suggested that marital tensions had played a large role in her departure. Kendall, meanwhile, is recently divorced. As of today, in fact, she is reverting to her maiden name, Megyn Kelly, for on-air use.

Moreover, getting involved with an underling is virtually par for the course for Fox higher-ups. Rupert Murdoch, chairman of FNC parent News Corp., embarked on an affair with his current wife, Wendi Deng, when she was an employee of the Star TV affiliate, and married her in 1999. Roger Ailes, now chairman of Fox Television Stations, divorced his second wife, Norma, in 1995 and went on to marry his current wife, Beth Tilson, who had been his second-in-command at *America's Talking*. And star pundit Bill O'Reilly famously described elaborate sexual fantasies over the phone to one of his producers, Andrea Mackris, leading to harassment allegations and a settlement of undisclosed size (reportedly around two million dollars).

As though begging for intervention, Kurtz added a second segment devoted to Tiger Woods. This time Gilbert Arenas, a basketball player who had brought a gun into the Washington Wizards' locker room, was brought on as an extra added attraction. This panel included two white men. Sports writer Mike Wise gave Arenas and Tiger some slack.

We're all flawed, he said. He was opposed by Buzz Bissinger whose *Vanity Fair* prose was used in an attempt to dignify a topless portrait of Tiger photographed by Annie Leibovitz, a woman who is obviously desperate to pay off her debts. Bissinger scolded both Arenas and Tiger for displaying "a false image," before Wise challenged him to take an "inventory" of his own life. Bissinger's comments show that separate but equalism exists even among the billionaire class, as evidenced by the media thrashing that Reginald Lewis, a billionaire, received as he was dying. A billionairess whom Dominick Dunne suspected of murdering her husband was able to get a story about Dunne's suspicions killed at *Vanity Fair*.

On February 21, it was Tiger again whom a woman sports writer from USA Today compared to President Obama, O.J. and Kobe Bryant. Extra added attraction in another black-men and domestic violence media sideshow was Gary Coleman being grilled by second-generation black-male basher, Lisa Bloom.

Given the fact that most of Woods' choices were Nordic types, could this be a case of shiksa envy on Kurtz's part, or maybe Kurtz should begin an Obama/Tiger recovery group. (Ironically, one of the sponsors of this particular show was National Car Rental whose pitchman was wife beater,

John McEnroe.) As though he were competing with Diane Dimond, the Tiger segments were followed by one about Warren Beatty's seduction count. Kurtz is becoming a regular old media ho.

Progressive Ed Schultz, a radio talk jock, could join the recovery. He wasn't the only commentator linking Obama to Woods to Chris Brown to Michael Vick in a sort of media chain gang of shame. *Media Matters* titled its December articles: "*Newsmax*'s Lowell Ponte compares Obama to Tiger Woods: 'eager to give cold cash to get hot love' at climate change conference," and "Fox Nation: 'Why Obama is Worse than Tiger?'" Fox's shock jock Glenn Beck compared Tiger with O.J. Simpson. (A black comedian appearing on a show sponsored by Shaquille O'Neal, the basketball star, said that during 2009, blacks got Obama and whites got O.J.)

And, of course, O.J. Simpson was tossed into the mix. While Tiger Woods was said by Frank Rich and others to represent the corruption at the end of this decade, O.J. Simpson was chosen to represent the end of the Millennium, no less, and while Rich associated Tiger with the Enron scandals, in 1997, the Institute of Contemporary Art in Boston put on an "End Of The Millennium" show curated by Christoph Grunenberg, in which O.J. Simpson was linked to Chernobyl!

The white progressives and liberals who had supported Obama in the beginning had begun sharing the right's enthusiasm for assailing the president. For progressive Amy Goodman, he was uppity; she criticized his "swooping" into the scene of the Copenhagen climate change conference. On January 1, during her annual retrospective program, Obama was subjected to withering criticism by her guests and this was followed the next day on progressive Pacifica radio, by Doug Henwood, a Marxist economist, who was just as unrelenting in his criticism of Obama. Even while admitting on his Pacifica show, aired on January 9, that manufacturing jobs were beginning to return, he, using the kind of language that slave masters used when trapping the movements of a fugitive slave, referred to Obama as "slippery" and like some others who are treating nonwhite voters as invisible, noted that Obama was "losing his friends."

Sam Roberts, who is a kind of Paul Revere for white nationalism, a man thrilled by the fact that whites with children are re-populating Manhattan and that Harlem no longer has a black majority, noted, maybe with alarm, that a coalition of nonwhites almost elected an obscure black politician over Mayor Bloomberg who spent over one hundred million during his campaign for Mayor of New York, yet white progressives still view themselves as Obama's base ignoring the fact that Southern blacks provided him with his winning margins in the South and Hispanics in the West. Both the mainstream and progressive whites have ignored this harbinger of things to come.

As an example of hypocritical posturing of media, white males who scold black men, like the divorcees and adulterers who praised Obama's lecturing black fathers, David Letterman poked fun at Tiger Woods' problems in his Top Ten Text Messages sent by Tiger. David Letterman still has his sponsors, without any protest from the white feminists at *Huffington Post* and *Salon.com*, progressive sites that are outdoing *The National Enquirer* in their obsession with Tiger Woods. Among Letterman's sponsors are Old Navy, Lipitor, H&R Block, Verizon, Direct TV and leading automobile and film companies.

The Kurtz panel decided that Letterman's exploitation of the women working for him was different from Tiger's relationship with women who were not employees of his, because Letterman confessed to his sexual transgression immediately, when some might argue that his extortionist forced him to do so.

When blacks complain that they are treated differently from whites, they might find confirmation during the last week in December. Charlie Sheen, a movie star whose face is recognized by millions the world over, was arrested for threatening his wife with a knife, an occurrence that wasn't mentioned during *The Reliable Sources* program that was aired on December 27, nor was there any discussion about his possibly losing his advertising contract with an underwear manufacturer. They dropped him, but CBS doesn't seem in a hurry to drop *Two and a Half Men*, starring Charlie Sheen, which, at the end of 2009, drew eleven million viewers.

In her autobiography, *A Paper Life*, Tatum O'Neal claims she was abused by her tennis-ace husband John McEnroe. She said that "the hot-headed sportsman regularly beat her up after his tantrums on the tennis court and claims he was a heavy cannabis smoker," yet National Car

Rental doesn't seem eager to drop him as a spokesperson. If Tiger had threatened his wife with a knife as Charlie Sheen had done or beaten her as McEnroe beat Tatum O'Neal would he still have his advertisers? Or if he had confessed his dalliances with other women when threatened by an extortionist?

When *The Wall Street Journal* asked me to comment about Tiger's situation I said that he should seek advice from Governor Arnold Schwarzenegger.

Women who were employed by Hollywood chose to remain anonymous when complaining about sexual advances against them by movie star Arnold Schwarzenegger. Though sportscaster Stephen Smith said that through his "antics" Tiger had alienated women, none of the complaints from women who had been sexually harassed by Schwarzenegger (Tiger's affairs were consensual), reported in a story from *The Los Angeles Times*, seemed to cause his alienation from women. On October 31, 2006, *Uprisingradio.com* reported:

> During Arnold Schwarzenegger's campaign for governor in the 2003 recall election, a number of women came forward to reveal their sexual harassment and assault by Arnold. *The Los Angeles Times* printed extensive reports just prior to that election. Now, just three years later, there is almost no mention of Arnold's sexist escapades. But some women are refusing to remain silent. More than a hundred women from across California have signed a letter to remind voters of the seriousness of the accusations of sixteen women against Schwarzenegger that surfaced during the 2003 recall campaign, and those that have surfaced since then involving minors.

Nevertheless, in 2003, he carried the women's vote and, after his election, family-values spokesperson Senator Orrin Hatch proposed that the laws be changed so that he could run for president.

Racists are identified as those who are unable to distinguish between members of one race from another. That certainly appeared to be the case of the media and the country's spreading Negro mania, mania being the word used by *The Philadelphia Inquirer*, which observed that Tiger mania was the biggest story to inspire mania since O.J. Simpson. One wonders which black male celebrity caught in a scandal will define the end of this decade.

David Carr is hipper than most white journalists. He was probably amused when he read a clueless column written by his colleague Frank Rich in which Imus-defender Rich said that the media's reaction to Tiger's problems had nothing to do with race. Tell that to *Vanity Fair* magazine, which ran a half-naked photo of Tiger Woods taken by Annie Leibovitz, who drew criticism for a previous photo of LeBron James that was based upon a World War I propaganda poster of a gorilla carrying off a white woman. Joan Walsh wrote on *Salon.com*:

> *Vanity Fair* should be ashamed of itself. The Thug Life photo of Tiger Woods that graces the magazine's February cover will go down in history with *Time's* "darkened" O.J. Simpson cover and *Vogue's* portrait of a brutish LeBron James carrying off a blond princess two years ago. I've always defended Woods' freedom to call himself Cablinasian, as befitting his mixed heritage. But *Vanity Fair* just proved the arguments of black people who dislike what they see as Woods' racial dodge. He'll always be black, but especially after he gets in trouble.

A black man exposed as a lover of Nordic-type white women has nothing to do with race? Rich hasn't read the sick disgusting blogs about Tiger's affairs written by white people who didn't go to Harvard.

David Carr on the other hand has been around and knows the streets. He knows for example that the media's description that crack is a black drug is false because he has smoked crack with white people (See: *The Night of the Gun: A Reporter Investigates The Darkest Story of His Life*). He was among the first to identify the media stories about widespread looting, rape and mayhem among black Katrina victims as being based upon exaggerations and lies. While complaints by blacks, Hispanics and Native Americans about media coverage for over one hundred years have been ignored or patronized, Carr at least acknowledges that the mainstream media have been accused of "pathologizing" black men, yet his explanation was in my mind unsatisfactory. (He also ignored the growing anger among blacks about the film *Precious*, which he admires). He wrote:

> Mainstream media have been accused of pathologizing the African-American male, but—let's face it—three men who happened to be black moved a lot of units this year. Just try to imagine this past year in media without President Obama, Michael Jackson and Tiger Woods. And lest you think it was all

pathology and politics, it is worth noting that on Twitter, the elections in Iran outranked Michael Jackson, who came in second, according to *What the Trend*, a site that ranked topics in 2009 (whatthetrend.com/zeitgeist). In an age that is ridiculed as chronically unserious, a life-and-death struggle for freedom on the other side of the world is the story that rang the bell on Twitter.

What kind of pathological behavior did President Obama engage in? Maybe the media's linking Obama to athletes involved in scandal might be pathological. And since when has Twitter become mainstream media? Mainstream media is *The New York Post* which had more cover stories (twenty) about Tiger than about 9/11.

Like the old puritan elders who condemned women who were manipulated by Hawthorne's black man in the forest, Frank Rich signed up for the Tiger mania when he coupled Tiger Woods with the Enron scandal and like the *Huffington Post,* which printed a piece linking Tiger's failure with that of Barack Obama's that was so outrageous that it was pulled. Rich, under the category of "they all look alike" wrote:

> Woods will surely be back on the links once the next celebrity scandal drowns his out. But after a decade in which two true national catastrophes, a wasteful war and a near-ruinous financial collapse, were both in part byproducts of the ease with which our leaders bamboozled us, we can't so easily move on. This can be seen in the increasingly urgent political plight of Barack Obama. Though the American left and right don't agree on much, they are both now coalescing around the suspicion that Obama's brilliant presidential campaign was as hollow as Tiger's public image—a marketing scam designed to camouflage either his covert anti-American radicalism (as the right sees it) or spineless timidity (as the left sees it).

Let's see. As a result of the Enron scandals, pensioners lost billions of dollars, twenty thousand people lost their jobs and some of those tied to Enron committed suicide. Isn't Rich's linking of Tiger Woods and Enron as strange as that of a white writer at the end of the 1990s nominating O.J. as the individual who defined that decade. But his noticing a right and left agreement was right on target.

While for Rich, Tiger is the most scandalous figure of the decade and indeed defines the decade, for Americans, when asked by a *Wall Street Journal*/NBC poll "What public figure disappointed you most in 2009?"

John Edwards came in at thirty-three percent. Tiger Woods came in at a distant sixteen percent. While Jan Crawford, chief legal correspondent for CBS, dubbed Caucasian Broadcasting for its lack of inclusion, said on January 3, *Face The Nation*, that Americans were beginning to question Obama's competency, according to a *USA Today*/Gallup Poll, Barack Obama, among American men, was the most admired.

On January 3 on CNN, Peggy Noonan, who claimed to speak for "the American people," criticized Obama's domestic programs while being allowed to dominate a panel that included black Princeton historian Nell Painter, and when Ms. Painter attempted to challenge Ms. Noonan's Republican talking points about higher taxes, blah, blah, with useful information, she was interrupted by Ms. Noonan whom Fareed Zakaria called a historian. Historian? Ms. Noonan is famous because she coined the phrase "A thousand points of light," which meant that individuals and charitable institutions should be charged with relieving the country's poor instead of the government, ignoring the fact that many of the main charities depended upon government support. On the Sunday that Ms. Noonan appeared, *The New York Times* reported that thanks to President Clinton's Welfare Reform Act, for six million people, food stamps were the only source of income.

Ms. Noonan, Tina Brown and Maureen Dowd represent the creeping Antoinettism that is affecting the upper-middle-class sisterhood, but at least Ms. Noonan, who believes that health care is a frivolous issue, even though millions of her white sisters are suffering because of a lack of health care, does not believe that her situation is worse than that of the black, brown, yellow and white male poor, which is what was implied when Gloria Steinem said that "gender" is the most "restrictive force" in American life. According to Peter Manso, in a forthcoming revised biography of Norman Mailer, Ms. Steinem's projects are backed by a Provincetown lesbian who is worth from two hundred to three hundred million dollars. Gender doesn't seem to be "restricting" Ms. Steinem.

The year ended with progressives risking the traditional charge that blacks and Latinos are "invisible" to them. This is what Ralph Ellison's *Invisible Man* was all about. A former generation of "progressives" abandoning domestic issues, like home foreclosures and the poor, for crises that were taking place overseas. For today's progressives, there is more interest in prison conditions in Gitmo than in Rikers Island, a few miles from where progressive Amy Goodman broadcasts *Democracy Now.* More concern about torture in secret prisons abroad than about torture in Chicago and Buffalo.

While progressive commentators insist that Obama is losing his base and that millions of progressives are abandoning the president his poll numbers among non-whites at the end of the year was a whopping seventy-three percent approving, twenty percent disapproving according to the Pew Research Center for the People & the Press.

On ESPN, a sports network, Barack Obama was linked to Michael Vick, another black male celebrity who was subjected to an endless Zapruder-like loop. To the dismay of sports writers, traditionally the most backward and racist contingent of the Jim Crow media, his team-mates, the Philadelphia Eagles, applauded Vick's courage by giving him an award and football fans gave him enthusiastic response upon his return to playing football.

Clay Travis of *Fanhouse* decided that he didn't need fellow white panelists to help him weigh in on the ten sports scandals of the decade. He decided that he would be the single judge of their actions. Seven out of ten scandals involved black athletes, including Kobe Bryant. The night before I read about the Travis verdict, I had watched a sizable segment of Sacramento Kings fans abandon their team to cheer Kobe's making a crucial buzzer three-pointer to defeat their team.

Travis is not the only one who is out of touch. The public that, when polled, found Obama to be the most admired of American men, disagreed with Frank Rich when he agreed with Rush Limbaugh that Tiger and Obama were "running neck and neck as the most unlikable frauds in the world."

About the pundits, both of the left and right, meaning white when they refer to Obama's "base," or "his friends" abandoning Obama, Jamison Foser of *Media Matters*, December 23, wrote under the headline: "Why does Howard Kurtz use white public opinion as the neutral baseline?"

When you get past Howard Kurtz's weird obsession with Tiger Woods, and his clumsy attempts to link Woods and President Obama, there's another problem with his piece today about Obama's race. (Take a look: www.washingtonpost.com)

"I have no doubt that no matter how deep a hole Obama digs himself, African Americans, who are already the most loyal Democratic group, will remain his fiercest defenders..."

In Kurtz's formulation, the fact that white support for Obama is at only forty-two percent means that Obama has dug himself a hole. White support for Obama, in this construct, is the impartial baseline against which Kurtz assesses Obama's "true" performance as president—he has dug himself a hole. And since African-American opinion of his performance doesn't reflect that "true" assessment, African Americans will fiercely defend Obama no matter what. Kurtz's formulation is simply a subtler version of Chris Matthews' tendency to use the phrase "regular folks" when he means "white folks."

He was right. On the January 5 edition of *Hard Ball*, Matthews said that Obama was being "hit by the right as well as the left. Where are his supporters on the Democratic side?"

Nobody from cable asked me to make a prediction for the next decade. Here it goes: Two thousand ten will see more cooperation between the white left and right. Frank Rich commented about this coalescing of interests when he left no degrees of separation between President Obama, Tiger Woods and Enron. This coalescing of the white right and left will continue. The white right will continue to try to break Obama. For its part, the white left from the time of the Abolitionist movement to today has never been comfortable with black leadership. Signs of cooperation between white right and left groups have become so visible that by the mid 2010s you might see a left-wing version of the tea party movement, with a Provincetown contingent waving banners along side one from South Carolina.

Why not? The progressive movement is now dominated by the white LGBTers and the white middle-class feminist movement. White, because black gays and lesbians say that they've been excluded from the mainstream LBGT movement and black women have been complaining about racism in the feminist movement for over one hundred years.

Proof that blacks and Latinos are excluded from the progressive movement comes in the form of a progressive like Ed Schultz warning President Obama that he is losing his "base," and Frank Rich writing that the president has "bamboozled us." On progressive Pacifica Berkeley's KPFA, two white Buddhist males were talking about how their generation had access to luxuries denied even emperors and kings of former time.

One of them said that "we" can walk into a supermarket and be exposed to a variety of goods. Which "base" and which "us" and which "we"? Moreover, did you ever think that you'd see Jane Hamsher from Firedog Lake signing petitions with Grover Norquist of Americans for Tax Reform, who says he wants to reduce government to so small a size that you can strangle it in a bathtub? Maybe it's not so surprising. While Norquist is called "a radical rightist," Ms. Hamsher might be called a radical leftist. Norquist, a right-winger so powerful that former President Bush sent representatives to his meetings, described President Obama as "John Kerry with a tan." Not to be outdone Ms. Hamsher thought it clever to alter the facial color of Senator Joseph Lieberman. Her blackface Lieberman was so outrageous that Arianna Huffington, of *The Huffington Post*, pulled the photo. Maybe if *The Huffington Post* employed more blacks they'd get some advice that wouldn't make it necessary for them to always have to pull things. Writer John Dickerson was outraged, he wrote:

> It pains me to no end that this appeared on none other than *The Huffington Post*, because I honestly can't believe Arianna Huffington would be a willing party to such racist trash. This may not make me any friends at the HuffPo but, seriously, someone at HuffPo needs to come out and address Hamsher's actions immediately.

But I guess that since "gender" is the "most restrictive force in American life," progressives like Ms. Hamsher are allowed to go blackface from time to time. An even more shocking alliance between the right and the left was a writer from the Revolutionary Communist Party, comrade Annie Day, agreeing with Barbara Bush about the merits of the movie, *Precious*. A movie that is being used to suggest that incest is a widespread practice in the black community. A movie that supports Draconian welfare policies and the sterilization of black women. For my criticism of the movie, Ms. Annie Day called me—are you ready for this—"a misogyn-ist," yet Ms. Day serves a white patriarch who has built a cult of person-ality around himself. At least white cultural nationalist outfits like *The Huffington Post* and *Salon.com* appear to have women in charge. Also, is this Maoist suggesting that I should use Mao Tse Tung as an example of how men should treat women? And given her attitudes toward black men, revealed in her article criticizing my *CounterPunch* essay about the film, *Precious*, her co-writer, Carl Dix, a black man, will never ascend to the leadership of the Revolutionary Communist Party. The Revolutionary Communist Party and Barbara Bush. Bizarre bedfellows.

As the domination of the country by an Anglo-Protestant culture, one that began in 1607, gives way to an American mosaic of cultures there will continue to be a merger of the white left and right. As the Obama administration continues on its course, Negro Mania will increase.

The year began with Barack Obama being hanged in jeopardy in a Georgia town. The tea baggers who came to Washington carrying signs of Obama as a witch doctor, Hitler, and The Joker, a socialist, a terrorist, etc., were up to their tricks. On January 5, Keith Olbermann's *Countdown*, footage was run of a tea bagger dressed in a black gown and hood like an Inquisition executioner, flogging a man with an Obama mask and a woman with a mask of Speaker of the House, Nancy Pelosi. They were covered with fake blood. Even with this kind of showing of racist imagery, which has become standard for the tea-party pageants, David Brooks of *The New York Times* gave them his grudging respect though he said he disagreed with them. He received a ton of mail for his remark after the earthquake that the problems of Haiti were cultural.

Is it the country that is addicted to Negro mania or is it the media, which believes that they are spreading the hysteria for profits? Up to their old tricks. Why else would extensive Michael Jackson stories be more important than news about the Iraq war, or why would *The New York Post* feel that news about Tiger is more important than news about 9/11 which resulted in three thousand lives lost? Reasons offered by David Carr don't quite explain it. There is something deeper going on. Susan Block, a psychologist tried to explain the Tiger mania by citing testimon-ies from her white male patients. I wish that she'd interviewed some of the white women at *Salon.com* and *The Huffington Post* to discover what excites them about Tiger.

One may disagree with Block's analysis but her bringing the subject of Tiger mania and yes Obama mania (MTV portrayed Obama as a sexual Mandingo in bed with Hillary Clinton—yes, they had to pull it) under a more sophisticated analysis than the one offered by Carr opens the door for further research.

Maybe we need experts from other professions to analyze Negro mania, an American sickness. I'm using "American" in the same way that the Jim Crow media use it. By the beginning of 2010, the Jim Crow media had done its job. By giving a small band of angry white voters a platform just for screaming and shouting and calling themselves tea baggers, a movement begun by a Fox News correspondent and supported by the insurance companies, a few billionaires and insurance-industry-backed phony "populist" organizations like Freedom Works, they had, according to commentators gloating over the election of a tea-bagger senator from Massachusetts, broken Barack Obama. An all-white panel on CNN was just about jumping for joy over the election of a man whom Keith Olbermann described on January 19 as "horrifically unqualified." Two of the most thrilled were Obama critics, Dana Bash and Gloria Borger, white women, and though the new tea-bagging Senator Scott Brown had a record that was unfriendly toward women's rights, without the votes of white women he would not have been elected. Keith Olbermann described him as "a homophobic racist reactionary sexist ex-nude model and advocate of violence against women." Rachel Maddow said that he campaigned "dishonestly." But Maddow and Olbermann were the exceptions. Because of low-intelligence commentators, or at least intellectually incurious commentators, resulting in low-information voters, fifty-two percent of Americans say President Obama has accomplished nothing or not very much after almost a year in office, according to a *Washington Post*/ABC News poll conducted January 12-15, 2010. (Forty-seven percent believe he has accomplished a great deal or a good amount). Those fifty-two percent probably got all of their information about Obama's record from *Saturday Night Live*, a comedy show written by uninformed white writers.

On January 20, Andrea Mitchell, a wealthy woman who socializes with the people whom she covers, grilled Obama aide David Axelrod about whether Barack Obama's health reform would fail as a result of the election of Scott Brown, who said he'd vote against it, even though he voted for similar legislation in Massachusetts. Left out of her exchange with Axelrod was any reference to the role her network played in spreading tea-bagger mis-information by endlessly featuring Sarah Palin's remark that health reform included provisions for death panels, which was called by *Politifact*, "The lie of the year," and although the media line was that Massachusetts voters were repudiating Barack Obama, a poll conducted by Republicans found him to be still popular in that state. *Motor City Liberal* reported: "Fabrizio, McLaughlin & Associates: Obama held a fifty-nine percent favorability mark and fifty-five percent job approval rating among MA voters. A January 20 *Politico* article reported that a Fabrizio, McLaughlin & Associates exit poll found that 'Obama's personal favorability remained high with voters.' The poll found that 'Obama boasted a fifty-nine percent favorability mark' and 'Obama's job approval rating even stayed at a respectable fifty-five percent as voters trekked to the ballot box to oppose the candidate he campaigned for just two days earlier.' The president even earned a passing mark on his handling of the economy (fifty percent approval) and received a clear majority's support for his work on the war in Afghanistan (fifty-nine percent approval). Fabrizio, McLaughlin & Associates is a Republican polling firm."

Andrea Mitchell, Chris Matthews and David Brooks have been given immense power to form public opinion, yet they don't always feel the need to study the facts. Both Matthews and Mitchell said that the United States played no role in Haiti's situation, a remark that many scholars and intellectuals would find laughable in light of a history of American-Haitian relations, which included invasions, a lengthy occupation under President Woodrow Wilson, a Klan admirer, and the recent abduction of an elected president and billions that Haitians had to pay to European nations that never forgave Haiti for ousting the colonialists. David Brooks, an Obama critic, was even more outrageous when he said of Haitians two days after the earthquake: "There is the influence of the voodoo religion, which spreads the message that life is capricious and

planning futile." For the stupidity of this remark Brooks was reproved
by a number of bloggers from different parts of the world. I asked Robert
Farris Thompson, Trumbull Professor of the History of Art at Yale
University, to comment. He wrote:

> I have worked for more than thirty years, doing, off and on, art historical
> research in Haiti. I have sat down with many priests and priestesses of vodun
> [not "voodoo" which to me is a Hollywood term, drenched with racism] dur-
> ing this period. And I never heard anything remotely matching the allega-
> tion that "life is capricious and planning futile." Who are his sources? Which
> voduist said that when, where, why? His is an outsider's assumption raised
> to the category of definition. In point of fact, to use an even deeper name for
> vodun in Haitian terms, sevi lwa [meaning the service of spirits under God}
> with its acts of charity and herbal healing, provides an island of art and car-
> ing within the larger world of Haiti. Wiser minds than mine have found this
> to be so, like the North American women scholars Maya Deren and Zora
> Neale Hurston, like the distinguished French ethnologist Alfred Metraux
> and more recently the Harvard-trained ethnologist Wade Davis. Vodun has
> inspired generations of superb painting. When Metraux said vodun was
> waiting for its Homer, Ishmael Reed responded to the challenge with a novel
> about the power and persistence and inherent beauty of vodun. All of the
> above distinguished researchers, not to mention the religious leaders and
> initiates of vodun themselves, are "called out of their name" by the false
> allegation that sevi lwa is essentially nihilistic. Things are bad enough in
> Haiti without maligning the national religion of the people. Gran Bois pa
> nan betise ave yo!

David Brooks found religion at the University of Chicago, a neo-con
temple whose presiding deity is the late Ayn Rand, the Queen of
Selfishness. His catechism includes slogans like "the free market," and
"cultural relativism." The difficulties of other nations, whose traditions
he doesn't feel necessary to give even a cursory examination, are due to
their culture. They should embrace the ways of the white man. His is the
kind of smug closed mind that confronts Obama, the internationalist, as
he starts his second year.

While white progressives and gays might lament the election of a tea
bagger who doubts whether Barack Obama's parents were married when
he was born and a man who is opposed to gay marriage and supports

water boarding, the constant carping against the president by both groups might have diminished the progressive and gay turnout of voters in Massachusetts. The white progressives spent the Wednesday after the Massachusetts election criticizing Obama and giving him advice.

Now look what they got. Since, for many white commentators, we live in a post-race period, they overlooked the money from racist groups that poured into the state from right-wing and racist sources. The total was thirteen million dollars. The insurance industry was there in the form of Freedom Works. Their goal, according to the January 21 *Times* was to "derail federal health care legislation."

The other panelist, Alex Castellanos, was licking his chops. Though he confessed to his profitable ties to the insurance industry, CNN's president Jonathan Klein has kept him on his job. That of criticizing President Obama.

Has President Obama been broken, which was the verdict of all-white panels appearing on January 19 and 20? Chris Matthews summed up the verdict of white progressives and their new buddies, the right, when he announced that President Obama's first year "ended badly." The next day, progressive radio talk-show host Thom Hartmann said that Obama had "pissed away a year."

On the same day, it was announced that because of the stimulus plan, which expands earned-income credit for certain workers in construction, permits for future projects rose eleven percent, indicating that the housing crisis was coming to an end, the economy in the United States was rebounding better than the pace in Europe, an economist, writing in *The New York Times* was congratulating Obama's proposed tax on big banks, and it was announced on January 21 that during December all economic indicators had surged: for the media, however, Obama's bad week had become a bad year, without any acknowledgement that it would have been worse had a depression occurred. Little attention was devoted to the day's economic news. Cable was fascinated with a rumor that Tiger had undergone sex therapy. Senator DeMint showed up to announce that Obama had been broken. He'd had his Waterloo, a reference that the younger generation of students would have missed. Again ignoring the sentiments of blacks and Latinos among whom Barack Obama's numbers are high, progressives continued to assert, arrogantly, that Obama's "base," which by now has become a code word, had deserted Obama. That remains to be seen. As this book has shown, they've been wrong before about Barack Obama, but a speech he made at a black church on Sunday, January 17, revealed that the criticisms of the first African-American president, the racist bile that was being retched by segments of some of the backward segments of the American population, were beginning to ruffle his cool demeanor. He said that "the words hurt," and "the barbs sting." But his "faith" kept him going.

For years, I've been asked the following question: what is the role of the writer? I've been reluctant to hamper any writer's creativity with any "role." But now I believe that there is a role for a writer whose group is being out-propagandized by moneyed opinion, and that is to pay attention. I have had the good fortune of living a life that has provided me with an opportunity to engage in contemplation, of reading and mulling over what I read, and discussing it with other intellectuals. I view myself as a one-man communication center that provides a check on the propaganda attacks on besieged groups and individuals who don't have the means to fight back. No, I don't wear a cape. One black intellectual told me that, "If it weren't for you, I'd think that I was crazy." That's how they've dismissed the black voices ever since a black writer picked up a pen. We're paranoid to them. In the words of Laura Miller, the kind of critic who fantasizes about being a character in a Jane Austin novel, we're "rowdy." We write "rants" and "diatribes." We're conspiracy theorists. We're controversial because we oppose the view of the world held by them. But now the paranoid community is expanding. Not only among blacks, Native Americans, Asian Americans, and Hispanics, which, for now, belong to communities where only forty percent are Internet users, but a foreign community of paranoids. My zine, *Konch*, draws readers from all over the world. So do my commentaries carried by *CounterPunch. org*. And I can also consult those ancestors whose experiences were similar to mine and whose witness was captured in slave narratives and folklore like the following:

Ole Sis Goose wus er-sailin' on de lake, and ole Brer Fox wus hidden in de weeds. Buy um by ole Sis Goose swum up close to der bank and ole Brer Fox lept out an cotched her.

O yes, ole Sis Goode, I'se got yer now, you'se been er-sailin' on mer lake er long time, en I'se got yer now. I'se gwine to break yer neck en pick yer bones.

Hole on derer, Brer Fox, hold on, I'se got jes as much right to swim in der lake as you has ter lie in der weeds. Hit's des as much my lake es hit is yours, and we is gwine to take dis matter to der cotehouse and see if you has any right to break my neck and pick my bones.

En so dey went to cote, and when dey got there, de sheriff, he wus er fox, en de judge, he wus er fox, en der tourneys, dey was foxes, en all de jurrymen, dey was foxes, too.

En dey tried ole Sis Goose, en dey 'victed her en dey 'scuted her, en dey picked her bones.

Now my chilluns, listen to me, when all de folks in the cotehouses is foxes, and you is jes er common goose, der ain't gwine to be much jestice for a pore nigger.

The Jim Crow media are full of Foxes too, and we are the Geese.

Ishmael Reed
Oakland, California
February 22, 2010

APPENDIX

Poll Shows the Jim Crow Media is Barack Obama's Chief Opponent

The Daily Kos conducted a poll from January 20 through January 31, 2010, which revealed the dangers of Americans receiving all of their information about the world from the Jim Crow media. All of the shocking responses to Barack Obama's presidency were inspired by the media, especially Fox News, which, also shocking, was found, in another poll, to be the network most trusted by the American people. Public Policy Polling found that forty-nine percent of Americans trusted Fox News, ten percentage points more than any other network. The poll also found that twenty-five percent of whites favor secession. A *Washington Post-ABC News* poll announced on February 11, 2010 found that seventy-one percent of those polled say that Sarah Palin is not qualified to be president. Even among Republicans her poll numbers are low, forty-five percent, yet, as the Daily Kos noted on February 11, 2010, the media were still pushing her as a viable presidential candidate, even televising a speech live from the Tea Bagger's convention, more evidence that the media is Barack Obama's chief opponent and that a non-elected talk show host is the leader of the opposition, something, which, as far as I know, is unprecedented.

QUESTION: Should Barack Obama be impeached, or not?

	YES	NO	NOT SURE
All	39	32	29
Men	43	30	27
Women	35	34	31
White	40	31	29
Other/Ref	31	41	28
18-29	38	33	29
30-44	38	32	30
45-59	40	32	28
60+	40	31	29
NE	34	35	31
South	42	29	29
MW	38	32	30
West	37	36	27
Def	40	31	29
Vote	39	32	29
Not Like	38	34	28
Def Not	37	35	28
Not Sure	37	35	28

QUESTION: Do you believe Barack Obama was born in the United States, or not?

	NO	YES	NOT SURE
All	36	42	22
Men	39	37	24
Women	33	47	20
White	37	41	22
Other/Ref	28	51	21
18-29	38	39	23
30-44	38	41	21
45-59	35	43	22
60+	34	43	23
NE	29	47	24

South	43	39	18
MW	33	43	24
West	31	44	25
Def	37	41	22
Vote	36	41	23
Not Like	35	45	20
Def Not	34	46	20
Not Sure	34	46	20

QUESTION: Do you think Barack Obama is a socialist?

	YES	NO	NOT SURE
All	63	21	16
Men	66	20	14
Women	60	22	18
White	64	20	16
Other/Ref	55	30	15
18-29	62	22	16
30-44	63	21	16
45-59	63	21	16
60+	64	21	15
NE	57	25	18
South	67	18	15
MW	61	22	17
West	60	23	17
Def	64	20	16
Vote	63	21	16
Not Like	61	23	16
Def Not	60	24	16
Not Sure	60	25	15

QUESTION: Do you believe Barack Obama wants the terrorists to win?

	YES	NO	NOT SURE
All	24	43	33
Men	27	41	32
Women	21	45	34
White	26	42	32
Other/Ref	9	51	40
18-29	23	44	33
30-44	24	43	33
45-59	24	43	33
60+	24	42	34
NE	19	49	32
South	28	39	33
MW	22	44	34
West	21	46	33
Def	25	42	33
Vote	24	43	33
Not Like	22	44	34
Def Not	22	46	32
Not Sure	22	46	32

QUESTION: Do you believe ACORN stole the 2008 election?

	YES	NO	NOT SURE
All	21	24	55
Men	23	22	55
Women	19	26	55
White	22	23	55
Other/Ref	7	42	51
18-29	19	25	56
30-44	24	24	52
45-59	21	24	55
60+	19	23	58
NE	18	28	54
South	23	21	56

MW	20	25	55
West	19	27	54
Def	22	23	55
Vote	22	24	54
Not Like	19	25	56
Def Not	18	27	55
Not Sure	17	27	56

QUESTION: Do you believe Sarah Palin is more qualified to be president than Barack Obama?

	YES	NO	NOT SURE
All	53	14	33
Men	55	13	32
Women	51	15	34
White	54	12	34
Other/Ref	45	31	24
18-29	52	16	32
30-44	53	14	33
45-59	53	14	33
60+	53	13	34
NE	47	19	34
South	57	12	31
MW	52	14	34
West	50	16	34
Def	54	13	33
Vote	53	14	33
Not Like	52	15	33
Def Not	51	17	32
Not Sure	51	18	31

QUESTION: Do you believe Barack Obama is a racist who hates white people?

	YES	NO	NOT SURE
All	31	36	33
Men	34	34	32
Women	27	38	35
White	33	35	32
Other/Ref	12	44	44
18-29	28	38	34
30-44	30	37	33
45-59	31	36	33
60+	33	34	33
NE	27	40	33
South	35	33	32
MW	30	37	33
West	28	39	33
Def	32	35	33
Vote	31	36	33
Not Like	30	38	32
Def Not	29	39	32
Not Sure	30	39	31

QUESTION: Do you believe your state should secede from the United States?

	YES	NO	NOT SURE
All	23	58	19
Men	27	56	17
Women	19	60	21
White	25	57	18
Other/Ref	7	66	27
18-29	21	60	19
30-44	22	60	18
45-59	24	56	20
60+	23	58	19
NE	10	66	24

South	33	52	15
MW	18	61	21
West	16	63	21
Def	24	56	20
Vote	23	58	19
Not Like	21	61	18
Def Not	21	62	17
Not Sure	21	62	17

QUESTION: Should Congress make it easier for workers to form and join labor unions?

	YES	NO	NOT SURE
All	7	68	25
Men	6	70	24
Women	8	66	26
White	6	71	23
Other/Ref	15	44	41
18-29	6	69	25
30-44	7	68	25
45-59	7	68	25
60+	7	67	26
NE	11	64	25
South	5	71	24
MW	7	68	25
West	9	65	26
Def	6	69	25
Vote	7	68	25
Not Like	9	67	24
Def Not	9	67	24
Not Sure	9	67	24

DKOS REPUBLICAN POLL 2010

The Daily Kos Republican Poll was conducted by Research 2000 from January 20 through January 31, 2010. A total of 2003 self-identified Republicans were interviewed nationally by telephone. Those interviewed were selected by the random variation of the last four digits of telephone numbers, nationally.

The margin for error, according to standards customarily used by statisticians, is no more than plus or minus two percentage points. This means that there is a ninety-five percent probability that the "true" figure would fall within that range if the entire self-identified Republican population were sampled. The margin for error is higher for any demographic subgroup, such as for gender or region.

GEOGRAPHIC BREAKDOWN

Northeast:
DC, ME, VT, NY, MD, PA, CT, DE, MA, NH, RI, WV, NJ

South:
FL, NC, SC, AL, MS, GA, VA, TN, KY, LA, AR, TX

Midwest:
IL, MN, MI, OH, WI, IA, MO, KS, IN, ND, SD, OK, NE

West:
NM, CA, OR, WA, AK, HI, MT, ID, UT, NV, AZ, WY, CO